Women in the
American Welfare Trap

Women in the American Welfare Trap

Catherine Pélissier Kingfisher

PENN

University of Pennsylvania Press

Philadelphia

Copyright © 1996 by Catherine Pélissier Kingfisher
Printed in the United States of America

Library of Congress Cataloging-in-Publication Data

Kingfisher, Catherine Pélissier.
    Women in the American welfare trap / Catherine Pélissier Kingfisher.
      p.   cm.
    Includes bibliographical references and index.
    ISBN 0-8122-3287-9 (cloth : alk. paper). — ISBN 0-8122-1515-X (pbk : alk. paper)
    1. Poor women—United States.   2. Welfare recipients—United States.   3. Human
services personnel—United States.   4. Public welfare—United States.   5. Aid to
families with dependent children programs—United States.   6. Welfare rights
movement—United States.   I. Title.
    HV1445.K57   1996
    362.83′8′093—dc20   96-19862
                                                                                   CIP

Language is also a place of struggle.

bell hooks

Politics is, essentially, a matter of words.

Pierre Bourdieu

Contents

Acknowledgments

This book, like most of life's projects, is a coproduction. It is, perhaps, a cultural peculiarity that we claim ownership of what we produce, and that we often privilege single authorship of books, poems, paintings, and songs over collective production. Even at the level of the actual writing, I did not produce this book singlehandedly, but was assisted by a barrage of editors, official and unofficial. Since "acknowledgments" is where we locate [and bracket] the fact of coproduction, however, it is here that I list my accomplices (none of whom, of course, bear responsibility for this work—sole responsibility being one of the hazards of single authorship).

First and foremost, the data in this book were coproduced by the recipients and workers who so graciously tolerated my various intrusions. They were dedicated and invaluable teachers. Their willingness to trust me, and, on occasion, to discuss activities that could have caused them considerable harm had they been revealed to others in the welfare system, indicates their desire to contribute to efforts to improve their situations. I hope that this study proves useful to them.

Robert Lovell of the Michigan Department of Social Services made this research possible by providing me with access to the Kenyon County welfare office. I thank him for his support and for his continuing interest in my work. I hope he finds this book helpful in his efforts to improve the working conditions of Assistance Payments workers in Michigan. In addition to Robert Lovell, I would like to thank the Director of the Kenyon County office for permitting my presence among her staff, a presence that no doubt was disruptive at times.

This book represents a substantially revised version of my doctoral thesis. My committee members, Ann Millard, Rita Gallin, Frederick Erickson, and Harry Raulet, were key coproducers of the original work. Aside from their various and invaluable expertise, I thank all of them for their patience, perseverance and good humor, all part and parcel of their remarkable skill as teachers. I would especially like to thank Ann Millard for her continuing collegiality, and Frederick Erickson for his willingness to continue a mentoring relationship over ten years and across great geographical distance. A number of colleagues who have contributed to the further development of this work, through either comments on drafts or conversations about specific points of interpretation, also deserve credit as coproducers. These include Eufracio Abaya, Lawrence Berg, Lois Bryson, Michael Goldsmith, Linda Gordon, Kai Jensen, Tom Ryan, A. R. Vasavi, and Anna Yeatman. I owe very special thanks to William Olszewski Kingfisher for his intellectual and personal friendship.

The Department of Women's and Gender Studies at the University of Waikato has provided an inspiring environment for my work, and I would like to thank Marion de Ras, Hilary Lapsley, Radhika Mohanram, Anna Yeatman, Helen Baird, and Lisa Whare for much needed collegiality and enthusiasm. Support staff outside the department, particularly in the IJK Word Processing Centre and the Computer Support Centre, were also invaluable, as were the funds provided by the University of Waikato Research Committee for word processing.

At the University of Pennsylvania Press, Patricia Smith, Alison Anderson, and Julia Sawabini were extremely helpful and encouraging throughout the review and production stages of the book. They make a great team. Three anonymous reviewers for the Press also provided useful comment and criticism.

Finally, while I was writing this book, I had the privilege of coproducing a beautiful little boy named Levi. In the two years of his life so far, Levi has given me a great deal of insight into the overriding concern for children shared by the women in this study. I thank him for his loving—and insistent—instruction.

Chapter 1
Producing the World in Everyday Talk

The thing that got me at the ((legislative)) hearing was ((the legislator who asked)) "why do ((women welfare recipients)) . . . have these children if they can't afford to raise 'em?" I was married. Sure my husband—he's 45 years old, 45 or 46—he ought to be working a decent job and making a decent living . . . Well I figured I could work and he could work together, you know, we could raise a family, we could have, you know, the little nuclear family, and everything would be hunky dory. (Rita Moore,[1] welfare recipient)

When you stop and think of it, this really is the lowly job in ((the Department of Social Services)), because the clerks (sort of) control what you do, the people above you control what you do . . . you are given all this responsibility and yet you don't really have any rights, I mean . . . you're responsible for people eating, and . . . paying their rent, and yet you really have no say in anything that goes on in the department, you have less say than any person in this department. (Judy Reynolds, welfare worker)

Rita Moore and Judy Reynolds sat on opposite sides of the table in the vast bureaucracy known in the United States as "welfare." Rita, a diabetic in her late twenties, had been on and off the welfare rolls for almost ten years; she had experienced battering, divorce, rape, and homelessness, and was currently fighting for custody of her son. Judy was in her early fifties, and had been a street level bureaucrat for eighteen years. Married twice with three children, she had been unable to continue her education beyond high school, as a result of which, she felt, she was "trapped" in her current job. Judy attributed her high blood pressure to workplace stress.

Judy's workplace was the Kenyon County office of the Michigan Department of Social Services (DSS), located in Webster, a small town in rural Michigan. Her position, Assistance Payments Worker (hereafter referred to as AP worker, or simply worker), was just above that of clerical

---

1. With the exception of the state governor and the director of the Michigan Department of Social Services, all personal, place, and organizational names are pseudonyms.

work in the department hierarchy and, along with clerical work, was not classified as "professional." Judy's primary job responsibility was to administer financial support programs, including Aid to Families with Dependent Children (AFDC) and food stamps, the programs most used by the recipients in this study. Specifically, the job entailed interviewing potential recipients, processing their applications, and opening, closing, and maintaining cases. Like her fellow workers, Judy was a member of her local union, which ostensibly was endeavoring to decrease workloads and increase pay.

Rita was a member of Low Income People for Equality (LIFE), a welfare rights group based in the city of Madrid, 30 miles northeast of Webster. Her work as a participant in LIFE consisted of educating the public about the plight and rights of low income individuals and families. To such ends, Rita took part in weekly LIFE meetings, worked on learning to "read" Department of Social Services policy manuals, attended legislative hearings, and participated in demonstrations at various government offices.

The experiences of Rita and Judy are both unique and typical of the experiences of the 125 welfare recipients and street level bureaucrats I worked with for seventeen months in 1989 and 1990. Like most of the women in this study, Judy and Rita have spent their lives in Michigan, a state that has in the past two decades experienced considerable economic hardship, and in which both economic opportunities and assistance for the poor have been steadily decreasing. In a population of approximately nine and a quarter million, 12.9 percent (over one million) received some form of poverty-related assistance in 1989. In 1990 the figure rose to 13 percent, and during the following year it reached 13.9 percent. Nevertheless, during this period the purchasing power of financial assistance dropped. In 1987 AFDC payments were at 61 percent of the federal poverty threshold[2] but by 1990 they were down to 55 percent; when food stamps are added, the figures are 83 percent and 80 percent respectively. In 1991 the AFDC minimum was the lowest in ten years (Michigan Department of Social Services 1991). All this occurred in a context of increasing unemployment, which, although down from the double digits of the early 1980s, rose from 7.0 percent in 1989 to 7.6 percent in 1990 (Michigan Department of Social Services 1993). More directly, with the 1990 election of Governor John Engler and the appointment of Gerald Miller as the new Director of Social Services, cuts were made in both public assistance and the staffing of the welfare department.

---

2. The poverty threshold for a family of four was $12,675 in 1989 and $13,359 in 1990 (U.S. Bureau of the Census 1992).

Rita and Judy are also typical of the participants in this study because they are women. At the time of my research, 87 percent of Assistance Payments workers and 94 percent of AFDC recipients in Michigan were women (Wertkin 1990; Michigan Department of Social Services 1990). The pattern holds at the national level as well. In 1989, for instance, while 12.8 percent of the U.S. population lived below the poverty level, 35.9 percent of those living in female headed households lived in poverty; the figures for 1990 were 13.5 percent and 37.2 percent respectively (U.S. Bureau of the Census 1992). Although poverty among women is on the increase (thus the concept of the "feminization of poverty"), there is also evidence indicating that women, and in particular single mothers and members of racialized minorities, have been disproportionately represented among the poor throughout U.S. history (Abramovitz 1988a; Handler and Hasenfeld 1991). They have accordingly comprised the majority of recipients of public relief, and, in particular, of AFDC, one of the most controversial and stigmatized forms of assistance in the U.S.

Women are also disproportionately represented among street level bureaucrats in the human services agencies through which programs purportedly designed to assist the poor are administered (Fraser 1989). In keeping with occupational segregation and the wage gap between men and women in the United States, front-line work in these settings is considered to be "women's work" and is accompanied by both high work loads and low pay and status (Ehrenreich and Piven 1984; Prottas 1979; Wertkin 1990; Wineman 1984). In general, then, the welfare system itself has become increasingly "critical in determining the lives and livelihood of women" (Piven 1984:15).

Language and Struggle

In their relationships to one another, to the welfare system, and to society at large, women welfare workers and recipients are situated in hierarchical and oppressed social spaces. To begin with, the women are subject to the constraints of the gender division of labor, which defines the substance and value of "women's work." The women must also contend with received views of poverty, its causes and meanings, as well as those of its opposite, economic success and security. More narrowly, recipients and workers move in a particular bureaucracy characterized by hierarchical organization and exclusionary and punitive policies.

Given the range of material and ideological forces arrayed against them, it is not surprising that women involved in the welfare system are often portrayed as powerless and given little credit as active agents struggling to define and improve their worlds. What is not always evident, and what I explore in this book, is the women's engagement in producing, reproducing, and contesting identity, ideology, institutional arrangements, and policy. I explore this engagement as it manifests itself in language. Language is the primary means by which we share our lives with others. It provides the means to typify and categorize experiences in ways that have meaning for ourselves subjectively and for others objectively in the same category of experience (Berger and Luckmann 1966). The use of language in interaction is a key location for the ongoing interpretation and construction of the social world, and is a significant and fundamental way we create meaning (Giddens 1984; Mishler 1986). Meaning, then, is not only imposed on individuals but also bestowed by them.

A great deal of workers' and recipients' construction of their meaning-worlds occurs in talk: in informal everyday conversations, and in more formal settings in which talk is organized around specific topics. In this book I analyze women's active production of their worlds by focusing on how participants in talk interpret and construct characterizations or classifications that help them "place" themselves and others in particular social spaces. These spaces, however, are contested and disputed. Recipients and workers are in continual struggle with themselves, one another, and the welfare system in their attempts to impose their view of reality; particular interpretations, stereotypes, ideologies, and policies are the site of these struggles. As Bourdieu (1990:137) has pointed out, the power to construct groups or categories is the power of "worldmaking," the struggle over which is part and parcel of an ongoing struggle over the perception of the social world. In this sense, "discourse as a political practice is not only a site of power struggle, but also a stake in power struggle" (Fairclough 1992:67).[3]

The notion of "worldmaking," as opposed to a view of individuals simply acting out an already created world, points to the dynamic and contingent nature of social structures and systems of meaning (Collier and Yanagisako 1989; Erickson 1975, 1986; Ortner 1984). Social reality is not "given" but rather continually produced and reproduced; the stereotypes, ideologies, and policies with which the women in this study are engaged are "accomplished" or "occasioned" by participants interacting in particular contexts (Erickson 1975; Erickson and Shultz 1982; Moerman 1988).[4] A key site for this accomplishment, or production, is talk, which does not so much reflect reality as constitute it.

3. "Discourse" is used variously in linguistics and social theory to mean samples of spoken or written texts, language particular to a specific social universe (here the discourse of welfare), or "different ways of structuring areas of knowledge and social practice" (Fairclough 1992:3). See Fairclough (1992) for detailed discussion.

4. Conceptions of the connection between "structure" and "action" (indicating a dualism which is itself problematic) are as numerous as the debates concerning its nature. For my purposes, Giddens (1984), who emphasizes "structuration," and Mehan (1979), who

This is not to say, however, that participants in interaction are free to construct anything they want. Society is not "the plastic creation of human subjects" (Giddens 1984:26), and a dominant system contains the power to "impose the principles of the construction of reality" (Bourdieu 1977:165; see also Gramsci 1971), thus placing limits on what is available for women to think with (D. Smith 1987). " 'The system' does in fact have [a] very powerful, even 'determining' effect upon human action and the shape of events"; the emphasis on "action and interaction is thus not a matter of denying or minimizing this point, but expresses rather an urgent need to understand where 'the system' comes from" (Ortner 1984:146). It is useful in this respect to think of cultural systems as simultaneously constraining and enabling (Collier and Yanagisako 1989; Giddens 1984), and to conceive of social structure and discourse in dialectical terms—in other words, of social structure as "a condition for, and an effect of" discourse (Fairclough 1992:64).

Talk, then, is both constrained and creative. When recipients label themselves as "working welfare moms," for example, they are strategically countering prevailing notions of women on welfare as immoral and lazy by positioning themselves as responsible, adult, and caring. In so doing, however, they are compelled to draw on what is culturally available: in this case, the ideal roles of "mother" and "worker." Rita Moore's references to marriage and the nuclear family, with which this chapter opened, provide a good example of this creative yet constrained use of language.

Women as Political Actors: Everyday and "Hidden" Forms of Resistance

Throughout the ages and cross-culturally, women of different classes and races have acted on their felt concerns whenever and however they were able. (West and Blumberg 1990:4)

The invisibility of women in many studies of political activity has prompted feminist scholars to question standard definitions of politics, calling for a broadening of such definitions to include "the everyday struggle to survive and to change power relations in our society" (Morgen and Bookman 1988:8; see also Moore 1988). There are many ex-

---

discusses the "structuring of structures" and "constitutive" ethnography, provide useful frameworks for thinking about this connection. Despite ongoing debates—most of which suggest either "micro" studies' neglect of connection to "macro" phenomena, or "macro" studies' neglect of illustrating what the phenomena look like at ground level—most scholars would agree that what are considered "micro" and "macro" mutually implicate and constitute each other.

amples of activities that fall outside the realm of electoral-representative politics but may nevertheless be considered "political." In her discussion of African American domestic workers, for instance, Dill refers to women's stories of using "confrontation, chicanery, or cajolery to establish their own limits within a particular household" as "stories of resistance" (1988:37). In a welfare-related context, it could be argued that "claiming benefits from public social programs is a political as well as an administrative act" (Nelson 1984:217; see also Gordon 1988). In this sense, the African American kinship and exchange networks described by Carol Stack (1974)—networks that challenge the welfare bureaucracy's construction of the family—may also be viewed in political terms.

In this book I borrow from Morgen and Bookman (1988) to define political activities as those that "are carried on in the daily lives of ordinary people and are enmeshed in the social institutions and political-economic processes of their society. When there is an attempt to change the social and economic institutions that embody the basic power relations in our society—that is politics" (1988:4). Social and economic institutions include ideologies, perceptions, and stereotypes among their key features. Conversation, in which these matters are continually renegotiated, is thus one location for attempts to change the world—that is, politics. Insofar, then, as the values and ideologies that in part comprise institutional practice are constructed in talk, talk is political activity.

As productive political activity, talk may be evaluated in terms of the extent to which it undermines or upholds particular social realities. In interpreting conversation within such a framework of resistance and accommodation, it is useful to draw on what Scott (1985, 1986) refers to as "everyday forms of resistance," meaning resistance in the mundane, day-to-day process of living, as opposed to more visible forms of resistance such as organized uprisings and insurrections. Included among everyday forms of resistance are "symbolic or ideological resistance," for example, "gossip, slander, rejecting imposed categories, [and] the withdrawal of deference" (1986:22). Everyday forms of resistance may also consist of "hidden transcripts" (Scott 1990), forms of resistance that people engage in "backstage," away from the view and hearing of the dominant group, or that are disguised so that members of the dominant group may only suspect their true meaning. Much of recipients' talk at welfare rights meetings, or AP workers' lunchtime talk, may be characterized as "hidden transcripts." Together with everyday forms of resistance, the notion of hidden transcripts provides a tool for exploring the activities of people who, for reasons of safety (ranging from the preservation of their employment to the preservation of their lives), are dissuaded from outright rebellion. As Moore (1988) writes, "Knowing when to give in is an integral part of knowing how and when to resist, if you happen to be poor and weak" (1988:180). Forms of resistance may further be limited by material options, and by what is considered " 'sex appropriate,' 'age appropriate,' [and] 'social-class appropriate' " (Cloward and Piven 1979:656; see also West and Blumberg 1990).

Compliance, then, is as important to understand—and as prevalent—as resistance. Accommodation may be strategic, "a choreographed demonstration of cooperation" that is in fact a form of resistance (Faith 1994: 39). It may also be unintentional, if, as I suggested above, the dominant system has the power to restrict people's thinking about their own situations. Struggle is situated within hegemonic relations, not outside of them (Faith 1994; Ong 1991).

Accommodation and resistance are, of course, analytically distinct concepts. In practice, however, they appear as opposite ends of a continuum, within which "mixed forms"[5] comprising both accommodation and resistance may occur. Each is often present in the other: resistance to a dominant discourse of necessity partakes of that discourse, while apparent accommodation may be a tool of subversion. Furthermore, the context of an action, in addition to its content, provides additional interpretive layers of (often overlapping) acquiescence and subversion. The stories and conversations of workers and recipients, while directly resistant to certain features of the welfare system, often accommodate aspects of the larger culture, reflecting mainstream ideologies and values. For example, in contesting the welfare system's work requirements, recipients often invoked ideals of family and motherhood that feminist scholars identify as patriarchal ideologies inimical to the interests of women (Ramazanoglu 1989; see also Warren 1990).

It is also useful to consider how welfare workers' and recipients' interpretations represent gradients of accommodation and resistance to dominant ideologies and the welfare policies of which they are part and parcel. The emphasis on gradients is crucial here because the women I worked with were neither full-time "zealous radicals" nor full-time "downtrodden poor folk trapped in 'worlds of pain' " (Bookman and Morgen 1988:viii). Rather, their talk was sometimes subversive, sometimes compliant, and often a little bit of both as they drew on one prevailing ideology in order to contest another, or vacillated between different positions in different contexts. Like ideologies and stereotypes, accommodation and resistance are accomplishments and occasions; they are at the same time patterned and unique.

5. I borrow the notion of "mixed forms" from Erickson and Mohatt (1982), who use it to refer to the communicative practices of communities in inter-ethnic contact.

The concepts of everyday and hidden forms of resistance resonate with feminist approaches to political activity. Feminists have criticized what may be grouped under the rubric of "male bias" in the social sciences—the emphasis on overt forms of political participation and resistance, and the rendering invisible, in masculinist discourse, of other forms of political activity. In taking as basic the notion that the personal is political,[6] feminism has brought into view the everyday, and has further argued persuasively for a review of many taken-for-granted assumptions, such as, in this case, what constitutes political activity. A focus on everyday and hidden forms of resistance also provides the means to circumvent dichotomies between intentions and consequences of resistance (Scott 1986), between pure self-interest (e.g., wanting more food) and resistance to structures of domination (e.g., food stamp policy).

Recipients and workers, then, do not simply internalize the views of the welfare system or society at large concerning their self-worth or place in society; rather, they interpret these views. In so doing they create and impose their own meanings, of which some may in certain ways accommodate those external images and others resist them. This action is accomplished, moreover, in the context of various material constraints, with implications for the reproduction or transformation of those constraints. The symbolic power of "worldmaking" is thus not removed from the "everyday." Indeed, the dichotomy of symbolic/practical is deceptive, leading to the erroneous conclusion that practical activities are not symbolic in nature and that symbolic activities are not practical (Collier and Yanagisako 1989). On the contrary, recipients' and workers' classifications of themselves and each other are accomplished in the course of the day-to-day activities of their lives as recipients and workers. In the end, whose view prevails affects the lived realities of both workers and recipients—for example, how long a recipient has to wait for her food stamps, or how often a worker is officially challenged by her clients.

Much of what occurs in the social world happens in language. The language of application forms and policy documents, the talk produced in worker-recipient interviews, and informal talk among various staff members are key constituents of welfare institutions. At a broader structural level, the languages of newspapers, radio talk shows, television sit-coms, and everyday chit-chat at the grocery store are the "institutionalization" of views of women and of poverty, while at the same time

---

6. "The personal is political," characterized by Philipson and Hansen (1990:6) as the "revolutionary battle cry of the women's liberation movement" of the 1960s, points to the connections between personal and everyday issues, such as sexuality and domestic arrangements, on the one hand, and politics and social structure on the other (see also Morgen and Bookman 1988).

being sites for the contestation of these views. Again, various discourses can support or subvert the status quo. In this sense, the talk that I examine in this book is more than just "talk"; rather, it is one of the means by which social structures and institutions are reproduced and transformed.

Situating Participants

Not only is recipients' and workers' talk productive political activity, so is this research on talk. The postmodern turn in anthropology has appropriately led to a new imperative for ethnographers to locate themselves in their work, to accept responsibility as active participants in the construction of a particular setting, event, or culture, and no longer to claim the status of disinterested recorders of "reality." Out of related concerns for the politics of research, many feminist scholars feel compelled to locate themselves in the social hierarchy, thus rendering transparent their perspective and its limitations. These efforts at self-location sometimes take the form of confessions which, once uttered, serve to absolve the sinner from all blame; or of simple, unexamined statements of fact which seem to raise obvious questions (what does "middle class" mean, specifically?). Perhaps most frustrating is a narrow focus on the researcher as an individual—or, to borrow from Richard Fox (1991:9), on the "myths that charter anthropology as artisanship," as if everything is within our individual power as producers of research, as if there is little need to examine history, institutional constraints, or the dynamics of class.

Given these limitations, simply stating that I am Anglo, heterosexual, and middle class, and that I was in my early thirties when involved in this research, in the end reveals very little. Instead, I offer a somewhat more telling and textured story of discovery.

I developed my interest in women and welfare while researching the Special Supplemental Food Program for Women, Infants and Children (WIC). A U.S. Department of Agriculture program, WIC is designed to meet the nutritional needs of low-income and poor pregnant women and young children. The program provides monthly coupons that may be exchanged for specific foods, such as milk and cheese. Our particular focus in the project was lactose intolerance (the inability to digest milk sugar), and how it was recognized or not recognized by staff nutritionists. Accordingly, I placed considerable emphasis on interactions between nutritionists and WIC participants and found that there were few opportunities for women to discuss problems with milk or turn down milk coupons in exchange for other, more appropriate, foods. Along with this institutionalized imposition of a particular model of physiology and culture, I encountered more overt abuses of power, for instance, cases in which staff expressed a desire to refer particular women to Social Services because of their unorthodox child-rearing practices. Some staff also made a distinction between the "working poor" and the rest—between those who deserved WIC assistance and those who did not. My experiences with the WIC program thus gave me a sense of the kinds of abuses of power, both unintentional and intentional, that can occur in institutions serving the needs of a poor and often stigmatized population.

A particularly painful incident during the course of the WIC study underscored my naivete for me and served to stimulate my curiosity and interest. One day, I encountered the partner of an acquaintance in the clinic. We chatted while Margo waited her turn. Although critical of the way in which the program imposed a particular diet, I was impressed with the fact that it provided pregnant women and young children with extra food. With this enthusiasm in mind, I commented to Margo that I thought highly of the program and that I had every intention of signing up for it if I became pregnant, to which Margo responded by narrowing her eyes and replying, in a voice thick with sarcasm, "maybe someday you'll be lucky enough to be poor like me."

The incident led me to reflect on what now seems obvious: that there is a difference between the temporary poverty of graduate school and the long-term poverty experienced by women such as Margo; that my views of programs such as WIC were inevitably refracted through the lens of a more or less privileged economic position that allowed me in effect to opt for the temporary poverty of graduate school, or for participation in the WIC program; that I had little understanding of what it might be like to be unable to provide for one's children and be forced to ask for food. This is what I mean, then, by "middle class." After recovering from my embarrassment, I moved on to guilt; after guilt I began to examine the experiences of women such as Margo in relationship to how they are constructed by others (e.g., policy makers, the dominant culture).

This story only hints at the positioning of the researcher to which I alluded above. My positionings are intended to be transparent throughout this book, though I have not always called attention to them. One way in which I hope to accomplish this transparency is by not editing my presence out of the conversations that provide the bulk of the data. Indeed, in some cases I am a co-producer of the constructions I analyze. Another way I endeavor to minimize silencing participants in favor of my own interpretations (Clifford 1986) is to work with material in which participants themselves make their meanings apparent to each other (Erickson 1979, 1986; McDermott, Gospondinoff, and Aron 1978). In keeping with the traditional goal of the ethnographic enterprise, my emphasis in this work is on "making contact" with locally relevant meanings, and on attending to what the participants themselves attend to (Blumer 1969; Erickson 1979; 1986).

As well as producing particular texts—the material representations of women's talk—this research produced particular kinds of relationships among and between participants. I was neither the only participant in this research nor the only participant with a stake in the project.

Poverty and welfare are not neutral phenomena in American culture. Nor is the relationship between women on welfare and AP workers particularly cordial. As a member of this culture, I could neither feign ignorance of issues surrounding public assistance nor claim "outsider" status. Throughout fieldwork, I made no attempts to be "objective"—to remain uninvolved in the political aspects of women's lives, or to avoid "taking sides" with them on important issues. Indeed, the women I worked with would most likely have been puzzled by such a notion of "objectivity"; rather, what they demanded from me was partisanship (cf. Oakley 1981).

Renato Rosaldo (1989) discusses at length Dorinne Kondo's fieldwork experience in Japan. As a Japanese-American, Kondo was subject to her hosts' cultural expectations about someone who looked Japanese. The experience was not as extreme for me because I was not, in fact, in another culture, but in my own. I was nevertheless crossing class lines, and found it curious that, because we were all American and all women, I was expected to share certain assumptions about the world held by workers and recipients, and to know about things they considered obvious, such as the nature of certain kinds of relationship problems or feelings of pride or humiliation. Like Kondo, moreover, I had trouble with "indelicate" questions, such as, for instance, those pertaining to workers' incomes.[7]

My partisan positions were an outgrowth of my involvement with the women and of my status as an active member of my own culture. I began the study more sympathetic toward welfare recipients than toward workers, since recipients are the poorer of the two groups, and since they fit into the category of the oppressed more than do workers (at least from the perspective of the popular left). I was touched and outraged by the plight of recipients, who, in addition to being overworked and stigma-

---

7. While income was not a taboo topic for welfare recipients—indeed, income insufficiency was a standard conversational topic—workers followed the more middle class notion that income is a more or less private affair. In the end, I gained access to information concerning workers' incomes by means of a confidential questionnaire. Although I wondered if my hesitation to ask workers about their incomes was simply a projection of my own middle class values, rather than a reflection of norms which they shared, I find it significant that I did not experience this hesitance with recipients. Perhaps this was because they themselves frequently initiated talk about money, or perhaps it was because poor people don't have the same social standing as members of the middle class.

tized, had to contend with not always having enough food to eat. This did not mean that I took sides against workers. As I learned with time, workers, like recipients, are women who suffer from both economic and social inequalities in U.S. society; moreover, they are also "victims" of the welfare system: while recipients are subject to both insufficient funds and stigma, workers are burdened with outsized caseloads and have low status in the welfare bureaucracy.

I was able to avoid some of the potential conflicts of my partisan positions by working with recipients and workers in separate counties. Although each group of women was aware that I was working with the other, I was not working with someone's particular worker, or with someone's particular client. The impact that working with recipients and their own AP workers might have had on my relationship with each group was quickly made evident to me through the attempts made by both to recruit me to their points of view, as, for example, when I was invited by a worker to agree with her characterization of a recipient as a child abuser or when I was invited by a recipient to agree with her that workers go out of their way to provide poor service to unsuspecting clients. Indeed, I was surprised at the degree to which I was expected to be partisan. This reflects, I think, a very important commonality among the two groups of women: their powerlessness and their politicization of their respective situations.

As part and parcel of their recruitment, both groups of women had high expectations of the results of my research. Since they themselves were relatively powerless, they expected me to express their concerns, to legitimize their cases. This was particularly so with the AP workers, who felt that they had no voice with administration and management. I, on the other hand, could document their predicament and thus force management to make long-needed changes. Workers assumed, of course, that management would disagree with my "findings." While in general less optimistic, recipients were hopeful that I could get their stories "out there," and that the public, once fully aware of the privations of public assistance, would be more sympathetic to their plight. The expectation that my study would vindicate the workers, or show the world that recipients were victims and not villains, indicates that the women did not consider me so much "one of them" as an outsider who could verify and legitimize their perceptions of reality.

Organization of the Book

In this book I explore welfare workers' and recipients' active construction of their world and its meanings in relation to the social and cultural constraints to which they are subject. I begin with a focus on welfare recipients. Recipients' stories and comments portray the experience of being poor, female, and on welfare, and provide insight into how women make sense of the welfare system and their place in it. Themes permeating the stories represent not only patterns of interpretation among the women, but also what they believed was most important for me, as an outsider, to know. Chapter 2 focuses on these stories told to an outsider, situating them within the broader historical and ideological context of the American welfare system.

Chapters 3–5 look more closely at what recipients said to each other, as knowledgeable insiders, within the context of welfare rights groups. The recipients in these chapters are not typical of all recipients, but rather of those among them who engage in explicitly oppositional activity: in this case, in welfare rights groups, which are organized for advocacy on behalf of people on public assistance. In Chapter 3 I outline the formal and informal organization and goals of two welfare rights groups, the Madrid Welfare Rights Organization (MWRO) and Low Income People for Equality (LIFE). I argue that while both groups emphasized opposition to the "system," they put considerable interactional effort into a related establishment of positive self-identities. Chapters 4 and 5 explore in greater detail the women's constructions of "them" (members of the "system") and "us."

In Chapters 6–8 I explore the world of Assistance Payments workers. Chapter 6 parallels Chapter 2 in emphasizing workers' interpretations of their jobs as AP workers within the context of the organization of street-level bureaucratic work. Chapter 7 focuses on workers' constructions of recipients, particularly with regard to the discursive construction of "deserving" versus "undeserving" clients. Chapters 7 and 8 deal with how this constructive work relates to department hierarchy and the pressures of everyday life in the welfare office, and thus its implications for policy production at ground level.

Women are not homogeneous. We come from different cultures, classes, races, ethnicities, nations, age groups, religions, and sexualities, among others. These multiple differences contribute to multiple positionings, which in turn have implications for how we see the world, and what we consider our interests to be. Recognition of this on the part of feminist activists and scholars has led to a call to go beyond the assumption of shared biology and oppression to a consideration of both difference and similarity—to a deconstruction of the singular category "woman" (Moore 1988; Ramazanoglu 1989). In order to accommodate the needs of all women, then, we must recognize and explore difference. Chapter 9 addresses this issue. Given the fundamental similarities *and* crucial differences in recipients' and workers' situations, experiences, and interpretations, moreover, I am interested in the conditions under which they recognize commonality and those under which they stress difference. My goal is to gain insight into both the obstacles to and the possibilities of comembership—the recognition and expression of an "us"—within the relationships of similarity and difference.

As I write this book in early 1995, Newt Gingrich and his Republican colleagues are singing the praises of the Personal Responsibility Act of the "Contract with America." Among the draconian measures included in the Act are cuts to medical services for AFDC recipients, increased work requirements, sanctions against women who give birth at an early age or out of wedlock, and severe restrictions on immigrants' access to assistance. The women who participated in this study—workers as well as recipients—are no doubt under greater pressure than ever before. What, then, are the implications of this study? And what difference does the women's talk make? I ponder these questions in the final chapter.

A Note on the Transcripts

My concern in this book is with the meanings the women make in their talk and with the processes involved in making meaning in talk. This content and process are best displayed directly, in quotes and transcripts. Transcripts are especially useful in that they provide a textual representation not only of what the women say but also of how they say it, giving us a particular (and, of course, partial) view of their worlds. In this book I take two approaches to presenting the women's talk. First, in the text itself I present the women's talk in quotes, some of which are embedded in vignettes, or in simplified transcripts. These modes of presentation are highly readable and allow the reader to focus specifically on the content of the talk. In the simplified transcripts, only speakers' words are included, along with several conventions: capital letters indicate emphatic delivery, parentheses bound uncertain or undecipherable words, and double parentheses bound my comments.

People do more than simply speak words when they talk, however. They also speak quickly or slowly, stressing certain words or phrases and de-emphasizing others, taking turns at particular times. Speed of talk, stress, intonation, turn-taking, pauses, false starts—all these may be relevant to an understanding of what is being accomplished in talk. There is thus a *process* by which the meaning of words in a particular context is conveyed. Accordingly, for those readers interested in process, I have included, in Appendix A, complete transcripts and analyses of ten instances in the text where talk is presented in quotes. This distinction between content and process is an artificial one I am making for purposes of presentation and readability.

Finally, talk does not speak for itself but must be interpreted. In providing interpretations of the women's talk, I draw not only on what is actually present in the quote or transcript, but also on my knowledge of the wider context of the talk, such as participants' personal histories, preceding events, and the specific relationships of the speakers.

Chapter 2
The Welfare Trap I: Recipients

I bust my ass trying to get off ((welfare)). (Susan Harrison)

The 79 recipients I worked with can be divided into two groups, reflecting the women's differing degrees of involvement with welfare rights and in the study. I spent the most time with (and thus focus my analysis on) 16 women, 6 of whom were core members of either the Madrid Welfare Rights Organization (MWRO) or Low Income People for Equality (LIFE). The second group of recipients consists of 24 occasional welfare rights participants and 39 recipients I encountered at the Kenyon County welfare office.

I conducted in-depth interviews with 12 of the 16 key participants; these interviews are the focus of this chapter. The 12 women ranged in age from 19 to 48 and had at least one child each (see Appendix B, Table B1). Eight of them had been married, and three had been married more than once. Three were presently living with men who contributed to household expenses. All of them were Anglo and heterosexual.

The women had both enduring and sporadic relationships with the Department of Social Services. Half of them had received public assistance continuously, for periods ranging from 18 months to 10 years. Maggie Fletcher, for instance, had been on AFDC for three years prior to entering graduate school, while Jody Dixon had been an AFDC mother for the nine years since her divorce. The remaining six women, who had been connected to the welfare department intermittently for an average of 12 years, referred to their experiences of "getting on and off welfare" as if it were comparable to going in and out of a bad relationship. Over the course of 25 years, Pat Graham had received various forms of relief for periods ranging from nine months to several years. And Mary McDonald, for her part, had been on the AFDC rolls for one to two years (she could not remember which), kept herself out of the system for two years, and then gotten back on the rolls for another five. The majority of the other recipients I encountered at welfare rights meetings and in the Kenyon County welfare office also had sporadic relationships with public assistance. According to the Michigan Department of Social Services, the average length of time recipients are on assistance is 34 months. In addition, 25 percent of recipients receive aid for from four to twelve months, while 40 percent are on assistance for over 24 months (Michigan Department of Social Services 1990). It is noteworthy that these statistics relate to recipients' "most recent period" of relief, an approach which recognizes that, like the women I worked with, individuals move in and out of the system as warranted by their personal circumstances.

When not on welfare, the women either received sufficient economic support from men or were in employment that paid enough for survival. Eleven of the 12 women had been or were currently in the paid workforce. Many of them had held numerous jobs, and many had earned an income while receiving public assistance. As with the often episodic nature of women's interactions with the welfare system, the fact that all but one of the women had worked to earn a living mirrors what we know in general about welfare recipients, namely, that many participate in paid labor (e.g., Zopf 1989).

The events that contributed to the women's initial and continuing relationships with the Department of Social Services are also typical. As they described it, poverty was not simply a problem of unemployment but was related to the gendered nature of their economic marginalization in U.S. society, a significant aspect of which is their financial dependence on men and their financial responsibility for children. In many cases, divorce was economically devastating because child support was insufficient or not forthcoming, a problem that seems to cut across socioeconomic class (Ehrenreich and Piven 1984; Folbre 1988). Coupled with the disadvantages they experienced in the labor market, then—only three of the women had been able to find employment paying more than the minimum wage[1]—the burdens of providing child care if they were employed left them financially vulnerable. Thus the *connections* between employment and relationships with significant others, rather than any single factor, were the key to the women's involvement with welfare.

The complexity of these connections and the burdens the women shouldered as clients of the welfare system come across clearly in the narratives that emerged from our interviews. First, however, I must outline two contextual features of these narratives: the historical and ideological context of public assistance, and the nature of the interviews in which the narratives were produced.

1. As of April 1990, the minimum wage was $3.80 per hour; it was raised to $4.25 per hour in April 1991.

Women and Public Assistance

Prior to the enactment of relief measures in the United States, poor
women had little recourse but to accept whatever paid employment was
available, enter the poorhouse ("indoor" relief, as opposed to "out-
door" relief, in which assistance is provided to recipients in their own
homes and communities), or place their children in orphanages.
Women were not excused from work by virtue of their sex or their roles
as mothers. On the contrary, during the period of industrialization,
single women and youth (of a certain class) were seen as a cheap and
necessary source of labor (Kessler-Harris 1982). With the rise in the first
half of the nineteenth century of the cult of domesticity and the ideology
of separate spheres, women's place was defined as being in the home,
where they could fulfill their "natural" roles as wives and mothers and
thereby do their duty to uphold the patriarchal family structure. Poor
women were still compelled to seek paid employment, however; the difference was that now they were socially condemned as somehow "lacking
in virtue" for doing so (Abramovitz 1988a). What is evident in accounts
of women and poverty in the United States since industrialization, therefore, is a history of contradictions and ambiguities surrounding women
and paid labor: while many women had to find jobs in order to survive,
their engagement in paid labor was seen as an affront to the preferred
family form (male breadwinner, dependent wife and children) (Handler
and Hansenfeld 1991).

The emphasis on women's roles as mothers provided the impetus for
the establishment of Mothers' Pensions, which provided small amounts
of cash to women bereft of male breadwinners to enable them to stay at
home with their children. Launched in forty states in 1911 and then in
an additional six in the 1920s and 1930s, Mothers' Pensions were in operation until 1935. Despite the publicity and rhetoric with which they
were surrounded, however, the programs were not, in fact, widely implemented; even at their peak they operated in only 50 percent of the counties in the nation (Abramovitz 1988a; see also Piven and Cloward 1988).

Mothers' Pensions reflected a social recognition of the importance of
children, specifically, a concern with "predelinquent" (i.e., poor) children who, if they were not properly socialized, would grow up to constitute a new generation of paupers and/or criminals (Handler and
Hasenfeld 1991). The focus on children, and on mothers as conduits for
care and the indoctrination of appropriate values and behavior (particularly work habits), is a theme that runs from Mothers' Pensions through
to Aid to Dependent Children (Abramovitz 1988b). At issue was the
long-term well-being of the child, not that of the mother, although the
mother could be "reformed" in the process (Gordon 1988). The status

of the mother was nevertheless crucial. In order to avoid encouraging single motherhood, for instance, Mothers' Pensions were to be provided specifically to morally upright families; in the context of received views of gender and race, this meant that the majority of recipients were Anglo widows (Abramovitz 1988a). Along with women of color, then, "never-married women, women who engaged in extramarital relations, used tobacco, housed a male lodger, lived in the wrong neighborhood, or did not attend church" were often disqualified (Abramovitz 1988b:294). While divorced, deserted, and unwed mothers were not automatically excluded in all states (Handler and Hasenfeld 1991), by 1930 only three states had instituted the provision of aid to single mothers (Abramovitz 1988b).

Handler and Hasenfeld (1991) summarize the controversy that may have contributed to the de facto meager relief provided by Mothers' Pensions:

The proponents and opponents both evoked the image of the traditional, patriarchal family, but differed sharply as to the impact of [Mothers' Pensions]. The proponents argued for the domestic code—men and women belonged in separate spheres; motherhood and the home were privileged, and should not be compromised by paid labor. Mothers' pensions, they said, removed the necessity for paid labor and would thereby reinforce patriarchy and domesticity. The opposition believed that pensions would weaken traditional family ties, weaken family (husband) responsibility, and encourage single motherhood. (1991:72)

The disjuncture between policies set at the state level, on the one hand, and local administration in which judges determined the worthiness of each applicant on a case-by-case basis, on the other, also added to the low rate of implementation (Handler and Hasenfeld 1991).

With passage of the Social Security Act in 1935, Mothers' Pensions were replaced by Aid to Dependent Children (ADC), a program all states had to implement. As its name indicates, however, and in keeping with Mothers' Pensions, ADC did not provide for mothers directly, but only for their children; it was also initially limited to single-parent families. Coverage for mothers was introduced in 1950; then in 1962 ADC was renamed Aid to Families with Dependent Children (AFDC) to reflect a targeting of families (including mothers) rather than individual children. In 1961 the program was expanded in approximately half the states to include unemployed parents (AFDC-UP), thus providing aid to intact families with an unemployed male head. The 1988 Family Support Act required that AFDC-UP be implemented in all states by 1994.[2]

The goal of AFDC is to provide for the basic needs of destitute families,

2. As of this writing, I do not know whether in fact the program has been implemented in all states.

in particular those related to shelter. Families that qualify for AFDC also automatically receive Medicaid for coverage of their health care costs. Finally, food costs are paid by food stamps, a separate program enacted in 1964 and administered by the U.S. Department of Agriculture. The latter provides recipients with coupons (as opposed to cash) that may be used to purchase food items only. In Michigan, these programs are administered through the county offices of the Department of Social Services, to which potential recipients apply for aid.

Although the Michigan Department of Social Services was not established until 1939, Michigan has a long history of public relief. Poor laws were enacted as early as 1790 and poorhouses established in the early 1830s, even before Michigan was admitted to statehood in 1837. The Department of Social Services that was established in 1939 had its origins in the State Welfare Department, established in 1921, and its predecessors, the State Board of Corrections and Charities, established in 1879, and the Board of State Commissioners for the General Supervision of Charitable, Penal, Pauper and Reformatory Institutions, established in 1871 (Michigan Department of Social Services 1989).

The funds for AFDC come from both federal and state sources. In the fiscal year 1990, 46.2 percent of the Michigan DSS budget came from federal funds, while 48.2 percent came from state funds (the remaining 5.6 percent came from "other" funds). The federal funding for AFDC was 55 percent and the state funding 45 percent. Of the department's entire budget, the greatest single portion, 39 percent, was spent on Financial Support Programs. Although the state shares administrative costs of food stamps with the federal government, funding for the actual food obtained through the program is 100 percent federal (Michigan Department of Social Services Biennial Report 1989–1990).

AFDC is a means-tested program, which requires applicants to meet federal and state criteria of eligibility in order to receive benefits. First, potential recipients must have at least one child. Poor adults without children are not eligible for AFDC. (Prior to fall 1991, when the program was terminated, single adults in Michigan could apply for General Assistance, a solely state-funded and -administered program.) Second, applicants' income and assets must fall below a certain limit established by the state. In 1990, for instance, Michigan asset limits for a family of three wishing to receive AFDC were $1000 plus $1500 in equity value on a car. Once enrolled in the program, recipients receive checks every two weeks to cover "basic needs" (rent and utilities) and "personal needs" (clothing, toiletries, laundry, transportation, and so forth). The amount of the check, or "grant," varies for different areas of the state, called zones, in order to reflect geographic variation in the cost of living; additionally, individual "grant" levels fluctuate to reflect changes in recipients' other sources of income. Food stamps are provided on a monthly basis.

Benefits are not "free," however. As mandated by the Family Support Act of 1988, recipients who are less than three months pregnant or who have children over three years of age must attend school or other job training programs, or find employment. In Michigan this requirement is embodied by the Michigan Opportunity and Skills Training (MOST) program.

The model for the Family Support Act and the MOST program is the social contract, in which there is supposedly an exchange between recipients and the welfare system. Specifically, recipients participate in training programs in exchange for a variety of services related to job placement and child and medical care. Recipients, in other words, are not "entitled" to benefits, but rather are subject to the "obligations" of citizenship (Mead 1986). The notion of contract, however, is somewhat misleading. First, sanctions are imposed on only one party (recipients) for failing to fulfill their part of the contract (Abramovitz 1988b; Handler and Hasenfeld 1991); second, it is difficult to portray the contract as free and voluntary "when one party lacks the barest means of subsistence while the other is the U.S. government" (Fraser and Gordon 1992:64).

The idea of contract, or exchange, nevertheless underlies current debate on welfare reform, much of which centers on various programs to reduce "welfare dependency." Some proposed reforms emphasize positive incentives, for example, promises to increase income "disregards" (the amount of a recipient's earned income that can be disregarded before reductions are made in her AFDC "grant") so that recipients can keep more of their paychecks. The logic is that with income disregards, recipients will be more inclined to seek and remain in paid work. Other proposed reforms are designed to provide negative sanctions for what is perceived as increased dependency on the welfare system. "Family cap" proposals calling for the imposition of financial penalties on recipients who increase their family size once they are on the welfare rolls are typical of this kind of negative reform. Finally, a number of potential reform measures combine positive and negative sanctions, such as those that would decrease recipients' benefits if they or their children fail to attend school and provide bonuses if they do (National Health Policy Forum 1992). In all cases, at both federal and state levels, emphasis is placed on the need for recipients to somehow "earn" their benefits, either by making money or gaining an education, or, at least, by learning certain "values," such as reproductive responsibility. This points to the third party in the Republican "Contract with America," namely, the "silent majority" which funds welfare programs. It is ostensibly in the interests of this silent majority that frugal, and in many cases punitive, policies are designed.

Underlying the emphasis on exchange is the ideology of "personal responsibility." This ideology stresses the accountability of individuals while discouraging analyses of social structure or economic organization. In a 1992 radio address, for instance, President Bush claimed that individuals on public assistance have a responsibility to pursue the means—that is, education or a job—to "get their lives in order," and that they need to establish "lifestyles that will enable them to fulfill their potential, not destroy it" (National Health Policy Forum 1992:3; see also Meucci 1992). In this formulation, the key actor—the key responsible actor—is the individual. The state should play a role in encouraging "personal responsibility," but it is up to the individual to move beyond dependency to independence. Although, in contrast to Reagan and Bush, President Clinton has conceded that macroeconomic forces do have an impact on poverty, he has, nevertheless, "joined . . . in the conservative attacks on 'welfare dependency,' accepting the view that the receipt of help must reduce one's 'independence,' that support for the poor should be minimized, that recipients should be moved off the welfare rolls and into 'work' as soon as possible, and that childraising does not count as work" (Fraser 1993:17). Echoing Bush's "lifestyles that will enable them to fulfill their potential, not destroy it" is Clinton's slogan that welfare should be "a second chance, not a way of life" (ibid.). The Clinton administration, then, provides little promise of positive change in the lives of poor American women. Indeed, there seems to be somewhat of a consensus about welfare reform that cuts across the political spectrum. In this light Handler and Hasenfeld (1991:241) compare Mead's (1986) discussion of the obligations of citizenship with that of Heidi Hartmann, who states,

In general, I believe that most [welfare] benefits should be tied to employment or participation in training programs. As working for wages increasingly becomes the norm for all women, the fact that poor, young minority women are "stockpiled" on welfare programs increasingly disadvantages them. They, like all women, need to learn labor market skills and progress toward self-sufficiency. Of course, not everyone is able to work, and social programs that provide a decent standard of living for those unable to work are needed as well. (1987:58)

Inextricably tied to this ideology of "personal responsibility" are the very real needs of the labor market. There has been an increasing shortage of low-skilled (and therefore low-paid) workers, a problem with serious implications for employers who may then be pressured to increase wage rates (Abramovitz 1988b). The 1988 Family Support Act thus provides one way of subsidizing the low-wage labor market.

In sum, the political climate is not a friendly one for poor women on relief. It is against this backdrop of an escalating war against the poor that the women's narratives must be interpreted.

Interview Methods

As I have stated, the women's welfare narratives were produced in interviews. I followed two approaches to interviewing. One was to schedule events called "interviews" with individual women, for the purpose of discussing their experiences with the welfare system. Although I orchestrated these events, I made every effort to follow Briggs's (1986:93) admonition to "listen before you leap," to conduct interviews in ways that capitalized on, rather than violated, received ways of communicating. Although I had sets of questions in mind, the order in which questions were discussed and how participants chose to address them were unspecified. In addition, other topics or approaches to topics introduced by the women were not glossed over but rather pursued. Mishler (1986) has claimed that people will often tell stories when not prevented from doing so by the asymmetries of power so often evident in standard interviews; stories and other narratives are, he points out, "one of the natural cognitive and linguistic forms through which individuals attempt to order, organize, and express meaning" (1986:106). The women who participated in this study often did respond to my inquiries with stories.

My second approach to gathering data followed Briggs's (1986:121) call to avoid what he calls "communicative hegemony," the imposition of particular forms of communication. Not only do standard interviews often constrain interaction to the classic question-answer format, they may also violate local norms of who gets to ask questions of whom, under what circumstances, and concerning which topics. To minimize the effects of communicative hegemony, I made every effort to ask questions informally, when they were topically and contextually appropriate. Opportunities to do this presented themselves both during "interviews," when I followed the women's lead in the introduction of topics, and on occasions when more than one woman was present (e.g., informal chitchat at someone's kitchen table). This approach has ethical as well as methodological strengths. Research ethics clearly go beyond merely gaining formal consent—which may be both a particularly western and class-based value, needless to say a legal imperative—to ongoing respect: in this case, respect for participants' time constraints and for received ways of communicating. Of course, I was not always successful in displaying this respect, and I may have neglected other forms of respect that I was unable to recognize.

In sum, the following themes emerged from the stories the women told in interviews and in more informal conversations. They represent not only patterns of interpretation among the women—how they made sense of their lives—but also what they believed was important for me, as an outsider to the experiences of poverty and welfare, to know.

Working Is Expensive

The uniqueness of women's poverty has prompted feminist scholars to criticize the "male pauper" model of welfare, which has as its subject the single able-bodied adult male.[3] As Pearce (1984:510) points out, "the traditional analysis of the problem of poverty for the able-bodied poor has been quite simple: their problem is joblessness, and the solution is to 'give' them a job. . . . The simple formula 'joblessness is the problem, jobs are the solution' does not work for women because their poverty is different from that of men."

Although they did not use the term, the women I interviewed clearly recognized the shortcomings of the "male pauper" model. They were unanimous in the conviction that employment was costly: it was a way to *lose* money, not make it. As with many women on welfare, a lack of educational credentials left the women restricted to minimum wage work, primarily in the service sector. Such work, while providing more income than AFDC, typically failed to furnish medical coverage, which the women strongly desired, or child care, which was a necessity. Minimum wage jobs, then, were considered a losing proposition.

Martha Hill had learned this lesson well. Her first encounter with public assistance occurred after her divorce, when she was awarded insufficient alimony to care for her five children. Her initial reaction to this encounter was to try to remove herself from the welfare rolls by finding employment—contrary to the advice of her AP worker at the time, who suggested that she focus on her education instead. Martha quickly discovered that she could not make ends meet, enrolled once again for AFDC, and decided to try the education route, with which she had been struggling ever since. Her response to a recent suggestion made by another worker that she seek employment illustrates what she learned from this experience:

You know, I had one ((worker)) who wanted me to go to a high school or adult education classes and I said, "I have all of high school and I have (a) really great grade point (average)," and she goes "well then why aren't you working?" I said, "I, I know I can go out and get a minimum wage job or two or three, in a, you know, this week. My problem is that whenever I go to work, I can't pay . . . rent. Now if you can tell me that I would be a couple hundred dollars ahead, you won't have a problem, but I have not, I've never yet come out ahead." I mean, it's not

3. See Gans (1992) for an example of the male pauper model of poverty.

like you can mark your money "made at Quality Dairy" ((a local convenience store chain)) (and it sounds) better, you know. (Martha Hill 8/8/90)

Other women echoed this sentiment. Mary McDonald, for instance, argued that the policy of deducting a certain amount from AFDC "grants" for each dollar earned "punishes" people who try to work. Janet Burns was penalized in this way when she increased her work hours only to be faced with cuts that would leave her unable to meet her housing and child care costs. Dee Cook also found that she was poorer when employed than when receiving AFDC and food stamps; it was, she said, "like I was just working for the experience of it" (Dee Cook 2/17/90). Dee, who had taken an economics course at the local community college, felt that welfare—or, as she called it, "wealthfare"—functioned to keep people poor so that the wealthy would be provided with a cheap source of labor. This claim of being poorer on the job than on welfare was, of course, a relative one, since AFDC, even when coupled with Medicaid and food stamps, was insufficient in itself to meet the women's basic needs (see pp. 2, 29).

Child care was a major factor in the women's negative views of employment and played a major role in their decisions to either avoid it or find under-the-table work. Without even the meager subsidies for child care provided by the welfare department, then, employment was something that the women could rarely afford to engage in: "it's just cheaper . . . to not work" (Katie Devon 8/16/89). Subsidies provided through the Michigan Opportunity and Skills Training (MOST) program did not hold out much promise either. On the one hand, the work requirement is coupled with various forms of support: education and job training, child care and medical support during participation in the program and for one year following the termination of AFDC benefits in favor of paid employment. On the other hand, shortages of jobs that pay enough and the inability of federal and state governments to meet the costs related to training and child and medical care mean that "the rhetoric" of programs like MOST "will not be matched by its operational reality" (Handler and Hasenfeld 1991:214). In fact, work program "success stories" are often in the long run stories of failure, insofar as a number of workfare graduates are forced into jobs that fail to provide adequate income and as a consequence find themselves back on the relief rolls after one or two years.

The women's talk about employment thus reflects material realities. Their narratives clearly subvert the work ethic: although they all initially attempted to conform to dominant views of work and economic self-sufficiency, they discovered that employment has little value in and of itself. Martha Hill, for instance, claims that, "it's not like you can mark your money 'made at Quality Dairy' (and it sounds) better"—in other words, money from a paycheck is no better than money from AFDC. She thereby counters the prevailing view that any kind of paid work (independence) is better than welfare (dependence). In addition, in refusing to engage in paid labor given the constraints of child care costs, the women indicted the welfare department's meager child care provisions; such a move contests official departmental claims that welfare recipients should be gainfully employed and that the system accommodates women by paying for child care. Unlike single able-bodied adult males, most AFDC recipients are mothers, with primary responsibility for the care of infants and children. This responsibility is usually ignored and rarely recognized materially or sufficiently by welfare programs or employers. The women's responses, then, provide a specifically gendered critique of the welfare system. The narratives they produce, in which they step out of the norm and reveal or challenge dominant views, provide examples of what may be referred to as counter-narratives (Personal Narratives Group 1989).

The women's stories were also sometimes mixed (Personal Narratives Group 1989), containing elements of acquiescence as well as subversion. Susan Harrison's story about the sexual molestation of her children is a case in point. Three years previously, Susan began working as a prostitute in the hopes of eventually removing herself from the welfare rolls. In response to pressure from her family, however, she left prostitution for a job paying $200 a week, much less than the $1,500 a week she sometimes earned as a prostitute. Since she no longer had enough money to pay for an adult baby-sitter, Susan hired some local teenagers, who soon after sexually molested her children. For Susan, trying to do things the "right way" by getting a "respectable" job turned out to be the wrong way. She learned that playing by the rules had numerous, and often unacceptable, costs. As she put it, "I put my kids' lives in jeopardy to try to get off it ((welfare))" (Susan Harrison 8/9/89). Both she and her children would have been better off if she had not tried to earn money legitimately and instead had simply accepted being a welfare recipient and/or prostitute.

Susan's story highlights the oppositions of legitimate versus illegitimate work, and the conflicts between motherhood and employment. She found that accommodating dominant views of appropriate work hindered her abilities to fulfill hegemonic models of good parenting. In her experience, the kind of job that allowed her to conform to models of both work (in itself, rather than in its appropriate or inappropriate forms) and parenting was prostitution, an illegitimate and stigmatized occupation. Susan's story thus runs counter to prevailing categories of appropriate and inappropriate work, yet nevertheless fails to question the idea that all "able-bodied" adults should earn a living; nor does she contest a mother's total responsibility for the care of her children. As such, her story provides an example of a mixed narrative.

Education Is the Way Out

In contrast to these mixed and counter-narratives, the women's talk about education represents a status quo approach. Protagonists in a status quo narrative accept and are willing to perpetuate the dominant system, of which they consider themselves to be potential, if not actual, beneficiaries (Personal Narratives Group 1989). In this case, the dominant system consists of mainstream models of achievement and success. In short, if a minimum wage job was not the answer to welfare, a well-paid job was, and the way to get a well-paid job was to get an education. Katie Devon was clear about this connection: "the only way to get off welfare is to go through school, that is the only way, because, you make more money living on welfare than you do at a job . . . at a minimum wage job—or even a four dollar an hour job" (Katie Devon, 8/16/89). The women's pursuit of educational credentials indicates that Katie's conviction was shared: Mary McDonald was taking courses in interior design and real estate, Tara Hope was trying to complete her high school diploma, Martha Hill was in a nursing program, Susan Harrison was enrolled in paralegal courses, Dee Cook was in her third year of pre-medical studies at a local community college, and Maggie Fletcher and Janet Burns hoped to end their short careers as welfare recipients when they entered graduate school.

As striking as the ubiquity of the perception that education was crucial to "making it," however, was the frequency with which the women began but did not complete educational programs. Pat Graham, Mary McDonald, Jane Thomas, Martha Hill, and Susan Harrison were all unable to finish their courses of study. As Jane put it, in response to the financial pressures involved, "I got sick of going to school, I said the heck with school, I dropped out of adult (education) six times" (Jane Thomas 3/12/90). The women nevertheless continued to trust in the value of an education. Although my data on this issue are sparse, it is reasonable to assume that the same financial and child care burdens the women experienced when employed also plagued their attempts to complete their educations. The difference from the women's perspective was that, while they could never get ahead on a minimum wage job, completing an education offered an eventual payback. Thus they did not criticize the meager child care provisions of the welfare department when discussing education as they did when discussing employment, although the amounts provided were the same. This gives testimony to the power of the idea that education is the means to advancement and economic security.

This status quo view of education was shared by all the women except Louise Black and Janet Burns, who had college degrees and thus knew from experience that education was not a panacea. Although Louise was eventually able to use her college degree to remove herself from the AFDC rolls, it was such a struggle that she finally accepted a post in Barbados, remarking that (paraphrase) "I have to go *overseas* to get a decent job!" Along with Janet, Louise disagreed with the idea that poverty was an individual problem that could be remedied through individual effort (such as the pursuit of educational credentials). The cause, rather, was systemic, reflecting an inequitable economic structure (MWRO 5/9/90). As such, the views expressed by Louise and Janet would provide examples of counter-narratives resistant to the status quo.

Dependence/Independence

Despite their differences, the "education is the way out" and "working is expensive" themes may be viewed within the context of a key binary in current welfare discourse, that of dependence/independence. As Fraser and Gordon (1994) point out, the meaning of "dependency" is historically specific: while at one point it referred to a constellation of social relations that were the norm and in most cases not stigmatized (as in being dependent on an employer for one's living), its meaning has now been narrowed to refer specifically to inherent, primarily negative, individual or group traits. In our current postindustrial society, social-structural dependencies have ostensibly been eliminated; thus, "whatever dependency remains . . . can be interpreted as the fault of individuals" (Fraser and Gordon 1994: 325). In fact, many social-structural dependencies have simply been obfuscated, as when the worker who is dependent on an employer for a living is defined as an independent and "free" wage laborer. Nevertheless, dependency is now individualized as pathology; it is "as if the social relations of dependency were being absorbed into personality" (331). Again, as with the ideology of "personal responsibility" discussed above, such discourse detracts from the structural aspects of poverty while focusing attention on the individual (or group) poor.

Dependency also has gender and race subtexts. The feminization of the term is related to the historical development of the "housewife" and the hegemony of the "family wage," also rooted in the industrial period. Dependency thus took its particular meanings in relation to its opposite, independence, particularly as represented by the free Anglo male earning a family wage (Fraser and Gordon 1994). The racialization of the term has its roots in industrial justifications of colonization and slavery. In current welfare discourse, "welfare dependency" evokes images of usually young and African American single mothers. Although seemingly less relevant to this study of Anglo welfare recipients, the race subtext of dependency is nevertheless important insofar as *all* recipients take on the negative attributes of the "dependent." Today's "welfare dependent" stands in opposition to the "independent" individual in every way, serving to both define the boundaries and constitute the particular meanings of dependence/independence.

In one sense, the "work is expensive" theme reinforces the negative meaning of "welfare dependency": all the women tried to become economically self-sufficient, and they all valued the status of "independent" wage earner. At the same time, however, the theme contests the idea that dependence results from individual pathology. The reason the women gave up their jobs in favor of welfare was that the jobs they had access to did not pay enough to meet their needs. This points to problems in economic structures rather than in individual personalities. In contradistinction, the "education is the way out" theme accommodates and reproduces the dependent/independent binary by coupling individual effort with success and security. Although Katie Devon claimed that she needed an education because minimum wage work didn't pay, neither she nor any of the other women were critical of the deficiencies of the minimum wage. Rather, it was up to them as individuals to acquire skills deserving of a livable income.

Welfare Inadequacies and Weighty Symbols

Although the jobs available to the women and the costs of child care often led them to "choose" public assistance over—or, in many cases, in addition to—paid labor, they also unanimously agreed that AFDC and food stamps did not provide sufficient resources for survival. Everyone experienced difficulty in meeting her family's basic needs, and comments about letting bills pile up, using "personal needs" funds to pay for heat, and being hungry at the end of the month were ubiquitous. Welfare "grants" failed to cover both the items for which they were targeted and numerous other necessary yet uncovered expenses. In 1990, for example, only 30 percent of Michigan recipients received enough in their shelter allowance to actually cover their shelter costs (Michigan Department of Social Services 1990).

The symbolic force of certain material shortages was particularly poignant for the women, and the absence of particular items, or classes of items, was acutely painful to them. Maggie Fletcher and her friends, for instance, recognized a powerful connection between milk and mothering, and their inability to provide milk for their children meant that they fell short of societal standards of motherhood. As Maggie put it:

and with a kid, and (you) know talking with other . . . AFDC mothers, you always feel if you have milk in the refrigerator, you know . . . then, you're meeting some kind of maternal need . . . . Milk is symbolic or something, it really is. (Maggie Fletcher 5/26/89)

Maggie also discussed how much she had missed toilet paper when she had been a welfare recipient. Now that she was no longer on AFDC, she claimed to be "phobic," always needing to have eight rolls in the house at a time. Her friends who were still receiving welfare remarked on her affluence when they saw her supply. Just as milk was symbolic of one's ability to provide for one's children, so toilet paper was symbolic of one's ability to meet one's own basic needs.

Christmas stories also highlighted the deprivations of poverty and welfare. On one occasion, for instance, Laura Baxter, Susan Harrison, and Susan's boyfriend, Fred Thompson, lamented their inability to provide their children with gifts at Christmas. Laura began by recounting how she "cried and cried at Christmas because I looked at my Christmas tree (and) there was nothing under it, my kids had nothing, my kids didn't have nothing." In the end she resorted to symbolic gifts: she borrowed presents from her mother to put under the tree so it wouldn't look empty. Susan then told her own story about using rent money for gifts and a pine tree limb in a bucket decorated with a child's cut-outs for want of finer ornaments:

When I was pregnant with her ((pointing to her daughter, Tiffany)), and I had to move outa my house, and sign my land over to my mom, so I could get ADC, in Virginia when Martin ((her husband)) left the second time, I was seven months pregnant with her, we had a pine tree limb in a bucket in the house, and what Jack made in first grade is what covered that tree, and I got three hundred dollars my first check, no food stamps, no nothing . . . but, I took my, my rental money, and I went to the store and I bought ten dollars worth of Christmas stuff, and that's what they had for Christmas. (LIFE 8/19/90)

What seemed most painful to the women was their inability to provide their children with a proper Christmas. This again indicates the importance of their identities as mothers, who, in order to be deemed adequate, are responsible for providing for all of their children's needs— needs which in U.S. culture include the delights of childhood as well as the basic necessities of food and shelter. The women thus experienced trouble meeting not only essential but also "extra" needs. These "extra" needs consisted of those material necessities crucial to adult identity in American capitalist society, but unrecognized—and, in a twist on a Marxist concept, perhaps deemed "false"—by the welfare system, and when it comes to poor people, by society at large. The inability to fulfill these "extra" needs left the women feeling doubly deprived, and doubly inadequate.

Despite the sense of defeat the women contested these absences and the associated feelings of inadequacy. Their defiance nevertheless included elements of conformity, resulting in the production of mixed narratives. For instance, in recounting her use of rent money for Christmas presents, Susan produces a story of resistance to both welfare regulations and an ideology that says that poor people shouldn't have "luxuries," especially at taxpayers' expense. In her resistance, however, Susan accommodates both consumerism and the dominant view that it is a parent's (in this case a mother's) responsibility to provide for all a child's needs and wants.

Stigma

The AFDC rolls increased dramatically in the 1960s. Rising by 17 percent during the period 1950–1960, they swelled by 107 percent during the period 1960–1969, with 71 percent of this growth occurring from 1964 to 1969 (Piven and Cloward 1971:186). According to Katz (1990),

Even though the cost remained a small and shrinking fraction of the total budget for social welfare,[4] it bore the onus of public hostility, which inflated popular conceptions of its relative cost and generosity (AFDC never lifted women over the official poverty line) and fueled myths about the poor women who turned to it for survival. AFDC clients fueled [sic] sexuality and welfare into a powerful image that touched deep, irrational fears embedded in American culture. As they refused to be grateful and demanded public assistance as a right, they provoked a transformation in the historic relation between women and welfare. Poor women now became the undeserving poor. (1990:68)

All the women in this study referred to the stigma of being on welfare, of being one of the undeserving poor. Food stamps, a visible marker of one's status as a welfare recipient—as Maggie Fletcher said, "you're branded by your food stamps"—were often the focus of stories of stigma:

I was living in this one apartment, and waiting and waiting for (them), you know you wait for the food stamps to come . . . and, for like three or four or five days . . . I hope our food stamps come, and this was when I first moved to Penrose, and was living in kind of a middle class . . . neighborhood. . . . I hated to go outside the door 'cause I felt so different . . . and I went through a whole thing there where I wouldn't even check my mail until after dark, you know, I just felt

4. In 1987, the federal share of AFDC accounted for less than 1% (0.76%) of the federal budget (Abramovitz 1988b:294).

so odd . . . anyway, so . . . it was one day, and the mailman came, and Dale, (he) was like three or something, and he was outside playing, he saw the mailman put the food stamps in the mailbox and he started screaming, "MOM! OUR FOOD STAMPS ARE HERE! OUR FOOD STAMPS ARE HERE!," like this ((laughing)) you know . . . and I was just so humiliated, I said, "GET IN HERE!," you know . . . and in one way it was real funny, but in another it was so pathetic . . . you know, and he was waiting so desperately for 'em too . . . you know, and, it was just, and that's how it was. (Maggie Fletcher 5/26/89)

Maggie's references to being "humiliated" and to feeling "different" and "odd" illustrate her experience of stigma. Other adjectives for feelings associated with using food stamps included "embarrassing," "horrible," and "degrading." Women related stories of "dirty looks" received from people behind them in line at the grocery store, and of cashiers holding up food stamps and yelling loudly to other cashiers for change (smaller denominations of food stamps). Ironically, while a U.S. one dollar bill has photographs of George Washington, the Great Pyramid, and the American eagle and flag, a $1 food stamp features photographs of the Declaration of Independence and the Liberty Bell, as if to illustrate those great American values and principles that recipients should be striving for, but have as yet failed to attain.

Most of the women developed strategies for minimizing these humiliating experiences. Maggie, for instance, told of friends who would only shop late at night, and of one woman who dressed in her fanciest clothes to shop, "for her pride"—a strategy that inadvertently may serve to reinforce stereotypes of food stamp "abusers" on which much stigma is based. These responses reflect a collusion with the stigma of food stamps, and are thus status quo narratives, despite the fact that the narrators clearly do not benefit from the status quo. The literature on public assistance contains many discussions of policies (some more implicit than others) designed to deter the use of public assistance by means of embarrassment, shame and humiliation (e.g., Katz 1986; Piven and Cloward 1971). In the case of food stamps, the public shame suffered by recipients deters other would-be recipients. Insofar as the women acquiesce in its effects, they are contributing to the efficacy of this policy.

There were exceptions to this conformity. Maggie's story of her friend who dressed up to shop is also a counter-narrative describing a form of resistance. In so dressing, the woman works against public disgrace, thereby mitigating the deterrent impact that seeing someone use food stamps might have on potential recipients. Two other women, Dee Cook and Mary McDonald, similarly refused to participate in public displays of shame. Dee's understanding was that AFDC and food stamps were "loans," and that, once she got a job, the social security deducted from her paychecks and the support payments made by her child's father would go directly to the state to pay back the loans. Consequently, she felt no need to be embarrassed about food stamps. For her part, Mary felt that, since no one else in her family had ever received public assistance and she was only temporarily "stuck" in the system, she had no reason to feel inferior: "I don't think that anybody treats me rude on it or anything like that but maybe, I really don't pay attention because it doesn't matter" (Mary McDonald 2/21/90). Mary's and Dee's responses represent counter-narratives, resistant to the status quo.

Regardless of their approach to it, however, all the recipients who participated in this study were aware of the stigma associated with being on welfare and felt compelled to address it in one way or another—by telling horror stories about it, by taking action to publicly identify themselves as other than "welfare recipient," or by refusing to give in to it. The stigmatized nature of public relief indicates that the discourse of welfare is directed at the non-poor as much as at the poor. With the symbols mobilized in welfare discourse, our world is constructed to include certain kinds of individuals, norms, institutions, and policies; within these constructions, individuals are accorded or denied social citizenship. The distinction in the Mothers' Pensions programs between those women who were viewed as "morally fit" and those who were not, for instance, provides an example of the power of deserving/undeserving, us/them dichotomies. In translating these distinctions into policy whereby Anglo widows (the "morally fit") were provided aid while the rest (women of color, deserted, divorced, and single mothers) were constituted as unfit and thereby denied aid, the idea and practice of "virtuous" women fulfilling their proper role was constructed and given symbolic and material force. According to R. Smith (1990), "Working-class and poor women were held to the same moral and social standard as middle- and upper-class women, but the purpose of the standard was to mark them as outsiders" (1990:223).

A similar argument may be made about contemporary workfare programs, which are "myth and ceremony, designed to affirm the modern, contemporary, middle-class employed mother by ensuring the failure and moral condemnation of the welfare mother" (Handler and Hasenfeld 1991:42). In the 1988 Family Support Act women's proper place is not in the home, but rather—or also—in the workplace. This view reflects current labor requirements and the fact that a large number of women with young children are in the paid labor force (Handler and Hasenfeld 1991). The construction of mothers as able-bodied workers harks back to the days prior to the Mothers' Pensions of the early twentieth century; the new morality is thus the old morality of the work ethic:

"Work is the providence of the modern peoples; it replaces morality, fills the gaps left by beliefs and is regarded as the principle of all good" (Foucault 1979:242, cited in R. Smith 1990:226).

In this sense, welfare policy is more than welfare policy. The moral degradation of recipients not only deters would-be recipients from seeking public assistance by making it more unpleasant than the lowest of the low-paid and degrading jobs, but also symbolically supports the economic order (R. Smith 1990:20). The existence of the poor, after all, questions current economic structures and the economic contract (Handler and Hasenfeld 1991), since they clearly do not work to everyone's benefit. This question must be answered, and it is answered by transforming the poor into the abnormal, and taking measures to prevent people from slipping from one side to the other. Thus Garfinkel (1956) points to the specifically *public* nature of "status degradation ceremonies," in which individuals are effectively reconstituted as specific types of persons. The message is directed not only at the object of degradation (the welfare recipient), but, perhaps more important, at the participants in the degradation, be they perpetrators or witnesses (see also Foucault 1979).

In addition to the economic order, narrowly conceived, the existence of the poor challenges the larger symbolic and conceptual order of liberal bourgeois society (R. Smith 1990). Put simply, liberal society makes a distinction between "good" or ordered nature and "bad" or disordered nature, the first under control and the second out of control. The poor, as representative of need and desire rather than autonomy and the rational pursuit of interests, are associated with disorderly "bad" nature, at the margins of ordered society and citizenship. The discourse of welfare thus provides not only for the control of the poor themselves, but also for "an ordered way for society to think about the poor that in turn stigmatizes the poor by the 'nonnatural'—that is, nonnormative—character of welfare institutions in a market economy" (Smith 1990:212). In constituting the poor as outside the boundaries of society, the discourse of poverty serves to define those boundaries, and thus to constitute liberal society itself. Again, Garfinkel's analysis of degradation ceremonies is useful here: the character of the denounced individual is always constructed in opposition to an ideal character (e.g., needy versus autonomous) and ritually removed from the legitimate order (1956:423). Women in particular, as well as the poor in general, represent "bad," disordered nature. Not only do women make up the majority of adult poor in contemporary U.S. society, but, like the poor in general, they are constructed as lacking autonomy and a capacity for the rational pursuit of interest. Instead, they are seen to be ruled by sexual passion and desire (perhaps akin to the neediness of the poor), and, as such, cannot hold the status of citizen (R. Smith 1990).

The stigma experienced by the women in this study also reflects the dual, or two-channel, U.S. welfare system (see Fraser 1989; Fraser and Gordon 1992; Nelson 1990; Pearce 1990). The first channel, the male channel, includes what are referred to as "contributory" social insurance programs, such as unemployment, workers' compensation, and Social Security. These programs ostensibly provide benefits on the basis of the contributions of recipients through their previous employment. Recipients are thus "entitled" to their benefits—they have earned them. The individuals targeted by these programs are accordingly positioned as "rights bearers" (citizens) and as "purchasing consumers" who may use their cash benefits as they see fit (Fraser 1989). Significantly, recipients—most of whom are men—are not subject to social stigma: they are not portrayed as "freeloaders," their privacy is not intruded upon, and they are not subject to rituals of degradation. Rather, they are deserving citizens who, *through no fault of their own,* are temporarily unable to care for themselves.

The second channel, on the other hand—the female channel—consists of "noncontributory"[5] programs, such as AFDC and food stamps. Referred to as public assistance rather than social insurance, the programs provide benefits on the basis of taxpayers' contributions, providing support for individuals who (at least the adults) have not fulfilled the "social obligations of citizenship" (Mead 1986). These obligations do not, of course, include unpaid housework or the rearing of children, but are constituted to include solely paid work. The majority of adult recipients of these programs, however, are women, who are most often the ones responsible for childcare and housework. In addition, and in contrast to the experience of social insurance beneficiaries, recipients of public assistance are stigmatized: they are subject to constant scrutiny

5. Fraser and Gordon (1992) reveal the misleading nature of the distinction between "contributory" and "noncontributory" programs by pointing to the contributory nature of all welfare programs. They state that:

all welfare programs are financed through "contributions," differing only as to where and how these are collected—through sales taxes or wage deductions, for example. Despite their official image as contractual, Social Security "insurance" programs depart significantly from actuarial principles, and benefits do not actually reflect financial contributions. And while the legitimacy of Social Security retirement pensions derives in part from the view that they compensate previous service, one might with equal plausibility claim that seemingly "noncontributory" programs like Aid to Families with Dependent Children . . . compensate the childrearing "service" of single mothers. (1992:61) and rituals of degradation—in short, to the suspension of many of their civil rights (Fraser and Gordon 1992). Recipients of public assistance are in a fundamental sense *noncitizens*; they are not "entitled" and they do not have the "right" to their benefits, and moreover, they often receive benefits "in kind" (e.g., food stamps, rent paid directly to landlords) rather than cash. They are not "rights bearers" but "clients" (Fraser 1989).

The distinction between the "deserving" and "undeserving" poor thus has very specific gendered features. The key attribute of a "deserving" male is his willingness to labor. Able-bodied men unwilling to labor because of alcoholism or some other moral failing are "undeserving." The case with women is different. Willingness to labor has been only one criterion in determining a woman's status as "deserving" or "undeserving"; the other has been her general moral stature, more specifically, her sexual behavior, which has in the past been discussed in terms of her "fitness" to raise children (Nelson 1990). Indeed, until 1968, welfare departments held a mandate to raid women's homes in the middle of the night in order to determine whether they were engaging in illicit sexual affairs. Called "man in the house" rules, such policies were ostensibly designed to ensure that women would be supported by the men in their lives rather than by the welfare department; they also barred men's access to welfare, thereby keeping them in the labor pool (Piven and Cloward 1988). However, "man in the house" rules are clearly also part and parcel of society's view of poor women as promiscuous. Indeed, if such couples were caught, it was the woman who was punished by losing her welfare "grant," rather than the man by being legally forced to provide financial support for his partner and her children. The "suitable home" rules enacted in the southern states, which penalized women with illegitimate children, reflected similar sentiments and served the additional function of coercing poor women of color into low-paid labor (Piven and Cloward 1971, 1988). Although suspended for a time, proposals for policies directed at regulating women's reproductive behavior are gaining currency. Clearly, the economic bases of such proposals also need to be considered. Piven and Cloward (1988:643) have claimed in this regard that "the preoccupation with family morality [is] deceptive"—that market forces have always been at the heart of welfare policy (see also Neubeck and Roach 1981), a claim supported by the work stipulations of the 1988 Family Support Act. The issue of morality nevertheless remains a powerful one in the discourse of welfare, and the provision of aid continues to have moral overtones. At a more subtle level than official policy, street-level bureaucrats' perceptions of recipients' moral characters have an impact, ranging from whether or not applicants receive public aid to how quickly their applications are processed to the amount of information they receive on other assistance programs for which they might be eligible.

Stigma is a key feature of this cultural and economic imperative to distinguish between the "deserving" and "undeserving" poor, a distinction which points to fundamental beliefs about poverty, wealth, and adulthood in the United States. Parker (1973) has pointed out that western views of poverty and wealth were transformed during the Industrial Revolution from phenomena associated with the workings of God to phenomena reflecting personal and moral character. The latter views were part and parcel of the European poor laws that formed the basis of relief measures instituted in the United States. As Polanyi (1989:153) claims in her grammar of American culture, "proper people" (adults) should be able to take care of themselves; those who cannot are less than "proper people." Senator Daniel Moynihan exemplified this basic tenet of U.S. culture when he stated that "[Dependency] is an incomplete state in life: normal in the child, abnormal in the adult. In a world where completed men and women stand on their own feet, persons who are dependent—as the buried imagery of the word denotes—hang" (Moynihan 1973:17, cited in Fraser and Gordon 1994:309).

Moreover, the deserving/undeserving dichotomy seems to lie at the base of welfare policy (Handler and Hasenfeld 1991:7). The key question around which relief policy and reform revolves—who may be excused from having to earn a living and under what conditions (16)—indicates that welfare and labor discipline are inextricably linked. Welfare policy is both "the institutionalized production of *symbols* whose primary purpose is to affirm the dominant social values of work, family and gender roles, and social status," and "a system of *regulation* [that] . . . reflects the structural demands of federalism, the political economy, and bureaucracy" (17). It is perhaps not so difficult in this light to understand the currency of programs directed at reforming individuals (the alternative, as R. Smith (1990) indicates, is to see the poor, and poor women, as beyond repair), and the recent popularity of Murray (1984), Mead (1986), and Gilder (1981) among right-wing politicians in particular, who prefer to locate the problem of poverty in individuals rather than in institutional or structural forces.

The Requirements of Structural Constraint: Manipulation Versus Hyper-Truth

I mean, if you go in there blankly and naive like I did and you think, you know, you work honestly with them and all that . . . that'll last about a month or two . . . and then you, you'll hit some crisis, and then you go to your friends, and they tell you how to handle it. (Maggie Fletcher 5/26/89)

AFDC mothers—ones I knew myself—would present that (compliant) face to them, like they're controlling us and regulating us, but when you go home, we make our own decisions about certain things, but it also is a matter of complying to get something, anything. (Maggie Fletcher 5/26/89)

The recipients in this study described two distinct strategies for dealing with the various inadequacies of public relief. The first was to manipulate the welfare system by means of certain kinds of impression management (e.g., deference to workers), or by withholding information (e.g., about extra income or household composition). The second tactic was to play by the rules, but with a vengeance. This approach consisted of providing the welfare department with all the required information *plus* some, occasionally policing other welfare recipients who break the rules, and most of all, being aware of and demanding one's entitlements. I refer to these two approaches as "manipulation" and "hyper-truth" respectively. Seemingly diametrically opposed, and leading to different solutions, both strategies reflected a perception of welfare provisions as inadequate.

Manipulation

Manipulation, the most common of the two approaches, was based on the assumption that total honesty in dealing with the welfare system would decrease one's chances of survival, while, conversely, manipulation would increase them.

Lying. Like getting a minimum wage job, telling welfare workers the truth was considered an expensive proposition. The most common lie the women told concerned extra income, most often generated by under-the-table work or by the contributions of another (undeclared) adult living in the household. The following account of a friend who had to apply for "emergency needs,"[6] told to me by Louise Black, underscores the need to lie in order to survive.

Bids for Burial
Sally Bennett's baby died from sudden infant death syndrome, and she asked Louise Black to help her to apply for emergency funds to pay for the burial. When they arrived at the welfare office, they discovered that all of Sally's assets had to be taken into account: "if you have anything over 50 bucks it has to go in there" ((to cover the costs of the burial)). In her distress Sally was prepared to

6. "Emergency needs" designates a particular category of aid consisting of one-time grants given in emergency situations. Items typically covered under emergency needs include security deposit and first month's rent for homeless people or recipients who have been evicted, and coverage of bills to energy companies that are threatening to cut off a recipient's heat or electricity. If all people seeking public assistance can be characterized as desperate, those applying for emergency needs are doubly so.

list all the money she had. Realizing that if Sally did so she would be left without rent money, Louise told her, "you don't have any money, you spent it all. Who cares if you got a check yesterday, you paid the rent." Louise then went on to comment, "they want you to spend your rent money and . . . what do YOU know? Your BABY died for God's sake!" The point here, according to Louise, is "you have to lie, you know you have to lie."

Following a discussion of assets, Sally was then told by her AP worker that she would have to get bids for the cost of the burial. As the worker put it, "we need to know how much people will charge and . . . we have to go with the least expensive." Louise was outraged by the requirement that women seek bids while in the midst of grief: "they shouldn't have to, it shouldn't be that way," she said, blowing her nose as she tried to hold back the tears. "People who are waiting to apply for emergency needs, have bad stories, you know?" (Louise Black 9/7/89)

This story illustrates the coldness and cruelty of the welfare system in the face of human tragedy: even a baby's death fails to evoke compassion. The juxtaposition of issues of death and survival in Louise's account highlights the imperative to lie: under the psychological pressure of coping with her infant's death, Sally must deceive her AP worker in order to save her rent; if she does not (one could conjecture), she could suffer the additional loss of her shelter. In addition, Sally has to be *told* to lie—it does not come naturally. This need to lie to survive in the system is inexorable, grief and loss notwithstanding; thus Louise's conclusion that "people who are waiting to apply for emergency needs, have bad stories." In effect, the system itself produces the liars and cheats it so readily condemns.

Impression management. Scott (1990:3) points out that "one of the key survival skills of subordinate groups has been impression management in power-laden situations" (see also Goffman 1969). In this context, apparent compliance, which included agreeing (if only implicitly) with workers' views of recipients or of the welfare system, was a performance women engaged in to get what they wanted.

Compliance was not the only possible "face," however. Louise Black, for instance, claimed that "it depends, I mean, sometimes if you get real threatening to them ((e.g., identify yourself as a member of a welfare rights group)), they'll give you more too, they'll follow the rules" (Louise Black 9/7/89). Both approaches, however—or any others that might exist, such as feigning ignorance—illustrate the same point, namely, that the women felt that they had to put on a particular "face" when interacting with workers. This assumes that AP workers are not simply implementing policy (although policy was presented as immutable at any given point), but that they have some leeway and, more significant, the *power* to help some people more than others. It also presupposes that welfare is structurally inadequate—that even at its best, the resources it provides are insufficient.

Manipulation is resistant in nature, and the examples I have provided here may be characterized as counter-narratives. Neither Maggie Fletcher, in the deliberate performance of compliance, nor Louise Black, in her admonition to her friend to lie about assets when applying for emergency needs, accommodates the rules of the welfare system. Rather, they play at compliance, or simply defy the regulations.

Hyper-Truth

This strategy entailed an exaggerated playing by the rules: telling AP workers every detail, reporting changes that did not need to be reported, and filling out every required form and getting it in on time. As with manipulation, the hyper-truth approach took it as a given that public assistance, in the form in which one typically receives it, is insufficient for survival. Accordingly, this approach had two additional features that worked to improve one's living conditions while staying well within the regulations of the welfare system. The first was to hold the system to its own rules: if recipients had to play by the rules, then so did the welfare system. The assumption here is that one typically does not receive all of one's entitlements; rather, one has to force the issue. Thus Dee threatened to sue the welfare department when she was inappropriately cut off, and Mary pressured the department for three years to get a new roof put on her house. Playing by the rules was not passive, but rather entailed a specific kind of confrontation with the system.[7]

The second feature of this approach consisted of policing other clients. This strategy may have been based on a particular interpretation of the welfare system as inadequate, namely, one that saw resources being depleted through individual abuse (by potentially undeserving people), as opposed to one that saw resource insufficiency as a characteristic feature of the system itself. If the former were the case, then eliminating abuse would be the way to increase the availability of resources for others. There were only two women in the group, Mary McDonald and Jane Thomas, who reported taking steps to police other clients. The phenomenon is important, however, given the fact that many of the women felt that "welfare cheats" did exist, and that the activities of such individuals had a negative impact on the well-being of other, more honest, recipients.

Jane Thomas was particularly angered by people who, she felt, abused food stamps. She worked hard to stretch her own stamps (by, for ex-

7. Forcing the welfare department to play by its own rules was part of Louise Black's strategy when she referred to putting on a "threatening" face (see above). In her case, however, this was not coupled with any need to be honest herself; in fact, in Louise Black's view, as represented in her "bids for burial" story, honesty is counterproductive.

ample, mixing powdered and regular milk and buying in bulk), and was incensed by people who used their stamps to buy "junk food" or who plotted to get cash change for food stamps in order to purchase alcohol or cigarettes. Jane eventually contacted the police to check on the legality of such behavior, but did not pursue the issue any further. Mary McDonald was more direct in her policing of abusers, and more explicit about her reasons for doing so:

Well, I think a lot of people abuse food stamps, too ((C: how do they, in what ways?)) . . . . Well, like when I worked at Quality Dairy they would . . . get something that doesn't cost very much so they can get the change and then try . . . to come back, but, that kind of, pisses me off, so I'd always ask 'em for their (food stamp) card, because you know, I'm struggling . . . and I don't like it when I see somebody abuse them ((C: right, so what, they would get the change and then use the change to buy something that you are not supposed to use food stamps for?)) yeah, this old man, he would come in there and . . . if there's two clerks, he would go to me and then go to the other girl . . . and then he'd come back in a few minutes later and go get a quart of beer ((laughs)) and I would, you know, and I would say "no" and then I'd go get the manager and stuff . . . and I seen that a lot and then . . . the people that send their kids in to get a candy bar and get the change and like that, and then I would ask them, you know, "you have to have your card to use them" and . . . "your name isn't on the card". . . . there's a lot of people abuse 'em and I think that probably is what makes it worse for the people who really do try. (Mary McDonald 2/21/90)

In her talk, Mary goes beyond complaining about food stamp abusers to claiming that she actively confronted them. And her reason for doing so is clear: food stamp abuse "probably is what makes it worse for people who really do try."

Mary's approach resembles the ambivalence towards one's own category of person (here, welfare recipients) that Goffman (1963) has claimed is typical of stigmatized groups. His basis for this claim is that, because they are members of the larger society, stigmatized individuals have, more or less, adopted the standards of which they fall short. One response to this is to create hierarchies within one's own group: "The stigmatized individual exhibits a tendency to stratify his [sic] 'own' according to the degree to which their stigma is apparent and obtrusive. He can then take up in regard to those who are more evidently stigmatized than himself the attitudes the normals take to him" (1963:107). In distinguishing between "good" and "bad" recipients and condemning the "bad," Mary and Jane elevate themselves from the bottom of the hierarchy.

In contrast with the strategy of manipulation, the hyper-truth approach thus represents complicity with the welfare system. Mary's talk about food stamp abuse is a classic example of a status quo narrative: not only does she help perpetuate prevailing stereotypes, she also assertively contributes to the policing function of welfare. In so doing, she perpetuates stereotypes of "welfare cheats." This collusion is not, however, simply a passive acceptance of current structures and regulations; rather, the hyper-truth approach is active in confronting both "welfare cheats" and a system that only gives recipients their due when forced to.

Significantly, the difference between the manipulation and hyper-truth strategies was not related to perceived insufficiencies of the welfare system, but rather to the perceived basis of such insufficiencies. In either case, the system was seen as inadequate. The cause, however, and thus the remedy, was different. From the perspective of the manipulation approach, the welfare bureaucracy was inherently insufficient; even if one were to receive all one's entitlements, it still would not suffice. From the perspective of the hyper-truth approach, in contrast, the problem did not lie with the system, but with individuals, whether welfare cheats or workers, who failed to follow the rules.

Summary

The themes that emerged from the women's welfare biographies reflect various degrees of accommodation and resistance to the views and structures of the welfare system. When the women accept the stigma of food stamps or police other welfare recipients, they actively collude with and reproduce dominant views of welfare recipients as prone to cheating, a proclivity which is seen to stem from an inherent laziness or lack of social conscience. Similarly, when they claim that "education is the way out," they reinforce the idea that economic success and security reflect individual effort and have little connection with larger structural forces. On the other hand, the strategic use of lying and impression management disrupts the smooth reproduction of prevailing views. As I discuss in the following three chapters, this resistance was even more marked in the context of welfare rights groups, in which, as Maggie Fletcher indicated, "you go to your friends, and they tell you how to handle it (the welfare system)" (Maggie Fletcher 5/26/89).

Chapter 3
A Tenuous Advocacy

In his work on stigma, Goffman (1963) notes that one approach to managing what he calls "spoiled identity" consists of aligning oneself with groups of similarly situated individuals. This allows the otherwise stigmatized individuals to construct a universe in which they have legitimacy. Among welfare recipients, the opportunity to form such alliances is provided by welfare rights groups. Welfare rights groups encourage women to work on their identities, and to counteract negative stereotypes that blame them for their own poverty by constructing theories that blame the system instead (Hertz 1977, 1981; Pope 1989). In comparing their experiences, the women engage in what Mills (1959) refers to as the "sociological imagination," thereby discovering that their situations are not unique. This permits them in turn to move from internal imputations of character defects to external explanations of structural failings.

What the women are accomplishing in the context of welfare rights groups is comembership, the recognition of similarity and commonality (Erickson 1975; Erickson and Shultz 1982; see also Shultz 1975). In the context of this study, comembership may be loosely defined as alliance or solidarity, the outcome of which may be viewed in terms of consciousness raising, or of a Freireian *conscientizacao* (Freire 1970). Erickson and Shultz (1982:35) focus on comembership based on "attributes of shared status that are particularistic rather than universalistic"; in other words, on attributes that are directly or indirectly determined by birth, versus those that are potentially achievable by anyone. Although I am using the term in the simpler sense to refer to recognition of any commonality, the dimensions of comembership I am most interested in do, in fact, concern particularistic attributes, such as gender and socioeconomic class.

Most of the evidence that women's self-esteem is improved as a result of participation in welfare rights groups takes the form of retrospective self-reports (Hertz 1977). While interviews reveal what individuals have to say to "outsiders" about how they make sense of the world, they fail to capture the processes involved in individuals' concerted, or collective, efforts to make particular kinds of senses of the world. We know very little, then, of how women accomplish the "management" of stigma in their interactions with each other in welfare rights meetings. This process is, accordingly, the topic of the next three chapters.

My analysis now moves from interviews to naturally occurring speech, speech which occurs for reasons other than that I, as a researcher, am present. My approach to gathering this kind of talk consisted of having a tape recorder running whenever possible. This allowed me both to be opportunistic and to minimize imposing my own definitions of what was important onto the event (by, for example, turning the recorder on and off when something I deemed "important" was happening—an action that no doubt would have been noted by the women) (Erickson 1986). Since a running tape recorder was a feature of my presence—indeed, it was a part of my body, as I wore it at all times on a shoulder strap—the women were able to get used to the recorder as they got used to me. I was nevertheless present as an outsider and researcher at the events tape recorded and so cannot claim that this method was completely unobtrusive. The women occasionally made comments either about or to the recorder, indicating an awareness of its presence (perhaps reflecting embarrassment, or a recognition of its utilitarian function in document-particular sentiments for posterity). However, references to and speech directed at the recorder diminished markedly over time; and it was always the case that conversational topics were directed and managed by the group as it went about the business of having a welfare rights meeting.

The two welfare rights groups I worked with, the Madrid Welfare Rights Organization (MWRO) and Low Income People for Equality (LIFE), were fragmented and tenuous, and struggled continuously to maintain cohesion. In the case of LIFE, the struggle was unsuccessful. Both groups, however, were part and parcel of the ongoing agitation for welfare rights in the United States, and they joined in a long history of protest against poverty and general economic oppression. As with many grass roots organizations, MWRO and LIFE suffered from shortages of time and money; in addition, they were restricted by the gendered nature of what West and Blumberg (1990:4) refer to as the " 'appropriate' boundaries of political behavior," what it is that women are, and are not, supposed to do. They nevertheless expended considerable energy in their counter-hegemonic projects, energy which most often took the form of talk.

I learned of MWRO through the telephone directory and, after speaking with one of its members, was invited to attend a meeting. In contrast, and in a reversal of traditional anthropological research in which a researcher solicits participants for a study, a member of LIFE heard of my study through an employee of the county health department, and invited me to include the group in my research. Permission to regularly attend LIFE and MWRO meetings was subsequently granted by the core members of each group. Since membership varied from meeting to meeting, however, I sought permission to tape record meetings on each occasion. The women never withheld their consent, although I was sometimes asked to leave the recorder off during "introductions," when they revealed their full names.

Access to research participants is clearly not something accomplished once and then permanent; rather, it is repeatedly negotiated over time as relationships develop and conditions change. Although a sympathetic ear was often claimed to be rewarding in itself by recipients who found little sympathy for their plight among the general public, I felt that I had to offer something, on a continuing and immediate basis, in exchange for the women's ongoing and practical contributions of time, energy, and confidence. Accordingly, I worked as a volunteer and contributed transportation, computer work, and, on occasion, food for individual women.

Overview of the Welfare Rights Groups

Madrid Welfare Rights Organization

The Madrid Welfare Rights Organization (MWRO) is a local branch of the National Welfare Rights Union. The original national group, the National Welfare Rights Organization (NWRO), was born in the context of the civil rights movement in the mid-1960s. Piven and Cloward (1977), who first outlined the idea of a welfare rights movement in a 1966 article in *The Nation*, summarized NWRO goals as follows:

If hundreds of thousands of families could be induced to demand relief, we thought that two gains might result. First, if large numbers of people succeeded in getting on the rolls, much of the worst of America's poverty would be eliminated. Second . . . we thought it likely that a huge increase in the relief rolls would set off fiscal and political crises in the cities, the reverberations of which might lead national political leaders to federalize the relief system and establish a national minimum income standard. It was a strategy designed to obtain immediate economic aid for the poor, coupled with the possibility of obtaining a longer-term national income standard. (Piven and Cloward 1977:276)

In its heyday, 1969, NWRO boasted 22,500 members. Its membership base quickly dwindled, however, as it turned from grass roots organizing and militant resistance (most prominently in the form of sit-ins at local welfare offices) to lobbying, and as civil rights and poverty waned in funding popularity (Piven and Cloward 1977). The national office closed in 1973.

During the 1980s, in the midst of increasing homelessness and economic dislocation, there was a resurgence of welfare rights activities. The contemporary Madrid Welfare Rights Organization was founded in 1982 by Louise Black, after a meeting with the head of the National Welfare Rights Union. At the time of this study, MWRO held monthly meetings at a local community center, where it had an office until financial and staffing problems compelled the officers (a chair, treasurer, and secretary) to shut it down. By the end of the study, the group had acquired free office space in the local Community Resources Center. As of early 1992, however, Martha Hill, a new core member, was still struggling to set up more or less regular meetings following the resignation of the most recent chair in January 1991 (Louise Black had resigned in July 1990).

The official goals of MWRO reflected particular assumptions about the operation of the welfare system. The first was that recipients rarely received all they were entitled to under existing policy. Specifically, it was believed that recipients were routinely shut out of particular programs or not assisted in a timely fashion. This was the result of either ignorance or malice on the part of Assistance Payments workers. Accordingly, a key goal of MWRO was to educate recipients in the use of policy manuals, so that they would have the tools with which to pursue their entitlements.

In seeking to gain access to the relief for which they qualified, recipients often had to confront the welfare bureaucracy directly. For instance, if a recipient felt that her worker was not treating her appropriately, she could appeal to the worker's supervisor; and if the outcome of that appeal was unsatisfactory, she could ask for a "hearing," in which more senior officials would be involved. In keeping with this need to challenge the system, a second assumption of MWRO was that, in confronting the welfare bureaucracy, any number of people together is better than someone alone, who might be less able to withstand the pressure of representatives of the system to withdraw complaints or settle for less than their due. Accordingly, a second goal of the organization was to advocate for individual recipients by accompanying them to meetings at the welfare office.

Finally, even if recipients were to receive all their entitlements under existing policy, they would still not be receiving assistance sufficient to meet their needs. The claim, in other words, was that, even at its best, welfare policy is inadequate. The third official goal of MWRO was thus to influence legislative budget allocations, a goal which entailed putting public pressure on legislators by testifying at legislative hearings.

Low Income People for Equality

Low Income People for Equality (LIFE) was started in 1990 by three women. Susan Harrison had been trying in vain to participate in a government program that would allow her to purchase a home. Feeling that she was getting a runaround from both the program coordinators and her state representative, Susan decided to write a letter to the governor. As she told her story to her daycare customers (she ran a daycare business out of her home), they decided to sign the letter with her. In the end she had 25 signatures. Armed with this letter, Susan and two of her friends, Janice Borup and Sylvia Hanson, decided to attend an MWRO meeting in the hopes of getting more signatures and help in confronting the system. The three women found that the meeting had been canceled for lack of participants, so they decided to start their own group.

LIFE members were drawn primarily from Susan's daycare business. They were all low income, and the majority of those who attended the weekly meetings—ranging from three to ten people—were welfare recipients. Like MWRO, LIFE had three officers: a president, treasurer, and secretary.

The concerns of LIFE overlapped with and extended beyond those of MWRO. Public assistance was a key concern, and the group thus shared the assumptions and goals of MWRO as outlined above. While welfare was a central issue, however, LIFE members felt that it was not the only problem faced by low income and poor women; rather, they saw welfare as part of the problem of a larger society that often restricted individuals' abilities to "make it." Issues of child care, housing, collusion among men in different socioeconomic classes, and the inaccessibility of many programs designed for low income people (not only AFDC and food stamps) were thus weighted equally with welfare policy. While MWRO members also made connections between welfare and the larger society, issues related to society in general were not on the official MWRO agenda and thus were never the target of MWRO activities. In contrast, activities contemplated by LIFE included not only advocacy regarding public assistance, but also lobbying for daycare programs for low income women, making a film to educate the public about poverty, getting involved in recycling programs, and pushing for pay freezes for legislators.

LIFE differed from MWRO in other respects as well. While MWRO members occasionally became friends as a result of their participation in the group, for many LIFE members LIFE was one among several activities that they engaged in together. They also socialized together, and topics of conversation at the meetings included relationships, children and family, and bar-hopping as well as welfare, housing, and collusion among men. The expanded agenda of LIFE when compared to MWRO, then, may have been related to the wider set of relationships among its participants.

The location and conduct of LIFE meetings reflected this wider set of relationships. While MWRO meetings were held in a location geographically separate from the rest of the women's lives (in an official meeting room), LIFE meetings were always held at a member's home. Although occasional attempts were made to mark the meetings (by sending children outdoors, announcing beginnings and endings), the meetings were by nature more integrated with the rest of life than were MWRO meetings. LIFE-related talk was accordingly punctuated by jokes about individuals' sexual exploits and by activities such as eating, smoking, and drinking; talking with children also was interwoven into official activities.

Overlapping Membership

In the summer of 1990, Louise Black, the chair of MWRO, took a job in Barbados. Earlier in the year, I had introduced Louise and Susan Harrison, and they had started discussing what their respective groups wanted to accomplish. Louise had also held a training session for LIFE members on how to interpret welfare policy manuals. Although Louise's suggestion that MWRO and LIFE merge was rejected by LIFE members, Louise did convince Susan to take over as chair of MWRO. Susan accepted this position in July 1990, and held it for eight months before resigning to move to Wisconsin in January of 1991.

While not officially merged, the two groups shared a number of key members. Most notably, Susan and several other LIFE participants began to attend MWRO meetings, although members from MWRO did not attend LIFE meetings. As a result, the agenda of MWRO meetings expanded over time to include some of the more generic concerns of LIFE.

Conduct of Meetings:
The Establishment of Comembership

MWRO meetings were typically devoted to discussing current legislative and policy issues, recruitment, and possible group activities. In addition, the final half hour or so of each meeting was put aside to help members sort through their individual problems with the welfare system. These were the official agenda items of MWRO, reflecting the purpose of gathering together in order to discuss problems and propose possible actions. Regardless of the particular content of these agenda items on different occasions, however, there was always an unofficial yet predominant orientation to ideology and identity. Although members did address such concrete and crucial issues as how to figure a food stamp budget and what can be applied for under "emergency needs," a key accomplishment of the meetings was the establishment of comembership among participants and the construction of shared critical interpretations of welfare and society.

The following tape index of the first twenty minutes of an MWRO meeting illustrates the overwhelming emphasis placed on comembership and critique. Despite the differences between the two groups outlined above, this index is also roughly illustrative of LIFE meetings. The index allows for a view of critique and comembership as they relate to official, explicitly welfare-related items. In contrast to the latter, which were formally marked as agenda items, the unofficial agenda was unmarked and therefore not explicitly recognized as having purpose and function in the meetings. In the following text, items dealing with comembership and critique are italicized; official agenda items are in boldface.

000   ((people arrive; shuffling chairs around))
086   Sandra reads a letter Sharon wrote to DSS about her **difficulties handling cuts in her food stamps**–cuts that were the result, moreover, of a previous error on the part of DSS.
111   Sharon responds to Sandra's reading of the letter by claiming that **when DSS makes a mistake, the client is the one to pay.** She tells her story about trying to make ends meet on $82/month in food stamps for three people, much of which consists of listing her expenses. She underscores her indignation by pointing out that people on welfare pay taxes too.
160   Sharon continues her lament with the claim that *DSS penalizes people for divorce and then wonders when clients don't report extra income.* She criticizes fraud referrals, and then makes the general claim that *when you're on welfare, you may as well be living in Russia or China.*
199   Louise **officially opens the meeting by suggesting that everyone introduce themselves.**
230   After a side sequence by Sharon on people on welfare using the concept of "tough love" to raise their children, Louise turns to **listing MWRO goals: advocacy and legislative work.**
244   Louise brings up **problems of membership**: MWRO doesn't have enough people working on advocacy.
260   Louise points out that **MWRO needs advocacy** workers because *DSS doesn't follow the rules it's supposed to follow.* Susan, a member of LIFE, says that she wants her group to **devise solutions to problems associated with welfare that can then be presented to legislators**. She refers to a recent TV program describing the welfare system in Wisconsin, and states that we need to find ways to address the issue of *runaway fathers.*
273   Louise points out that *education* ((a commonly cited solution to the welfare problem)) *is useless if the jobs are not out there*, and offers a critique of *a "free" labor force.*
286   Louise again brings up the **problem of membership**, and lays out her claim that people join, get off welfare, and then leave the group.
289   Proposing that **all welfare programs be combined**, and referring to the fact

that this is supposed to be *a free country,* a woman starts discussing the *rights of homeless people and how we have our priorities wrong:* we don't allow abortion but don't take care of babies once they're born, and we have fancy technology to keep people alive but mistreat the aged. She then tells a story about a decrepit old man she knew when she worked at a hospital.

324   Louise picks up on this topic and talks about *poverty and health,* and outlines how *children on welfare are dying* and how *the rich are getting richer while the poor are getting poorer.* Group participants then start discussing *what they have to live on.*

350   From this, participants start discussing *how legislators think about welfare recipients.*

368   This brings up the topic of *attempts to control women's reproductive capacities,* which is followed by a discussion of *why women get on welfare* (e.g., following traditional models of marriage and motherhood).

388   The discussion moves to **why people on welfare won't fight the system: fear.**

415   After a discussion of trash bag price hikes (another example of *how difficult it is to live on welfare*), the topic returns to **membership problems.** (MWRO 4/4/90)

The most striking feature of this sequence is the extent to which critiques of the system predominate. This is typical of both MWRO and LIFE meetings. In the course of approximately 20 minutes, the women make the following claims:

- recipients are the ones to pay when DSS makes a mistake[1]
- you cannot live on what DSS gives you
- DSS forces you to lie
- if you're on welfare, you may as well be living in a communist country
- DSS typically doesn't give people what they are entitled to
- education and job training programs are a farce in the face of current economic trends
- poor people (especially children and the aged) are not well taken care of in this country
- there is an increasing gap between rich and poor
- people in power make erroneous assumptions about poor people and intrude into their private lives and rights

These criticisms of welfare and society underscore the women's comembership as victims (and angry ones at that) rather than as failures. They also help the women to build a common interpretation of their situations. Although it could be argued that the official business of the meeting to this point—discussing advocacy, legislative work, and mem-

1. The mistake most often made is "overpay," giving recipients more than they are officially entitled to. When the error is recognized, the welfare department must recoup the overpay; this is usually done by reducing the recipient's "grant" by a certain percentage (usually 5 percent) each month until the total amount has been recovered.

bership—is subsumed by this larger project, the project of establishing solidarity and a common understanding of what is wrong with welfare and society are what provide the grounds for the conduct of official business. Following Scott (1990:191), such critiques may be considered "a condition of practical resistance rather than a substitute for it."

The clear connection between unofficial and official agenda items— perhaps indicating the difficulty of making such a distinction—can be seen at segment 260, when Louise Black claims that MWRO needs advocacy workers because the Department of Social Services fails to adhere to its own regulations. The perception that the department does not follow its own policy, and shared agreement on that perception, is crucial to then establishing and acting on the goal of advocacy.

A key activity in establishing comembership and shared interpretations entails jumping from individual situations to generalized assertions and sometimes back again. For instance, Sandra begins segment 086 by describing Sharon's experience with food stamp cuts. Sharon uses this story to make the general claim that the welfare department makes recipients pay for its own mistakes, and then reinforces this assertion by outlining her own personal struggles. During segment 289–324, a woman makes a general assertion about the way old people are treated in this country and, again, backs it up with a specific example. Finally, Louise's assertion in segment 324–350 concerning the gap between rich and poor is picked up by all the women, who each start listing what it is that they have to try to live on. This jumping between individual and general levels was a ubiquitous feature of both MWRO and LIFE meetings.

Manual Training Sessions

Manual training sessions, during which the women learned how to interpret and use official Department of Social Services policy manuals, illustrate the importance of comembership and common interpretation as practical activity.

During the course of my research there were three manual training sessions, two attended by MWRO members exclusively, and one attended by both MWRO and LIFE members. There were several reasons for the relative rarity of this event. One concerned the difficulty of scheduling— the logistics of regular meetings were difficult enough. Second, policy manuals are cumbersome; the five regularly used state manuals contain hundreds of pages of policy, and the frequent updates (there were over twenty sets of updates from March 1990 to March 1991, some of which were over fifty pages in length) require constant re-learning. Third, manual training implies at least the possibility of commitment to advocacy work, something that few of the women were willing to engage in given its outright confrontational stance and the large amount of time that it takes.

In a manual training session, participants construct a view of the system while learning about welfare policy. As the instructor lays out various welfare programs, opportunities are provided for interpreting and critiquing the rationale behind the programs and how the welfare department routinely interprets and implements them. This in turn justifies learning to use the manuals. While learning to "read" the manuals is fairly straightforward (although cumbersome) given sufficient patience—a matter of learning how they are organized, and of getting used to a particular, albeit obfuscating, language—the reasons for using them, and the ways in which one might want to use them, are not given, and must be established.

The following segment is from a training session on food stamps, run by Louise Black for a new MWRO member, Kathy Simpson, and myself. Louise opened the meeting by demonstrating how to look up various aspects of food stamp policy in the index, and then began to read excerpts from the manual, explaining what she read as she went along. Her focus was on expedited food stamps, a program that allows people in emergency situations to receive food stamps within five days, rather than the normal thirty days. Louise reads from the manual, and then goes on to interpret and qualify its meaning.

((*quoting from the manual*)) "If the application is filed in person the interview must be held the same day. If the . . . client qualifies for out-of-office or telephone interview, it must be conducted no later than the first working day."
((*interpretation*)) Okay . . . so they have to interview you right away
((*referring to the manual*)) They need to have the following minimum verifications:
((*interpretation*)) See . . . the problem is, you're playing lawyer, you're playing lawyer with this stuff . . . because . . . they're not gonna read on, the department doesn't read on, the department doesn't apply (all) kinds of things. (MWRO 1/17/90)

In this segment, Louise interrupts her reading from the manual to explain why recipients should pay close attention to what is written in the manuals. As she is getting ready to read the list of minimum verifications (of an applicant's identity or financial status), she stops to explain that knowing the list is important because welfare workers are "not gonna read on," meaning that their familiarity with the manuals is superficial. For instance, the types of verification (e.g., of address) workers most often ask for are at the top of the list in the manual (e.g., driver's license). If you "read on," however, you find that there are a number of alternatives (e.g., a letter from a neighbor). Also, at the end of each subsection addressing a specific program, there is a section on exceptions to the rules. The assumption—and the rationale for playing "lawyer"—is that workers are ignorant of or unwilling to learn the details of welfare policy. It is up to the recipient to do her research and use the information she gets to press her worker to give her something (here, to process her food stamp application quickly).

The following provides an even clearer example of how Louise establishes the need to learn the manuals:

> believe it or not, EVERY program and EVERY move that DSS makes, they have rules and regulations about how they need to proceed, and what their time limits are, what their rules are, everything they do is totally bound by law, and all of that is stuff that you can know, all of that is stuff that is accessible to people, they don't necessarily tell you, they certainly don't break their backs trying to let you know that . . . but all of it is that way. (MWRO 1/17/90)

There are two key phrases here: "believe it or not, EVERY program . . . ((has)) rules" (delivered in a sarcastic tone), and "they certainly don't break their backs trying to let you know that." That there *are* regulations and that workers don't feel that they have to educate recipients about the *range* of rules are sufficient reason for recipients to educate themselves.

Resistance, and Recruitment and Retention of Membership

At their height MWRO meetings were attended by up to twenty people. The group never had very many members, however, and as of early 1992 there were fewer than five core members. I sometimes went to meetings where I was one of only three people present, and sometimes meetings were canceled for lack of participants. Often, individuals attended only one or two meetings before disappearing. Despite the high turnover, however, MWRO has nevertheless continued.

In contrast, LIFE was unable to maintain even a minimal level of involvement. In September 1991, only seven months after its establishment, LIFE died a quiet death. My speculation is that, while the group suffered from some of the same membership problems as MWRO, the nature of the relationships between its members added an additional burden. Specifically, as friendships waxed and waned, so did group membership. On one occasion, for instance, Janice Borup, one of LIFE's founding members, threw a birthday party for a girlfriend. She hired Fred, Susan Harrison's boyfriend, to dance, since this was cheaper than taking her friend to a male striptease bar. Later, Fred had sex with Janice's friend, and after Susan found out, Janice never attended another LIFE meeting. To provide another example: as LIFE was forming, Rita Moore moved into Susan Harrison's house because she was homeless.

Living in close quarters put pressure on their relationship, and several times Susan threatened to kick Rita out; at one point, Susan even accused Rita of stealing money. One result of this friction was that Susan actively blocked Rita's bid for an official position on the LIFE board by having members vote when Rita was not present. Eventually, Rita both moved out of Susan's house and dropped out of LIFE.

Despite their differences, the problem of recruiting and maintaining an active membership was a fundamental one for both LIFE and MWRO and was frequently discussed at their meetings. The women had a number of explanations for this problem. First, they felt that the material and logistical constraints of time, transportation, and lack of telephones made regular, ongoing participation in the groups difficult for most members. Second, they believed that many participants lacked what they referred to as "community values": there seemed to be a pattern in which people joined the group when faced with a particular problem with DSS, and then abruptly dropped out after receiving help in solving the problem. This, perhaps, was one reason why MWRO meetings were organized to raise individual problems last. Finally, participants recognized the subversive nature of their activities—and of the mere existence of the groups—and often cited fear as a major cause of membership shortages. In confronting the system, they felt, one risked being punished by it. Interestingly, the women never mentioned the constraints of motherhood as contributing to low membership. Their identities as mothers were a fundamental feature of their relationships with the welfare system and with welfare rights. Indeed, the women routinely brought their children with them to meetings, and they felt that the presence of children at, for instance, public demonstrations was a strategic advantage.

The strong need to establish comembership and shared understandings points to this fundamentally resistant nature of the two organizations. As outlined above, contestation took the form of critiques that countered individual deficit explanations of poverty. It also took the practical forms of efforts to learn more about how the welfare system operates (manual training), attempts to change the system (testifying at legislative hearings), and, until it could be changed, help for those trapped in the system (advocacy). Building comembership was crucial to this enterprise and can be seen as an act of resistance in and of itself. Moreover, the women's interpretations of the welfare system, and the activities that they planned on the basis of those interpretations, were subversive insofar as they confronted a system that was not only powerful in its own right, but which also had the support of the wider society. The sheer amount of time devoted to establishing comembership and to constructing particular interpretations is thus understandable.

Whether as a result of fear or logistical constraints, most of what was accomplished by MWRO and LIFE was talk, the majority of which occurred during group meetings. Very occasionally, this talk took place in legislative hearings (two occasions during the course of the research), private meetings with legislative aides (two occasions), and public demonstrations (one occasion). It is to this talk, as both counter-hegemonic and complicit, that I now turn.

Chapter 4
"Us"

A former public health nurse comments that people on welfare "don't need to have call waiting, they don't need to have TVs." She adds that it's frustrating to see people living in filthy houses and using their welfare money to buy cigarettes and pop.

A waitress in a working class bar tells of a woman she knows on AFDC who took a weekend trip to Las Vegas. She says that welfare makes people lazy.

An apprentice hair stylist tells a similar story: his friend's mother takes weekend vacations at Florida resorts on AFDC. Moreover, she won't allow her son to get a job because she doesn't want to lose her welfare money.

A female educational researcher quips, in imitation of "welfare" reasoning, "If I have another baby, I won't have to work at all!"

A social worker tells the story of a woman on welfare whose daughter got in an argument with her about money and said, "well, I'll just go out and have a baby so I can get a check of my own."

A businessman states that women need to be more responsible for their reproductive behavior. He is in favor of programs that financially penalize women who give birth after they are on the welfare rolls.

The above are typical of the negative responses I received from acquaintances when I told them about this study. The key issue in all of the responses is abuse of the system. The second and third examples, for instance, portray a flagrant misuse of funds intended for basic necessities. Trips to resorts, moreover, represent the unfulfilled desires of many people (thus such reactions as, "*I* can't afford to do that and I'm *working*!"). The funds that welfare recipients receive ultimately come from "us," so such trips are an abuse not only of the welfare system but also of the taxpayers who support it. The protagonists in the resort examples, as in the last three examples, which allude to the inappropriate use of reproductive capacities, are women. Only the first example is gender neutral.

The recipients I worked with contested the kinds of negative views expressed by my acquaintances. They countered stereotypes of women on welfare both directly and indirectly, by challenging the validity of the stereotypes on a number of grounds, and by mobilizing culturally valued attributes to posit alternative identities for themselves.

A Further Note on Methods

At the beginning of Chapter 3, I made a distinction between interview and naturally occurring talk, claiming that the latter provides access to participants' co-construction of their meaning-worlds. In collecting and analyzing the naturally occurring talk produced at MWRO and LIFE meetings (and, in Chapters 6–9, at the Kenyon County welfare office), I drew on the methods of microanalysis. Microanalysis, or microethnography, is concerned with fine-grained analysis of the moment-by-moment production of social reality, including perceptions and classifications as well as various kinds of institutional arrangements. The basic claim of the approach is that social "facts" such as the existence of deserving and undeserving poor are socially constructed and that "the objective reality of social facts [is] an ongoing accomplishment of the concerted activities of daily life" (Garfinkel 1967:vii). What goes on between people in interaction is seen as a key location for the construction and expression of meaning and social structure (Erickson 1975, 1986, 1992; Erickson and Shultz 1982; McDermott and Roth 1978)—thus my emphasis here on naturally occurring talk.

In this and the following chapters, then, the evidence I present for the points I argue is in the form not only of quotes, but also of transcribed segments of talk produced in welfare rights and welfare office related contexts. By attending to these transcripts with care, we—outsiders—can witness social construction in action.

"It's not true—at least not in the way most people think": Challenges to Stereotypes

The women challenged negative stereotypes of welfare recipients in three ways: by admitting their reality, with the qualification that the stereotypes did not apply to *them*; by claiming that the negatively valued activities they engaged in were the outgrowth of relationships with a welfare system that taught—indeed, forced—them to behave in such ways; and by categorically denying their reality.

Bad-People-Exist-But-I'm-Not-One-of-Them

In my discussion of the "hyper-truth" approach in Chapter 2 (see pp. 40–42, I argued that recipients themselves sometimes reproduced the distinction between the worthy and undeserving poor. The bad-people-exist-but-I'm-not-one-of-them strategy entails precisely this kind of collusion and was the most common tactic employed by MWRO and LIFE participants in their challenge to negative stereotypes. In essence, the strategy entailed acknowledging the existence of "bad" individuals—dividuals who were lazy, who lied and cheated, or who were promiscuous or otherwise morally lax—while simultaneously claiming that they themselves did not belong in this undeserving category. As well as providing a means to exempt themselves from negative stereotypes, the bad-people-exist-but-I'm-not-one-of-them approach provided grounds for arguing against punitive policies which the women felt were inappropriately constructed on the basis of such stereotypes.

The following exchange on forced sterilization provides a good example of the working out of this position. The participants are Susan Harrison, Janet Burns and her mother Marge, and myself.

```
 1   J:   um, I'VE heard it before, I've heard RUMORS of this before, of
 2        women who've had some—certain amount of kids
 3   S:   I have too
 4   J:   and been forced to have a tubal litigation [sic], NOW—
 5   S:   well, Ashley Potter, my, my uh, ex sister, well she's my sister-in-law, she
 6        had six kids and they MADE her tie HER tubes
 7   M:   who made her? welfare?
 8   S:   their welfare did, either she tied 'em or she didn't get benefits, and
 9        that's in Virginia. Six is enough for the welfare rolls, but, THIS
10        woman literally DID, she IS a welfare (degenerate), when she was
11        fourteen, she started having BABIES, she never finished SCHOOL,
12        her MOM, it was generation, down
13   M:   you can unders—
14   S:   and HER kids is also gonna be welfare AGAIN, and that's how they
15        were raised
16   M:   well, THAT, they'll use THAT kinda instance to justify it
17   S:   yeah they do
18   C:   yeah EXACTLY
19   S:   they DO
20   M:   and ARE they justified in it then?
21   S:   no NO because the MAJORITY of us out there on it is NOT like that.
22        I bust my ass trying to get off
23   M:   yeah
24   S:   I don't want to be on it no, no more, no more than I have to, but when
25        it, when I HAVE to be on it, I don't want to feel like some
26   M:   yes
```

27 S: you know CRUD coming in the door
28 M: I know
29 S: or leavin' the door
30 J: or feelin' like—
31 S: or not being able to DO so—you know GET off of it, I don't LIKE
          that   (LIFE 4/8/90)

Susan's story about her ex-sister-in-law Ashley brings to life the stereotype
on which policies of enforced sterilization are potentially built. Not only
is Ashley reproductively irresponsible, but, as Susan rhythmically lists
them, she exhibits a range of negatively valued behaviors: she started
having babies when she was only fourteen, she dropped out of school,
and her mother was also a welfare recipient (lines 10–12). Ashley reproduces welfare dependency as well as human beings (note the phrase
"generation, down," line 12).

   In her comment "Six is enough for the welfare rolls" (line 9), spoken
slowly and in a low voice, Susan indicates agreement with the welfare
system's ultimatum—*in Ashley's case.* By not calling into question the legitimacy of forcing Ashley to have a tubal ligation, Marge's comments
immediately following the story (lines 13 and 16) support Susan's evaluation. No one questions that the system has the right to coerce a woman
such as Ashley to be sterilized. What *is* challenged is the idea of transforming the legitimate application of forced sterilization in Ashley's case
into a generalized policy applicable to all women receiving public assistance. As Marge points out at line 16, the welfare system will use cases
like Ashley's to justify creating such policies; a position with which Susan
and I agree. In her next turn, during which she asks "and ARE they justified in it then?" (line 20), Marge provides the opportunity for rebuttal.
Susan takes this opportunity, arguing that most women on welfare are
not like her ex sister-in-law, that she herself has been working hard, and
that she is not willing to accept the disgrace of being placed in the same
category as Ashley. In making this argument, Susan invokes "working"
(as opposed to simply producing a lot of babies) as something to be re-
spected and rewarded, and challenges not only a policy of forced sterilization, but also the stigma that would be attached to her and other
"good" recipients as the result of such a policy. Marge's comments at
lines 23 and 26 ("yeah," "yes") help Susan along in this argument.
Janet's bid at line 30, although unsuccessful, also reinforces Susan's position insofar as she seems about to name another negative feeling to
back up Susan's feeling like "crud."

   Together, then, Susan, Marge, Janet and myself criticize both the inappropriate application of stereotypes and the construction of policies
based on stereotypes. Simultaneously, however, we reinforce mainstream
views of generational welfare mothers. There was no objection in prin-

ciple to punitive policies. Indeed, the women sometimes suggested punitive policies that could be applied to other segments of the "welfare" population, most notably men. Susan, for instance, reacted strongly to a television documentary (entitled "Stuck on Welfare") describing a Wisconsin program that forced women on AFDC to work or attend school on penalty of losing their benefits. Susan, whose children had been sexually abused by babysitters while she was at work, felt strongly that women should be permitted to stay at home with their children. In her view, much of the problem rested with men who were delinquent on child care payments. Nothing was done to punish these men, however; the targets of punitive policies always seemed to be women. Therefore, to hold men accountable for the children they fathered, Susan proposed that they be placed in half-way houses, required to work, and forced to wear wrist bands that would alert the police if they wandered off. This strategy for resistance, then, was dependent on the construction of a category of individuals deserving of punishment.

Susan's response to one woman's view of welfare cheats provides another example of this strategy. At a LIFE meeting Dara DeLuca, a close friend of Susan's who had never received public assistance, voiced her disdain for people who abuse the system because they are too lazy to look after themselves (a transcript and analysis of this interaction are included in Appendix A as Case #1):

I understand the people that have kids, and that can't get a job, yes I understand, but I (don't) understand people that CAN get a job and that are on WELfare . . . you LOOK AROUND and you see these people driving these nice cars and you know damn WELL they're on welfare because of the way they LIVE, you know damn WELL, or they've TALKED about it with you, so how the hell'd you get this nice CAR if you're such a, you know, on WELfare, who are YOU screwing ((laughs)) you KNOW, and I don't agree with that, hell NO, I don't ((laughs)). (LIFE 5/6/90)

Susan's response to Dara was to concede that lazy people exist, but to claim—as in the discussion of forced sterilization—that they comprise only a small proportion of welfare recipients:

But see that's, THAT'S just a FEW . . . . There's fifty percent working, working welfare moms, there's twenty-five percent I think that would LIKE to work but they don't have no HOpe and then we've got the twenty-five percent that just don't GIVE a damn, go out there and do it FOR me, you know type shit. (LIFE 5/6/90)

Here Susan argues, in scientific parlance, that the ones who "don't give a damn"—the undeserving—comprise only one quarter of all recipients. A full 50 percent of welfare recipients are employed; they are, moreover, also mothers ("working welfare moms"). Those who work, and those who want to work (the 25 percent who "don't have no hope") are deserving, and should not be penalized for what the 25 percent who "don't give a damn" do (or, more significantly, don't do[1]). Meg Irwin made a similar argument at a Senate hearing, when she said, "you got your percentage of some welfare people that are lazy . . . but . . . the majority are not lazy" (LIFE 5/8/90). Interestingly, Susan's figures were not questioned; the mere recitation of percentages lends an authority to her argument that Dara seems unwilling to contest.

In sum, the bad-people-do-exist-but-I'm-not-one-of-them approach involved simultaneous criticism of "bad" people and of welfare policy. When the women deprecated individuals who purportedly engaged in stigmatized activities, they afforded validity to and thereby reproduced the stereotypes. However, the claim was that those who engaged in the stigmatized activities were a minority, and that to thus base policy on stereotypes was to punish innocent recipients. Just as the bad-people-exist-but-I'm-not-one-of-them argument did not question the validity of the stereotypes, so the critique of policy generated by the argument did not question the appropriateness of punitive policies per se; they just had to be applied to the right people. There are, therefore, elements of both mixed and status quo narratives in this talk—mixed insofar as the women seem to simultaneously reproduce and challenge certain ideologies, and status quo insofar as they are willing to participate in the perpetuation (and even the extension to new categories of people) of punitive policies that have their roots in such ideologies.

Welfare-Made-Me-Do-It

The second most common way the women challenged negative stereotypes entailed admitting to "bad" behaviors, with the proviso that such actions arose not from the women's personalities but rather from the nature of their relationship with the welfare system. The implication is that the responsibility for these behaviors rests with the welfare system, not the women.

For instance, a common belief about welfare recipients is that they are dishonest. "Welfare cheat" is ubiquitous both in everyday conversation and in official debates about welfare reform. The presence of welfare fraud hotlines in many cities provides further testimony to the prevalence of this view. In response to the accusation of deception, MWRO

---

1. This is similar to the argument Mary McDonald offered about food stamp abuse in the discussion of the hyper-truth approach pp. 40–41. It is not clear, however, that Mary McDonald would consider welfare cheats to be in the minority.

and LIFE members routinely claimed that the welfare system itself generated dishonesty, a response which implies a latent structure of the welfare system: lying is required in order to survive. Susan Harrison explained the process in the following way:

I don't lie to people, unless I ABsolutely HAVE to lie I don't lie. I just avoid the question or go around it another way ((laughs)), I don't actually LIE lie ((laughs)). If you're gonna pin me to the wall you better make sure you ask it JUST the right way, 'cause I'm gonna go AROUND it ((laughs)) if there's any way I CAN, but HELL, you learn that from welfare. Yep, my aunt told me that one time, years and years ago, 'cause I always wondered how could she get . . . you know, things that I couldn't get . . . and she said "Susan Harrison, you don't go in there and tell them the truth, ya ASShole," you know. (LIFE 4/20/90)

Despite her aunt's advice, Susan continued in her honesty. She could only bring herself to break her habit of telling welfare workers "anything they wanted to know" after she experienced homelessness. As she put it, "I don't like to LIE, I was raised never to LIE." Rita Moore, who was present at my interview with Susan, shared Susan's disposition: "it goes againt MY grain, I am NOT a liar." That a predisposition to honesty was a problem was clearly the argument being made in the "Bids for Burial" story I recounted in Chapter 2 (see pp. 38–39).

The argument, then, is that "you learn that ((lying)) from welfare," and that you have to lie to get the basic necessities, such as shelter, and the extra "things" that Susan's aunt managed to finagle. What to lie about, and how to go about it, however, is not always clear; rather, because workers are unpredictable, recipients must develop skill in "winging it." As Rita put it, "after so many times of going in there and talking to them you just sorta get a feel for the situation." Once having been forced to lie, though, the strategy can be employed in trickster-like fashion to subvert the system. Again: "if you're gonna pin me to the wall you better make sure you ask it just the right way, 'cause Im going to go a-ROUND it ((laughs)) if there's any way I CAN, but HELL, you learn that from welfare." Even this trickster element is attributed to the welfare system.

The stories about learning to lie (or engage in some other negatively valued behavior) usually followed the same format: when I first got on welfare, I told my worker everything (I was honest). Pretty soon, however, I figured out that that didn't pay (I was penalized for telling the truth), so I got smart (started lying). This was usually followed, or preceded, by some evaluative remark to the effect that the teller believed lying (or some other negatively valued activity) was wrong: "It's a shame to have to do that, you know, it really is." The narratives produced were clearly mixed, containing elements of both accommodation (by admitting to lying, cheating, or whatever else was at issue) and resistance (in claiming that such behavior was in essence required by the welfare system).

A second area to which the "welfare-made-me-do-it" argument was applied concerned spending habits. According to received wisdom on the right (see, e.g., Gilder 1981; Mead 1986; Murray 1984), recipients of public assistance do not budget wisely, they spend money on things they cannot afford, and, like children or "primitives," they are incapable of deferring gratification. The idea here is that public assistance creates dependency and poor spending and work habits. To some extent the women agreed with this assessment: when you don't know when you'll get your next welfare check (that is, if you get one at all), or how much it'll be for, you tend to spend money while you have it. There is a difference, however, in the underlying assumptions of the two positions. From the point of view of the right, the welfare system is lax, thus making it easy for recipients to avoid economizing. From the point of view of the women in this study, the system both fails to provide for basic needs and is unpredictable—in other words, it is *irresponsible*. The agreement on outcome yet disagreement on cause holds as well for recipients and workers, a topic I explore in Chapter 9.

In sum, women who drew on the welfare-made-me-do-it argument transformed accusations against themselves as recipients into accusations against the welfare system. It was not they who were abusing the system; rather, by forcing them to engage in behavior which went against their principles, the welfare system was abusing them.

Denial: The Convenient Ideologies Argument

A final discursive strategy for resisting negative stereotypes entailed a categorical denial of their reality. This approach was most clearly articulated by Louise Black, who claimed that negative stereotypes of poor people were little more than convenient ideologies used by those in power to maintain the status quo. She argued that the priorities of legislators who determined the state budget did not include taking care of poor people, despite their awareness of the hardships suffered by their impoverished constituents. Claiming that "there's no doubt in their mind what's going on," Louise described the legislative agenda and its consequences as follows:

. . . they're deciding that the state of Michigan has some priorities and those priorities are increasing, and one of the things Wenger ((a Democratic politician considered friendly by MWRO)) talks about ((is)) increasing tax expenditures, increasing tax write offs for businesses, that is extremely important, that is what ((the priorities are)) gonna continue to be, and when they do that, they will let a certain number of, at this point, black, primarily black youth between eighteen and twenty-five, die, there is no problem with that, they will have, a certain number of children who are born to poor people who will die, or who will be permanently disabled as a result of living in poverty, and that is acceptable to them, that's the choice they make. (Louise Black 9/7/89)

Later in the conversation, Louise describes legislators' claims that they are trying to provide opportunities for the "underclass" through their JobStart program (which was designed to remove people from the welfare rolls by giving them steady employment) as a "straight out lie."

Not only were legislators aware of the fact that the poor would suffer and perhaps die as a result of budget priorities, but they used negative stereotypes of welfare recipients to make these facts more palatable to themselves and the general public. According to Louise, politicians justified leaving "whole groups to die" by invoking a "crisis of morals"— meaning a crisis in individual morals or in family structure—or distinctions between worthy and unworthy poor. The "attack" on the poor is accomplished through division:

the move is to . . . picking some kind group that they think is deserving and protecting that group, which means that that it's okay to kill folks, that it's okay to leave whole groups to die, and that that has become okay and acceptable, and they call it, you know, being politically realistic, or something like that. (Louise Black 9/7/89)

The false distinction between the deserving and undeserving poor was all the more salient for Louise, given her conversion, after her own experiences with AFDC and food stamps, from someone who had been unsympathetic to welfare recipients into someone fighting for welfare rights.

The accomplishment of the convenient ideologies approach to stereotypes is illustrated in the following exchange between Louise, Naomi Anderson, and Bobbie Bradford at an MWRO meeting (the previous two exchanges are from an interview I had with Louise). Bobbie had been describing an encounter with an African American worker who had been "real snippy with me," to whom she had responded by asking, "what the f((uck)) do I have to do? paint myself to be a nigger?" This remark was challenged by Naomi, who argued in favor of greater racial integration. Louise then interjects her claim that racism is a divisive tactic used by the powerful to keep the poor from uniting.

1 L: the way that they get OVER with trying to FEED us all these CUTS is
2   trying to do EXACTLY that same THING, is trying to separate this
3   BLACK-WHITE stuff
4 N: that's what they're doing and if you go into a big city like Chicago it

5   IS RIDICULOUS, it is AWFUL in Chicago
6   L: and they TRY to get us to BUY it, but we have to say, we HAVE to say,
7   EVERYbody, EVERYbody needs enough money to live on, if YOU can't
8   give us jobs
9   B: right
10 L: WE have to live, WE have to feed our kids, WE have to have a house
11   to live in, NObody in this country needs to die in the street and that
12   means ALL of us
13 B: right
14 L: whether anybody's black white
15 B: and green purple
16 L: old YOUNG, WHO CARES
17 B: yeah
18 L: nobody needs to die in the street and WE need to be about SAYIN'
         that   (MWRO 3/7/90)

Louise argues that when the poor agree that some people deserve more help than others—when they take a tack similar to bad-people-exist-but-I'm-not-one-of-them—they are serving the interests of those in power. As is made clear in the first half of the exchange, both Louise and Naomi have strong feelings about racism. Bobbie, the speaker to whom Louise and Naomi are addressing themselves, eventually voices agreement. Not only does she begin to respond, "right," "right" (lines 9, 13), but she adds to the argument by producing some of the features typically listed when referring to the range of human variation (line 15). Louise and Naomi together produce an anti-racist message, then, in which Bobbie eventually participates by correcting herself.

The argument Louise makes at line18 is a "bottom line" argument: everybody has the same needs (food, shelter), and everybody has the right to have those needs met. To accept any of the stereotypes about people on welfare—or even to reinforce ideologies that ostensibly have nothing to do with welfare, like racism—is to collude with those in power in denying certain people the right to live. The talk produced in this exchange therefore counters the status quo. There was no place for accommodation to *any* feature of the dominant ideology, insofar as the claim was that the dominant ideology was "ideology" in the sense of false, distorted belief erected and perpetuated to serve the interests of the dominant classes.

"I work harder than anybody I KNOW of": The Challenge of Positive Constructions

In addition to, and often co-occurring with, direct counters to stereotypes, the women produced positive identities that drew on mainstream values concerning gender roles and the achievement of economic success and security. In so doing, they portrayed themselves as clearly something other than lazy, dishonest, and promiscuous. Rather, they constructed identities as good, ordinary, hardworking women and mothers trying to do "the right thing."

Hard Workers

A very powerful counter-construction to the lazy recipient stereotype was that of a hard worker. All the women claimed that they worked hard, and that if they were unemployed, it was not by choice. In her testimony at a Senate hearing, for instance, Janice Adams described how she had tried to work two jobs while raising three children, but had been unable to make ends meet because of child care costs. This echoes the theme of "working is expensive" discussed in Chapter 2.

In the following exchange, Susan Harrison, Meg Irwin, and Janet Burns discuss how the welfare system undermines people's efforts to succeed. Susan has just been recounting how she was homeless for five months because the welfare department would not provide her with any assistance. As the segment opens, Meg and Janet agree with her point that "there's no right to live here ((in the U.S.))." Janet then brings up the topic of work, which, along with the idea of being "stuck" on welfare, provides the focus for the remainder of the exchange. The participants are Susan, Janet, Meg, and myself.

```
 1   S:   they are refusing us a right to LIVE
 2   M:   right to live
 3   J:   right to live, and that's not saying that we're not working
 4   S:   that's IT
 5   J:   you know, that's just IT you know
 6   S:   I work harder than anybody I KNOW of
 7   J:   uh huh
 8   B:   and to,to be on ADC ((laughs))
 9   J:   yeah
10   S:   I mean you know I pull some hellacious hours
11   J:   uh huh
12   C:   sounds like it
13   S:   there's no getting OFF of it
14   J:   exactly (      )
15   S:   if you get off it, what're you LOOKing for, there's no HELP out there
16   J:   and and talk about, you know, that's just IT you know they think well
17        you're lazy this or that you know, like well where's my, um, where's my
18        time that I've gone out and partied all night? you know
19   S:   that's it, they think we have such a wild life you know
20   J:   yeah
21   S:   we're single moms we're hot in the ASS ((laughs)) I mean that's what
22        they SAY, we can get some money, you know, but yet we get out there
```

23		and try to MAKE money we get arrested, oh WOW there goes ours
24		kids bye-BYE
25	J:	right, exactly
26	M:	mmm, huh
27	S:	you know, but you HAVE to do it, you have to
28	J:	((to child)) are you eating that?
29	S:	so you're breaking one law after another trying to make it
30	J:	RIGHT
31	S:	and which is basically your right, as a tax payer if nothing else as a
32		human BEING
33	J:	well you know a lot of times people will say things like, well, this per-
34		son, you know, like um, some of the, uh, like Vietnamese and things
34		like that
35	S:	yeah
36	J:	that come over and they start with nothing, and they work and work
37		and get things done—well YEAH, they work and they, GET some-
38		where okay—
39	S:	they're also, quote, a minority
40	J:	yeah
41	S:	they get a lot a help me and you aren't even QUALIFIED for
42	J:	that's true and I DON'T even think they have to pay TAXES
43	S:	none
44	J:	not that I'm saying this is WRONG or anything, BUT, it's not saying
45		that we you know
46	S:	it's wrong in the aspect that they can get it and we're not eligible for
47		it and it's our own damn COUNTRY (LIFE 3/11/90)

Early in the exchange, Susan states, "I work harder than anybody I KNOW of" (line 6), claiming an identity as industrious rather than lazy. Janet participates in this construction by debunking the stereotype of "lazy" welfare recipients: "where's my time that I've gone out and partied all night?" (lines 17–18). Susan then makes the transition from "partying" to another negative stereotype; namely, that of the promiscuous welfare mother. Not only does she ridicule this stereotype (line 21); she also turns it against the welfare system by claiming that women receiving public assistance are forced to engage in prostitution in order to survive (lines 22–24, 27). The final topic of the exchange is "foreigners." Janet brings up the stereotypical hard-working Vietnamese for a reason that she is unable to voice immediately (later it comes out that she was trying to argue that she, too, is "industrious"); instead, Susan uses Janet's example to complain about "minorities" who get more help than Anglo Americans do (lines 39–47)—a perspective that reinforces her claim that she and the others present are being oppressed.[2] In sum, the interpretation that Susan and Janet produce is one that portrays

2. This resembles the view initially expressed by Bobby in the exchange on race discussed on pp. 64–65, and helps to explain the racial/ethnic homogeneity of MWRO and LIFE.

women on welfare as victims: despite their efforts to fulfill the work ethic, they cannot extricate themselves from the system; and they continue to suffer from stereotypes that in no way represent their actions or desires.

Just Ordinary People/Women

Many of the women also stressed that they were just like anyone else: they had the same dreams and aspirations as other women, and did what any-one else would do to fulfill those dreams. The "anyone" referred to was, as can be gleaned from the aspirations and dreams discussed, a middle class woman;[3] and the dreams had to do with marriage, motherhood, and economic security.

The women often invoked cultural models of marriage, motherhood, and economic security when discussing claims that promiscuity is char-acteristic of women on welfare. Recall, for instance, the quote by Rita Moore at the beginning of Chapter 1, in which she refers to a legislative hearing during which a Senator had accused AFDC recipients—mean-ing women—of being reproductively irresponsible:

The thing that got me at the hearing was, "why do they have these children if they can't afford to raise 'em?" I was married. Sure my husband—he's 45 years old, 45 or 46—he ought to be working a decent job and making a decent living . . . Well I figured I could work and he could work together, you know, we could raise a family, we could have, you know, the little nuclear family, and every-thing would be hunky dory. (LIFE 4/1/90)

Rita claims pursuing the ideal of the nuclear family. If the traditional arrangement of husband-as-breadwinner was not possible, then husband and wife could both work in paid employment to maintain the family. In either case, no one could accuse Rita of either irresponsibility or immor-ality. She was only trying to do what a good woman should, and only wanted what other women wanted.

Susan Harrison also drew on the model of the nuclear family when she testified at a legislative hearing on the welfare budget:

((People end up on welfare)) because something happens in their life, not be-cause you wanna be, you have your kids—you meet your husband you get married you have your kids or whatever, you got the KIDS what'd ya wanna DO? Just, you know? It's, it's not like you're TRYing to have kids to stay on welfare, it's

3. As Ortner (1991:188) points out, "It might be argued that 'middle class' is not a class term at all, since it is not generally seen as part of a class structure, that is, as a positional or relational category vis-à-vis other classes. In ordinary discourse it seems simply to mean a general allegiance to the nation and to large, overarching values like freedom and individu-alism." I am using middle class in this loose sense to refer to the dominant ideologies with which the women in this study were engaged.

not like that. You GOT your percentage of some welfare people (that) that ARE lazy, okay? (but that's not your maJORity). (LIFE 5/8/90)

The point Susan endeavors to make in her testimony is that women are not on the relief rolls because they choose to be, but as the result of unfortunate circumstances. At least, this is so in the majority of cases. A more detailed analysis of this plea, in which Meg Irwin participated, comprises Case #2 in Appendix A. In summary, according to Susan and Meg, most AFDC recipients have their children the way women are *supposed* to have their children—through marriage. The majority of women on public assistance are, moreover, hard workers. In this view, welfare mothers are simply ordinary citizens, both hardworking and morally upright, who have suffered some set-back, such as desertion by a husband.

Summary

The women's talk explored in this chapter illustrates varying engagements with dominant views of welfare recipients. These engagements may be situated in the immediate contexts of their production, MWRO and LIFE meetings and the specific topics of discussion at those meetings. The task at hand—contesting forced sterilization, racism, or accusations of promiscuity—influenced the kind of argument produced. In resisting workfare programs, for instance, it may be useful to invoke the sanctity of motherhood, while a challenge to the charge of immorality, on the other hand, might call for an alignment with the values of hard work and responsibility.

The women's talk may also be situated in the wider context of the welfare system and society at large. This would provide insight into the connections between accommodation and resistance and reproduction and change at the level of culture and society. When read from this perspective, only the convenient ideologies argument is truly counter-hegemonic: it does not enter into conversation with dominant views but rather denies their validity altogether. The other strategies employed by MWRO and LIFE members are mixed in nature and all, to some extent, reinforce ideologies and stereotypes that contribute to the specific oppressions they are resisting. For example, the bad-people-exist-but-I'm-not-one-of-them argument reinforces and in effect reproduces received views of lazy, dishonest, and otherwise irresponsible welfare recipients. In using this strategy, the women did not question the validity of the stereotypes, as long as they were not included in the categories at issue; nor did they present any argument against the use of such stereotypes in the construction of punitive welfare policies (e.g., forced sterilization), as long as they were only applied to those who fit the stereotypes. Although extricating themselves from negative characterizations, the women left mainstream views of welfare recipients intact. The women's invocation of the work ethic may also be detrimental to their interests in the long run. As Abramovitz (1988a) has pointed out, the work ethic is a crucial aspect of welfare ideology; welfare policy and efforts to deter people from seeking public assistance have been based, both historically and currently, on various aspects of this ethic (see also Katz 1986; Piven and Cloward 1971). While resistant to accusations of laziness, the women's constructions of themselves as hard workers reinforce the view that all able-bodied people should be gainfully employed, with the implication that those who are not (for whatever reasons, including motherhood in the case of poor people) are undeserving—a view, along with the need for cheap labor, fundamental to workfare programs. The women also support the idea that mothering is not "work."

In appropriating dominant views, however, recipients were not simply reproducing them. What is culturally available to think with is enabling as well as constraining (Collier and Yanagisako 1989), and provides opportunities for resistance as well as accommodation. In their confrontations with the dominant system, LIFE and MWRO members used the words, categories, and values of the dominant system to their own advantage. Such acts are superficially accommodating, insofar as they partake of dominant views. Insofar as they appropriate dominant views for subversive purposes, however, they are acts of resistance. For instance, in the welfare-made-me-do-it argument, the women deployed mainstream values of honesty and frugality to claim that lapses in their honesty or financial responsibility were the direct outcome of welfare policy. Policy, not recipients, should be held to blame.

The women's positive constructions of themselves also drew on dominant ideologies and confronted the system with its own contradictions concerning, for instance, women's roles as mothers, workers, and dependents. Weedon (1987) following Foucault refers in this regard to "reverse" discourses, discourses that draw on the very vocabulary or categories of dominant discourses in order to make a case for oppressed groups. In this case, the contradictions inherent in the welfare system concerning women's role as mother versus worker provide a discursive space within which recipients may challenge the system. This discursive space is perhaps where the struggle over "worldmaking" to which Bourdieu (1990) refers takes place.

In sum, in MWRO and LIFE talk, accommodation and resistance interact to produce views which may be read as complicit or counterhegemonic or both depending on the interpretive perspective. Generally, however, the metamessage of much of the women's talk was something like the following: "I'm doing my best to be a good woman and mother and to take care of myself and my family, but the welfare system will not allow me to succeed." In other words, the women expressed belief in the American values of motherhood, the nuclear family, and the work ethic, but saw all their efforts to fulfill those values as futile in the face of the constraints of the welfare bureaucracy.

Chapter 5
"Them"

. . . they ((legislators)) ARE an aggressive kind of GROUP, they will—you'll be AMAZED at the kind of things they will SAY, I mean they will come out with ALL of the myths that you think that only ignorant people have about welfare. (Louise Black, MWRO meeting)

The women in MWRO and LIFE resisted their stigmatized social positions by contesting not only negative stereotypes of welfare recipients but also what they saw as the privileged social positions of particular "others" in their lives. In so doing, they constructed these others as specific types of people—most often as individuals who did not evince integrity or principled behavior. The "them" in these constructions sometimes referred to a particular category of person (such as AP workers or politicians), and sometimes to an amorphous group that shared certain characteristics, such as extreme self-interest, or ignorance.

The women's constructions of others were part and parcel of their constructions of themselves; in other words, the "us" explored in the previous chapter and the "them" explored in this chapter are relational categories, mutually constitutive and interdependent. Moreover, in constructing "us" as "good" and "them" as "bad," MWRO and LIFE members reversed the deserving/undeserving distinction, elevating themselves to deserving status while lowering the supposedly worthy to the category of the undeserving.

Assistance Payments Workers

The women's characterizations of Assistance Payments workers were overwhelmingly negative. Attributes they assigned to workers, listed in order of frequency, included the following: workers are arbitrary; they don't explain things; they are nice and helpful; they punish you if you confront them; they are lazy; they are concerned with their own status; and they are inaccessible, ignorant, and always say no. Workers as nice and friendly, while third in frequency, was a relatively rare characterization when set against the long list of negative attributes.

MWRO and LIFE members most often characterized workers as arbitrary. In this sense, the women saw workers as practicing the type of personal domination discussed by Scott (1990): while workers' official authority was based on their status as representatives of the Department of Social Services, and although they invoked rules over which they ostensibly had no control, from the point of view of recipients they were unpredictable. This sentiment was reflected in remarks to the effect that "it depends on who your case worker is," and "discrimination against personality ((on the part of workers)), that's a major problem" (LIFE 4/29/90). The following story, told by Joan Ryan, points to the implications of this for recipients' material well-being:

> When I got cut off, the reason why I got cut off is because I went down to the food stamps (office) three times and she ((the AP worker)) . . . couldn't get my name into the computer so she just told me I was cut off. It was ten dollars, but I went down there three times, which is more than ten dollars worth of food stamps ((for transportation)), just to get cut off. (LIFE 4/20/90)

Joan's claim is that the AP worker involved did not know how to work the computer and so, at her whim, decided to dismiss the case. The problem is seen to rest not with policy, but with people.

The discussion about lying included in Chapter 4 also illustrates the view of workers as capricious. As Susan Harrison points out, recipients have to take their chances; and as Rita Moore explains it, "after SO many times of going in there and talking to them you just sorta get a feel for the situation" (LIFE 4/20/90). The image is one of unpredictable circumstances, rather than of a fixed, immutable system that can be learned and accordingly manipulated.

The women gathered evidence for workers' despotic nature when they compared their cases at welfare rights meetings and discovered discrepancies in their "grant" levels. Why did a woman with one child get almost $200 per month in food stamps while another woman with three children got almost the same amount? Why was one woman given child care funds while another had to fend for herself? While there were a number of possible explanations for such discrepancies, including policy differences between counties and differences in recipients' earned income, the women's favored explanation was that the workers who represented the system were arbitrary.

Not only were workers erratic; they also failed to provide clarification. Specifically, they often neglected to explain the purpose of the various forms they had applicants complete, and they rarely provided information on the different options available to recipients. This view is expressed in the following exchange between Janet Burns and Rita Moore (the beginning of Janet's turn is not included on the tape):

```
 1  J:   with um, case workers being much less than helpful
 2  R:   yes, not being, I don't know, I I I won't say DISHONEST so much, just
 3       not telling me everything
 4  J:   well they won't—it's like they won't tell you ANY, you know ((sighs
 5       loudly))
 6  R:   um, like it, the RULES, seem to CHANGE, um, I mean it, it's all the
 7       same RULES but, the case workers don't tell—aren't HONEST with
 8       you, they don't, they aren't HELPful, they, um, they don't tell you that
 9       you can have your child care vendored, you know they say oh no no
10       no no
11  J:   yeah, see I don't even understand that even after you guys have said
12       something about it, I don't understand about like having your child
13       care vendored and all this, stuff    (LIFE 4/13/90)
```

Janet's display of ignorance concerning child care vendoring (in which DSS pays child care facilities directly) provides the example that proves the point: workers do not systematically inform their clients of all the options available to them.

One of the interesting aspects of this exchange is the difficulty Rita has getting started in her criticism (lines 2–3). Perhaps this suggests the ambivalence recipients may feel toward workers who sometimes do provide them with at least some of what they need. Such hesitancy in criticizing workers was rare (and later in the exchange Rita does come out and accuse workers of dishonesty). Nevertheless, there were occasions when recipients told stories of workers who were "nice," or who went out of their way to be helpful: Leslie Lash, an occasional LIFE participant, told of a worker who processed her food stamps immediately and gave her more than she had originally asked for; and Stephanie Diamond, who attended one LIFE meeting, claimed that her worker was never anything less than very helpful. Both claims, however, were made during discussions of workers' negative attributes. Interestingly, they seemed to reinforce the view of workers as unpredictable. And clearly, as indicated in the above exchange, it is the workers, not the system, who are to blame for recipients' misfortunes. Note how Rita begins by indicting the "rules" (welfare policy), but quickly switches to a focus on workers: "it's all the same RULES ((i.e., policy remains constant)) but, the case workers don't tell—aren't HONEST with you, they don't, they aren't HELPful" (lines 6–8). Just as recipients were categorized as "good" or "bad" and "deserving" or "undeserving," so they in turn assigned workers to "good" and "bad" categories. As in workers' constructions of their clients, MWRO and LIFE members placed the majority of workers in the "bad" group. I explore the relationship between recipients and workers in more detail in Chapter 9.

Politicians, the Rich, and Men

Although MWRO and LIFE members spent a considerable amount of time discussing AP workers, they placed the greatest emphasis on politicians, the rich, and men. This grouping of politicians, the rich, and men reflects the connections the women made between their actions and intentions. Politicians, for instance, were often portrayed as rich men concerned with maintaining their own power, and rich male politicians were seen to help other men before addressing the needs of women. Indeed, the women often employed the categories interchangeably, using "politician" or "rich" to refer to the same people or similar sets of characteristics.

The following descriptions from an MWRO meeting illustrate how the women constructed (wealthy and male) politicians. During the meeting, MWRO members responded to the negative stereotypes of recipients invoked by legislators by constructing their own negative stereotypes of politicians. One topic of discussion, for instance, was legislators' claims that recipients are lazy. In rebuttal, Donna Day, Sandra Barrett, and Gayle Adkins characterized legislators as privileged and ignorant:

D: all of 'em are set for THEIR nice fancy housing, THEIR nice fancy (gardens), they don't WANNA hear about ANYthing else
S: they have their real nice meals three times a day
D: OH YEAH and have everything served to 'em on TOP of it
G: well if they're saying all the ignorant myths ((about welfare recipients)) then they must be ignorant.   (MWRO 5/2/90)

Donna's, Sandra's and Gayle's talk was in keeping with the confrontational tone of the meeting:

Attacking 'em back
Louise was describing Senator Jones, a right wing legislator who responded to women's pleas for assistance for their children by accusing the women of laziness: "well why don't you do something about it? why don't you get off your lazy butt?" the Senator would attack. In Louise's view, legislators weren't interested in hearing about recipients' struggles. "I've SEEN them," she said, "If there's too many recipients in the room they will just not have the meeting." In fact, on one occasion when MWRO had organized a large contingent of recipients to attend a legislative hearing, the meeting was simply canceled.

The women responded to Louise's complaint with a call to "attack 'em back." Returning the legislators' attacks, was, moreover a relatively simple affair: it required only the presence of recipients. Louise, for example, told the story of how

Nancy Green had managed to make a legislator squirm simply by *sitting behind him:*"I've seen Nancy sit there and stare Jones right in the back. And this man, he . . . just kept, TRYING TO MOVE AWAY FROM HER YOU KNOW BECAUSE HE'S TALKIN' ABOUT ALL THESE CUTS AND HE LOOKS AROUND AND SHE'S JUST *DEAD* LOOKING AT 'EM, his WHOLE HEAD just turns red, right, he gets real NERvous about it." Donna Dey's description of her meetings with Representative Wenger, a relatively "friendly" member of the Legislature, confirmed Louise's assessment: "he'll sit right there and you would've swore somebody put a snake in his pants." When pitted against politicians, welfare recipients were clearly the moral victors. (MWRO 5/2/90)

In thus working to criticize politicians' negative stereotypes of recipients, the women produced their own constructions of politicians as ignorant and uncaring. By implication, they also portrayed themselves as fundamentally different from what the legislators claimed them to be. A detailed analysis of how the women's constructions of "us" and "them" co-occured in the meeting is included as Case #3 in Appendix A.

In addition to a marked callousness, the women claimed that wealthy male politicians supported the interests of men in general over those of women. Members of LIFE, in particular, argued that men of various class backgrounds colluded to maintain male privilege. Male judges, for instance, enabled other men to avoid paying child support. The reasoning behind this was clear:

This world is, men's GOT it, man. Look how many men we got in the White House. Why ain't there more women up there?—'cause they don't want us, they don't want to SHARE with us. (LIFE 4/1/90)

As Susan Harrison put it:

if you ain't paid your RENT they're gonna put mother and kids and all out in this fuckin' cold STREET, you KNOW, they're HARD on us, they're hard on the WOMEN, they're easy as hell on the MEN. ((C: why do you think that is?)) Because there's MEN up there running this COUNTRY and they don't GIVE a shit, if they can pay you two hundred dollars to get in your damn pants buddy, while their wife don't know about it, they'll do it, beLIEVE me THEY'LL do it. (LIFE 4/1/90)

The men these women referred to "don't any of 'em know what it's really like. They've never had to ask anybody for help." Men in positions of power, then—landlords, government figures—neither understand nor truly care about women. Their focus on women is, rather, unidimensional: women are there for the men's sexual pleasure. And because powerful men were "easy as hell" on other men, women were left with full responsibility for children—responsibility that often forced them onto the welfare rolls. Indeed, the men with whom the women had the most direct experience typically reneged on their fatherly responsibilities, and were considered less than useful. Thus Janice Borup's comment that "I'd STILL be on welfare ((if I lived)) with my kid's dad" (LIFE 4/1/90). Moreover, men sometimes tried to take advantage of the women's financial vulnerability. In this regard, Janet Burns told of a man who approached her for sex after she had purchased milk at a convenience store. She felt that her food stamps had signaled her potential availability:

I paid for my . . . milk with food stamps . . . and that was the only thing I could see that might have led him . . . to believe that I would've done anything for some money. (LIFE 4/29/90)

On another occasion, Rita Moore spoke of having sex with her landlord in order to avoid eviction.

In sum, the women felt discriminated against by politicians because they were rich and thus had no interest in the trials and tribulations of the indigent. In general, whether wealthy or not, men had little understanding of women's needs, and no sense of their own responsibilities, whether as legislators or as fathers.

The gender and class features of this construction are interesting. Significantly, the women produce the idea of men colluding across class (the issue of race was not raised as the legislators and other men in question were all Anglo). Regardless of the differences between legislators and indigent men, their gender provides the basis for an alliance that works against the interests of women. As I discuss in Chapter 9, however, the women did not entertain the idea of a similar gender alliance with welfare workers; rather, differences in social position superseded the similarities of their sex. A second noteworthy feature of this construction relates to the women's views of gender roles. Men, like women, should fulfill their roles—as leaders of society and heads of families. Dissent, in this case, is not in relation to societal norms, but in relation to the men's unwillingness to abide by those norms.

Discussion: Empowerment and Welfare Rights Groups

The official purpose of welfare rights groups is to organize recipients for specific actions in order to change the system. Participation in these groups also provides women with the opportunity to work on their own identities by replacing personal deficit explanations for poverty with explanations based on social structure or the interests of the dominant classes. Indeed, the welfare rights conversations in these last two chapters illustrate the extent to which this identity work was a key feature of the meetings, and, indeed, of the groups' activism. Insofar as it exonerates recipients, this work can be called empowering. The women may at least develop a sense that they are doing the best they can, or even that they hold the moral high ground. Given the negative image of welfare recipients in U.S. society and the ways their morality is questioned, occupying the moral high ground is a considerable accomplishment.

The collective nature of the sense-making produced at the welfare rights meetings may have contributed to this accomplishment. To defy mainstream explanations and stereotypes while standing with others is, after all, a less fearful enterprise than to do so while standing alone. A comparison of the exchanges in welfare rights meetings with those in interviews uncovers differences in both tone and content which highlight the empowering nature of this collective activity.[1]

I would argue that the immediate context of the meetings—the presence of other recipients—provided the means of expression and joint empowerment. LIFE and MWRO members produced constructions that were either absent or only nascent in the interviews. While elements of resistance were clearly evident in the welfare biographies, the comembership established at welfare rights meetings strengthened this resistance and provided grounds for the development of new perceptions. The meetings also provided greater opportunity for participants to explore and either appropriate or dismiss mainstream models of, for example, women's roles, or the nature of economic success and security. In drawing on conversations among multiple participants as well as on individual biographies, however, I am not claiming that the former are more authentic or real, and thus more valuable than the other. Both interviews and naturally occurring conversation provide insights into how the women construct their worlds. Both, moreover, are social productions—productions of an interviewee and interviewer in the one case, and of multiple participants with relatively similar status in the other. An exploration of the two kinds of talk does, however, allow an opportunity to compare the constructions that occur in these two very different interactional contexts. This provides insight into the range of the women's views and allows for an understanding of these as fluid and emergent rather than static. Moreover, I am not claiming that women were transformed by their participation in welfare rights groups as in a before-after sequence, although I would not deny this possibility. Rather, I am arguing that the meetings provided a context conducive to expressions and constructions that differed in both content and tone from

1. It is important to point out that the two groups of women did not overlap entirely. I interviewed five women who had never been active participants in a welfare rights group; however, their names were on a group mailing list, indicating that they had either attended a meeting or called for help or information. The remaining seven women were previously active (two), current core members (four), or occasional participants (one) in one of the two welfare rights groups.

those found in the interview data. Again, this highlights the fluid, emergent, and context-dependent nature of the women's constructive work.

In comparing interview and welfare rights talk, it is evident that the tone of welfare rights meetings was more animated, as indicated by the frequency of overlaps, and by loud and sometimes speeded-up speech. This difference in tone mirrored differences in the range of emotions expressed. Women were more likely to express anger and to employ sarcasm and ridicule in welfare rights meetings, and less likely to express shame or embarrassment. This is in keeping with differences in the content of the two kinds of talk, which, although sometimes similar across the two contexts, differed in striking ways. Stigma, for instance, played a much larger role in the interviews than in welfare rights conversations. While the women I interviewed reported resisting stigma in their own, individual ways, they seemed more or less resigned to it and did not, with the exception of Mary McDonald and Dee Cook, question its validity. This was not the case in LIFE and MWRO meetings, during which members were more likely to scoff at negative stereotypes. Ways of talking about key others, most notably welfare workers, also differed in the two contexts. For instance, the view of AP workers as arbitrary and unpredictable—a view commonly aired in LIFE and MWRO meetings—was not voiced in interviews, despite the frequency of negative comments on workers in those contexts. This may have been the result of discovering, during the course of conversations with other recipients, that people were being treated differently. Similarly, getting together with other women may have enabled participants to disparage men as a group, something which did not occur in the interviews. Finally, talk about employment and "hard work" also differed in the two contexts. Both contexts saw efforts to accommodate the work ethic and critiques of how the welfare system prevented economic success, but there was a greater emphasis in the welfare rights meetings on the women's identities as "hard workers."

A key difference between interviews and welfare rights conversations is that, in the former, the women seemed less resistant to negative stereotypes, while in the latter they more often appropriated dominant values to contest the same stereotypes. Again, MWRO and LIFE members argued that it was the welfare system which did not allow women to fulfill their obligations as mothers (by forcing them to find employment), which forced them to engage in illegal behavior (e.g., prostitution), and which kept them from securing financial independence (by penalizing them when they reported employment income). In other words, recipients were prevented from being what society expected of women—and what they themselves professed wanting to be. Instead, they were forced to become what they and society looked down upon. In using the tools (values, ideologies) provided by those in power (Scott 1990), the women produced a number of reversals, whereby their accusers, such as legislators, were constructed as, for example, "irresponsible," which the dominant discourse on welfare associates with recipients. The women thereby reconstituted dominant notions of responsibility to reflect well on themselves and poorly on those who would call them irresponsible.

The following exchange exemplifies the moral positioning that occurred in welfare rights conversations. Susan Harrison, Rita Moore, and myself are the participants; we are discussing a meeting that Susan and Rita had had with the aide to a local legislator.

```
 1   S:  I told him, I said EVERY child NEEDS a safe environment, NOT the
 2       RICH, NOT the MIDDLE class, but ALSO WELfare mothers
 3   R:  yep
 4   S:  and we're having to leave our kids with ANYbody and everybody that'll
 5       TAKE 'em
 6   C:  yep
 7   S:  THAT'S not right
 8   C:  no, it's not right
 9   R:  'cause they're our FUTURE
10   S:  ye—THAT'S WHAT I TOLD 'EM TOO ((laughs))
11   R:  THESE CHILDREN, these children are growing up after being abused
12       and, uh
13   S:  sexually assaulted
14   R:  YEAH, and
15   S:  you know
16   R:  and
17   S:  the HELL with that
18   R:  there IS gonna be no future
19   C:  right
20   S:  and for the FIRST time in my ENTIRE life, I ACTUALLY sat down in
21       front of this high honcho and asked—DELIBERATELY, came right out
22       and told him the truth, I said you know what really burns my ass is
23       that ya'll spending all this money on this drug shit and gettin' women
24       off the streets and stuff, we HAVE to be there
25   C:  mm huh, you said that to him?
26   R:  he—she told him she—
27   S:  I told 'em
28   R:  prostituted
29   S:  that whole four months, yes SIR, that welfare didn't help me
30   C:  what did he say about it?
31   S:  he just ((laughs)), you know
32   C:  whoa
33   R:  yep
34   S:  he just didn't know WHAT to say, he didn't realize that THIS SHIT is
         going ON you know    (LIFE 4/20/90)
```

In this exchange, Susan and Rita claim that welfare mothers are equals of, and have the same rights as, members of the more privileged classes. They also make general statements about right and wrong: it's "not right" to leave the care and upbringing of children to just anybody, because "they're our FUTURE" (line 9). The "our" in "our future" refers to society as a whole; in other words, if we collectively fail to provide adequate care for all of our children, we will all suffer the consequences.[2] The concern, then, is not an individualistic one, but a *societal* one. This clearly provides some moral standing. Susan's recounting of how she confronted "this high honcho" with the reality of misguided policies that compel prostitution provides evidence of her conviction that she holds the moral high ground (lines 20–24). The entire segment is characterized by tones of outrage at the state of affairs and accomplishment at having confronted a representative of the system.

The kind of empowerment expressed in this exchange is also evident in the MWRO discussion of legislative hearings referred to above (see pp.75–76). The women in the group manage to find some power for themselves in the face of both legislators' failure to see beyond their own wealth and the power they have to silence recipients' voices. Not only can recipients see through politicians' deployment of negative stereotypes and thus characterize them as "ignorant"—again, note the reversal—but recipients also have the ability to make legislators uncomfortable, in that they have to work so hard to avoid recognizing recipients' plight.

What happened when women got together, then, was different from what happened when I spoke with them alone. When interviewed, the women were relating their experiences to an outsider—to someone who had no idea what it was like to be a welfare recipient. When they got together at welfare rights meetings, however, they were sharing their experiences with others who did know what it was like. Accordingly, at the meetings there were expressions of solidarity with other recipients that were not evident in the one-on-one discussions, regardless of my partisan position. To be sure, this sense of solidarity had its boundaries, as when women divorced themselves from other categories of recipients who were not as worthy as they. Mostly, however, the women were able to pull together in the face of much more powerful opposing forces, and to construct themselves as more worthy than their adversaries. That they drew on moral issues and principles in their work is reasonable and strategically sound, given that it is precisely on such bases that they are most often condemned by those in power. The views of one such powerful group—AP workers—is my focus in the following three chapters.

2. Similar arguments were advanced by welfare reformers in the late 19th and early 20th centuries, particularly by those reformers who advocated removing children from poor homes so that they could be raised properly. Some have argued that calls for the proper raising of children were in actuality calls for the proper training of a docile work force (Abramovitz 1988a).

Chapter 6
The Welfare Trap II: Workers

I THInk that might be part, of everyone's PROBlem, is you are . . . trapped. We can't go ANYplace and get paid as much as we get paid ((here)), out of the benefits and the job security. (Anne Jensen, DSS)

Just as poverty is feminized, so the majority of front-line workers in the U.S. welfare system are women (Ehrenreich and Piven 1984; Fraser 1989; Gordon 1990; Withorn 1984). Women's associations with public assistance in this study were thus not limited to receiving it, but included working for the Department of Social Services as Assistance Payments workers. Women, in fact, have been at the center of the U.S. welfare system since its inception (Mink 1990; Sklar 1993) and their continued role as workers reflects both occupational segregation and cultural views concerning women's roles as caregivers (Ehrenreich and Piven 1984; Fraser 1989).

The AP workers who participated in this study included the 17 women who made up the AP staff of the Kenyon County welfare office and 30 workers who attended a three-day training course for new department employees. The Kenyon County workers gave me permission to tape record both their interviews with applicants (contingent on each applicant's consent) and their informal conversations with each other, up to and including comments passed in the women's restroom. It is therefore their work lives and talk that provide the data for the following three chapters, although I make occasional reference to the workers in the training course.

Most of the women in the Kenyon County office came from working class backgrounds; their parents were factory workers, cashiers, truck drivers, waitresses, and the like. Only five of the seventeen had parents who held what are typically considered to be middle class jobs in management, education, and business. Ranging in age from 25 to 59 years, 12 of the women had children, and only two had never had a male partner (see Appendix B, Table B2). Like the recipients in this study, all of them were Anglo and heterosexual. Also like the recipients, they did not have many educational credentials. In keeping with statewide statistics (Wertkin 1990), only three of the women (18 percent) had Bachelor's degrees. Two of them (12 percent) had attended college for three years, and an additional four (24 percent) had attended for two years. Two others had gone to community college, one for one year, and the other for six months (6 percent each). Finally, two of the women (12 percent) had attended technical-vocational schools (business, secretarial) for two years and six months respectively. The remaining four women (24 percent) had high school diplomas. As outlined in Appendix B Table B2, all the women's work histories provide clear evidence of occupational segregation by gender.

By virtue of their affiliation with state government, then, the women earned more money than they probably would have otherwise, given their work backgrounds and educational credentials. The majority—eleven of seventeen—earned $30,000 or more per year, and five earned between $24,000 and $28,000 per year; only one new worker was earning a low salary of $20,000 per year. Most of the women experienced a marked jump in wages on becoming an AP worker. The women's awareness of this fact is illustrated in the first theme discussed in this chapter, "Trapped in AP Work."

The women had been AP workers for periods ranging from one to 18 years, with an average of 11.5 years. In their positions as welfare workers, they were street level bureaucrats, sharing with their kin—police officers, emergency room clerks, and teachers, among others—a particular institutional position and function. Specifically, they sit at the boundary between human service bureaucracies—in this case, the Michigan Department of Social Services—and the citizens making claims on those bureaucracies. They regularly meet the public face-to-face and must, in a direct and practical sense, mediate between the needs of the organization and the demands of its constituents (Erickson 1975; Erickson and Shultz 1982; Lipsky 1980; Prottas 1979). This mediation consists in part of transforming these constituents, who are otherwise complex human beings, into categories/attributes that can be processed by the organization. It is this transformation that allows the organization to fulfill its function, by providing a basis on which services are rendered to individuals now constituted as "clients."

Despite their pivotal role, however, AP workers are at the bottom of the department hierarchy. Their work as the official executors (as opposed to designers) of policy, and as those who administer (which is different from provide) care for recipients, is low in status. It is also high in repetition, in the need to attend to detail, and in requirements for output. As such, AP work reflects the gendered organization of many government bureaucracies (see Witz and Savage 1992).

A Note on Methods

In previous chapters, I made a distinction between interview and naturally occurring talk. In the case of AP workers, however, this distinction is blurred. Although I conducted individual interviews with each worker, the informal talk I tape recorded often took the form of semi-interviews, falling somewhere between interview and naturally occurring talk. Unlike welfare rights meetings, in which I participated but did not directly elicit information or introduce topics, my participation in the informal conversations at the Kenyon County welfare office was sometimes more direct as, following Briggs (1986), I raised questions at contextually appropriate moments. On occasion, informal conversations during breaktimes resembled group interviews, as the women jointly responded to an issue that I had raised.

This difference in data partly reflects the spatial and social organization of the data collection sites. Whereas naturally occurring and interview talk were kept separate in the case of recipients—the first taking place in welfare rights meetings and the second in events officially designated as "interview" and occurring elsewhere—in the welfare office the distinctions between public and private, official and unofficial were marked differently. Distinct types of talk were not separated geographically; rather, the main distinction was between the presence of recipients, staff meetings, and everything else, all of which could occur in the same place. Moreover, except during break-time walks through the surrounding neighborhoods, I did not interact with the workers outside the welfare office, or outside the normal working day. In contrast to recipients, workers did not invite me to their homes. Perhaps this reflects an ability on their part to "keep work at work," while for recipients welfare clearly permeated every aspect of their lives.

Thus far, I have referred to women on welfare as welfare recipients, since this, along with "welfare mother," is how they preferred to refer to themselves. In the next three chapters, I follow the practice of workers and refer to recipients as "clients" when discussing workers' perspectives. It is significant in this regard that, in the context of the welfare system, "client" suggests a relationship of dependency not implied by the term "recipient" (Wineman 1984).

Trapped in Assistance Payments Work

With the exception of Fran Knight, who had earned a high salary prior to starting her job with the Department of Social Services, all the women believed that they could not find other employment that paid them as well as AP work. A conversation I had with Sally Blake and Ann Jensen illustrates this perception (see Case #4, Appendix A). One day, the two women were explaining how the structure of their job prevented them from doing good work: they found it impossible to keep up with all the paper work and were thus unable to give their clients sufficient attention. When I asked them why they then remained in their jobs, Ann responded that, "we can't go ANYplace and get paid as much as we get paid ((here)), out of the benefits and the job security." Sally explained part of the reason for this: "I don't have a four year degree . . . I have REAL limited options. I have a STUpid two-year degree which is the same as the other guys with a ((high school)) diploma." This sense of restricted opportunity is what Sally and Ann were referring to when they described feelings of "resentment" and of being "trapped," sentiments that they believed were shared by their fellow workers. They sneered at the notion that "it's your choice to be here," listing as their job alternatives working at K-mart (a discount store), or being a motel maid or housemaker—all low status, low paying jobs (with the exception of housemaker, which is unpaid) typically held by women. This despite the fact that, in their view, they had developed as much expertise over the years as anyone with a college degree. Their resentment was further heightened by the fact that they drew on numerous skills to perform their jobs. According to Ann and Sally, AP workers "have to know so much about everything," including law, marketing, and management. As the more detailed analysis of this conversation included in Appendix A indicates, the two women felt that, even though they deserved better, they had little option to but settle for their unrewarding jobs as AP workers (DSS 8/3/90).

As Sally and Ann claimed, other workers also felt "trapped" in their jobs. Edith Saunders, for instance, regretted the decision she made in 1974 to move from clerical into AP work: despite the better pay, in AP work there was "no more ((career)) ladder," and positions such as supervisor or trainer were "almost impossible to get anymore" (DSS 8/24/90). Like Sally and Anne, Judy Reynolds and Gilda White felt financially restricted. Like Sally, Gilda explained that "I don't have a college degree and I couldn't earn this type of money ((in another job))" (DSS 8/24/90); Judy simply stated that "I cannot afford to quit the job" (DSS 8/10/90). Others, like Karrie Holmes and Diane Kane, were constrained by motherhood and geographic location: AP work provided the only lucrative employment in Webster, where they felt compelled to remain because of their child care concerns. The women's decisions concerning AP work, then, reflect the intersection of economic and role (motherhood) concerns and responsibilities. The goal was to get the best possible locally available job. For married women, the husband's job determined where the family would live, thus further limiting their options.

With two exceptions, all the AP workers in the Kenyon County welfare office claimed to have applied for their jobs because of the pay, benefits packages, and security. Many of them, in fact, had no idea of what AP work involved before they took the job. Emma Nichols, for instance, "never knew nothing about it when I came into it" (DSS 8/13/90); Diane Kane "had no prior interest in it" (DSS 8/13/90); and Valerie Wood "knew nothing, nothing, nothing about this job at all when I took it" (DSS 8/13/90). Valerie, moreover, like Gilda White, told me that she had simply taken the first state job she could get, just to get her foot in the door. The workers I spoke with at the training session I attended echoed this view: when queried, they said that they wanted to work for the state because the money was good; if nothing else, AP work was a stepping stone to more attractive administrative positions, either in the Department of Social Services or elsewhere in the state system. Public service, then, was not the women's primary motive. Indeed, for most of the women, public service had not even been a consideration.

The two exceptions to this were Nora Ryan and Harriet Eaton, both of whom applied for AP positions because they wanted to help people. Prior to becoming an AP worker in 1974, Nora had worked for the Office of Economic Opportunity as a community aid and home maker. Although she, too, was interested in the income from AP work, she was eager to help people, and saw herself as a "people-oriented person" (DSS 8/10/90). Harriet also had strong convictions about helping those in need. Because of the overtime she had been able to earn in her previous job, she actually took a cut in pay when she moved into AP work. She was amenable to this, however, because "I really thought it would be something new and I would be helping people" (DSS 8/13/90).

Although Nora and Harriet were the only workers who chose AP work out of an explicit desire to do good, many of the other workers claimed that being able to help people—a possibility they discovered once on the job—was one of the rewards of their position. While not as frequent as references to money, the women did make comments such as, "every once in a while you actually feel like you do some good" (DSS 8/17/90); and most workers took pleasure in helping someone who they really felt was in need.

In sum, the women's educational credentials and employment backgrounds placed limits on their economic opportunities, with the result that AP work was their most lucrative option. The need to support themselves and their families was their central motive for pursuing and remaining in their jobs. AP work also allowed some of the women to be close to home, thus accommodating their roles as the primary caretakers of their children. This compelling need to remain street level bureaucrats was reflected in the sentiment of being "trapped."

Powerlessness

A second major theme that emerged from the workers' talk was what they referred to as "powerlessness," "helplessness," and "frustration." The women expressed these feelings with regard to four particular areas of their work lives: workloads, policy, relationships with their managers and clients, and the mundane details of day-to-day life in the welfare office.

Workloads

All the women, without exception, complained about the size of their case loads. Such complaints are best understood within the context of actual workloads, exemplified by the following figures for the months of June and July 1991. During each month workers averaged:

- Ongoing (continuing) case loads of 169 and 168 respectively. While many ongoing cases lay dormant most of the time, they are cases which workers may be required to work on at any moment.
- Ten new eligibility determinations or dispensations. Eligibility determinations entail interviewing applicants and processing their applications; dispensations involve processing paperwork.
- Six reviews. These are annual redeterminations of eligibility to receive assistance, and are similar in procedure to initial eligibility determinations.
- Twenty-four income reports. Recipients whose income changes must file income reports. In response, workers run new budgets for the cases and alter assistance allocations accordingly.
- Seven emergency needs applications. The process is similar to that for new applications, with, however, additional time pressures.

Workers estimate that interviewing applicants takes from twenty minutes to over an hour, while processing each application or review takes approximately four hours. Prottas (1979) points out, however, that the length of interviews in street-level bureaucratic work is quite unpredictable. Recipients in unusual or complicated situations invariably take longer to interview; their paperwork may also take more time to process. As the women work, moreover, they are frequently interrupted by other clients and AP workers, their supervisors, clerks, the office director, and employees in other departments of the office, such as child protective services. It is clear, then, that AP workloads are extremely strenuous. Indeed, according to Wertkin (1990) case load expectations for AP workers in Michigan exceeded 130 percent in 1990. Comments such as, "it's just physically impossible to keep up" (DSS, 8/13/90) were ubiquitous in the Kenyon County welfare office. As Emma Nichols, an AP worker of 17 years, put it:

I really liked it in the beginning, but . . . I can't handle all this paper work and ((policy)) manual changes . . . I don't like to say I'm a perfectionist, but when it is something, I like to do it right, and I just don't feel that I'm doing it right now, before it seemed like I was . . . I just can't keep up with (changes in the manuals) anymore. I just (don't) have the time to sit down and read all that material when I'm trying to do everything else, and it . . . really makes you feel incompetent. (DSS 8/13/90)

Planning for vacations put particular pressure on workers, as they frantically tried to get ahead of themselves in order to avoid finding themselves far behind when they returned to work. Nora Ryan, for example, stopped me in the restroom one day to complain about having to come to the office on the weekends in order to prepare for a one-week vacation she was taking in three week's time. The women gave the general impression of running to stay in place.

Policy: Knowledge, Input, and Appropriateness

Public assistance policy is in a constant state of flux. Although I have no figures for the period of this research, Wertkin (1990) refers to a study reporting that in 1976, AP workers received an average of 22 pages of interoffice memo or new policy material each week. Given the increasing complexity of policy since that time, it is reasonable to assume that that average has increased. One outcome of this deluge is that workers are unable to keep abreast of policy changes and as a result feel incompetent. Edith Saunders, in AP work for 16 years, lamented her loss of knowledge over the years:

There's too many manuals, you . . . can see all the manuals we deal with and we're supposed to know all the programs when we virtually can't. Budgeting is so complicated now that you can't look at something and—before we could look at something and sorta know if they were eligible or not, now you can't. (DSS 8/24/90)

Edith was referring to what Wertkin (1990) calls "proletarianizing," a process which reduces the skills required of workers to perform their jobs. The process of proletarianizing began in 1972, when, by federal mandate, social services were separated from income maintenance programs—a separation that was maintained in Michigan despite rescission of the mandate in 1975. This separation has resulted in the deprofessionalizing and deskilling of AP work: applicants are required to meet fewer educational and training standards to qualify for the position, and they are given little official leeway in implementing policy. Rather than making assessments themselves, based on their knowledge of policy—something that Edith remembered doing when she started her job—workers have become dependent on computers to determine recipients' statuses, and are increasingly unfamiliar with what the computer does with the numbers they give it. Proletarianizing has effectively removed knowledge and understanding from workers, who have been officially designated as mere executors of policy. It is not surprising, then, that workers felt excluded from the framing of policy. This might have been more acceptable if policy makers took account of workers' needs and expertise, but they did not. Debbie Brown, for instance, a worker of 15 years, argued that current policies were not responsive to either workers' or clients' needs. When I asked her what, if anything, she would change about the welfare system given the opportunity, she produced a lengthy discourse on the need for consistency, so that people would not "fall through the cracks"; and for flat grants (in which benefits are determined by income and number of family members, rather than by assets or expenditures), so that recipients could save money if they chose and workers would have less paperwork to process. In Debbie's view, current policy suffered three shortcomings: it was financially unsound, it placed unnecessary burdens on workers, and, finally, it did not adequately respond to the needs of the population it was supposed to serve. Debbie also felt that, as a worker at the street level, she had gained some insight into the needs of poor people and of how to best approach satisfying those needs. The rigid division between the work of policy formation and the work involved in its execution—between management and labor—left AP workers ignorant of the workings of policy, yet responsible for implementing programs they felt were designed with little understanding of either poverty or AP work.

Managers and Clients

It should be clear by now that AP workers believed management (including their immediate supervisors as well as those higher up on the department hierarchy) "really (don't) know what it's like" to do AP work.

There were two main features of this view: (1) people in management have it easy, that is, have "cushy cushy jobs . . . where people are sitting there doing nothing" (Harriet Eaton 8/13/90); and (2) managers have no idea of the stresses suffered by AP workers and thus make decisions that only place additional burdens on them, as Debbie Brown indicated in her remarks on policy, above. Workers who left AP positions to write policy—an extremely rare occurrence but one with considerable salience for the workers—soon forgot, it was felt, what AP work entailed, and eventually took the side of management in claiming that AP workers had nothing to complain about. The women felt that their clients, as well, "don't have a real good picture of what goes on," especially with regard to the work entailed in processing applications (Sherry Nelson and Harriet Eaton 6/13/90). Workers thus felt pressed from both sides—from administrators who structured their work lives and from recipients who required their services—and believed that neither group fully understood or appreciated the demands of AP work.

Workers frequently complained about the constraints they faced in their interactions with recipients. Two examples I discuss in greater detail in Chapter 7 illustrate this claim. In the first, policy specifications permitted an applicant to assert that she did not share meals with her live-in boyfriend, thereby effectively eliminating his income from her welfare budget. The end result of this was that she received more food stamps than she otherwise would have. While the applicant's worker was convinced that the two people did indeed share their meals, she could not do anything about it because, as she put it, "I have to take it for what they say" (DSS 6/19/90). In the second example, a worker was convinced that one of her clients was abusing her children; rules of evidence, however, prohibited her from fully pursuing the case (DSS 6/19/90). There were limits, then, to workers' abilities to reprimand their clients for what they felt was inappropriate behavior.

Workers also expressed frustration when they encountered restrictions but wanted to do *more* for a client than policy would allow. Harriet Eaton gave voice to this frustration when she told me of her discovery that she could not help everybody:

I . . . will never forget when I went into . . . Orange County. I had, I had this, when I hadn't been there very long and this woman and her son came in, and I think—I don't remember if I had to deny her or she didn't like whatever I said, that she went, she just tore out of the building, well, I went tearing out after her, and this one woman said to me, "yeah, you came in here like a big bird thinking you were gonna take everybody under your wing, but you can't do it" . . . I still, I feel frustrated, I can't . . . when I can't help 'em, and yet I know that sometimes people are . . . suffering because I haven't gotten the cases open, and it's the—but there are people that . . . there're old people out there that don't ever apply, that should, and that get, you know, maybe they got a little too much in assets and they're not eligible, so I'm, I'm beginning to think, and I've always been against socialized medicine, totally against it, but I'm beginning to think that the money they pay us to sit here and say you're eligible, you're not eligible, if that money was put into medical care for people I think it would be good, because I'm sure there are people that . . . like I said, probably do without medications and do without things they need because they can't afford it. (DSS 8/13/90)

Harriet was in tears as she told me this story. She later excused herself by saying, "I think I'm tired, that's why I'm so weepy."

Even in cases where policy allowed for some flexibility, however, such as emergency needs (one-time allotments given in emergency situations), workers' decision-making powers were circumscribed by those of their supervisors. In the following exchange, Karrie Holmes tries to convince Ester Dove, her supervisor, to ask the central office for money to repair a roof for Myra Goodwin, a 76-year-old client who spends her time caring for 30 abandoned cats. As Karrie discovered when she visited her, Myra's mobile home was in shambles: not only was the roof in need of repair, but a number of windows were broken and boarded up, the electricity was not working properly, there was no hot water, and the furniture was falling apart. Nevertheless, Karrie felt that Myra could get by with just a new roof, which was all that Myra had asked for. Ester, however, had no desire to put money into a "bottomless pit." The following discussion takes place after Ester has asked Karrie a number of questions about Myra's situation. Note that length of pauses, in seconds, is indicated in parentheses.

1	E:	I don't know (1) if there's anything we can do to save someone like that
2		(1) um, from themselves (2) 'cause I can't see us pouring the money in
3	K:	mm huh
4	E:	and the fact th—
5	K:	YET, wh—wh—when you were GONE, we SPENT, close to two thou-
6		sand dollars on a MIGRANT family, but, you know, they came up here,
7		looking for a job, they didn't HAVE any job, they didn't QUALIFY,
8		because they were not legal aliens. We spent close to two thousand
9		dollars just putting them up for a week and sendin' 'em back to Texas
10		where they came from
11	E:	because they, they meet the, criteria
12	K:	yeah
13	E:	right, and she's falling through the CRACKS
14	K:	and she's falling through the cracks
15	E:	and ((sigh)) (2) if we can GET—what's the—the landlord sayin'?
16	K:	((name of landlord))
17	E:	yeah, what she's sayin' as to (1)
18	K:	she said that she'd be willing to give her a life lease on the trailer but
19		not the land, but she's not going to pay any legal expense, she's not
20		putting ANY more money into it than what—

21 E: I don't BLAME her
22 K: I mean, 'cause it's, I mean she's got—
23 E: MAYbe—
24 K: the land free and EVERYthing
25 E: maybe THAT'S what (6) I, yo—you know, I'll TELL ya, I'm not real
26   THRILLED about putting the MONEY in it, mySELF (2)
27 K: I don't know, you got a human RESPONSIBILITY ((laughs)) I mean
28   she's a HUMAN being out there and, and—
29 E: I underSTAND that, but she's also making ch—CHOICES   (DSS 6/
        27/90)

Karrie and Ester are arguing two opposing perceptions of Myra's case. Ester, who feels that Myra (and the welfare department) would be better off if she gave up her cats and moved elsewhere, claims that Myra is responsible for the choices she is making; thus her statements that "I don't know if there's anything we can do to save someone like that" (line 1) and "she's also making ch—CHOICES" (line 29). Karrie, on the other hand, admires Myra's dedication to the cats and feels, moreover, that caring for the cats is necessary to Myra's health and happiness. She argues, accordingly, that Ester should at least try to convince the department to fix the roof: "I don't know, you got a human RESPONSIBILITY ((laughs)) I mean she's a HUMAN being out there" (lines 27–28). The only thing the two women agree on is that Myra is "falling through the cracks" (lines 13–14).

Karrie's reluctance to confront Ester is clear at lines 5: she cuts in on Ester's turn, voice raised, but then falters as she starts to make her argument. This hesitancy might have been related to the fact that Ester was her supervisor, to Karrie's strong feelings about the case, or to her awareness that the department would be unlikely to fulfill her request. (Karrie is not arguing with the department here, however, but with Ester's unwillingness to try to push the case through.) Later in the discussion, Karrie makes it clear that she is concerned about both policy and her own standing as a worker:

((Myra)) is of the opinion that anybody from this office that doesn't come and see her that it's just a worker that sits on their fat ass and works five days out of the month . . . I was telling the girls on the way ((to the home visit)), well, I can come out of this smelling good or bad ((laughs)), either I'm one of the bad asses ((laughs)) or, or else I'm gonna help her. (DSS 6/27/90)

Karrie here reconstitutes the distinction between the deserving and undeserving poor as one between good and bad workers.

For her part, Ester's frequent pauses (at lines 1, 2, 15, 17, 25, 26) might also indicate a certain hesitancy, perhaps related to her understanding of the limits to welfare policy, to her discomfort with the moral force of

Karrie's position, or to the fact that I was present (I did not interact with supervisors on a regular basis). In examining the entire exchange of which the above excerpt is just a part, however, it becomes clear that supervisors as well as workers are subject to a number of constraints. On three occasions, Ester points to her limitations: "I don't think that I could talk fast enough to get this one to pass ENP" (Emergency Needs Program), "I cannot see that we are going to get ENP to do anything on this," and "I'm willing to bend the rules, but I'm not willing to break them all to hell." While the first two statements indicate the limits to Ester's power, the latter testifies to her discretionary power. It is to this discretionary power that Karrie is appealing, perhaps in the same way that recipients appeal to a related discretionary power on the part of workers.

Karrie's and Ester's differing conceptions of this case underscore what Lipsky (1980) refers to as the "intrinsically conflictual" nature of the worker-manager relationship. Managers, on the one side, want to exercise tight reign over their workers and are concerned with total output. Workers, in contrast, prefer to be unencumbered in their efforts to deal with clients on a one-by-one basis. In the end, both the real and chosen limits to Karrie's and Ester's discretionary powers resulted in a search for free (voluntary) rather than official aid for Myra.

Karrie's efforts on behalf of Myra and Harriet's story of not being able to help everyone suggest how workers transform the individuals who come to the welfare office into particular kinds of clients. I discuss this process in detail in Chapter 7. For now it is sufficient to note that in these examples Harriet and Karrie transform the two women they encounter into the "deserving" poor. In so doing, they are both constructing and policing the discursive boundary between the mutually exclusive yet mutually constitutive categories of "deserving" and "undeserving."

The Day-to-Day

From the workers' point of view, management's attempts to control their work lives could reach ridiculous extremes. Consider the following field-note entry:

Peggy Stewart broke two of her toes, and consequently was wearing slippers to work. During a cigarette break outside, she announced to the other workers that Edna, her supervisor, had told her that slippers were inappropriate attire in the office, and that she should at least wear a regular shoe on her healthy foot. The workers laughed heartily at this, one of them calling Edna a "chicken shit" because when she had had to wear special shoes for health reasons, she had brought in a doctor's note to justify it. As indicated by their derisive laughter, Edna's focus on shoes seemed ludicrous to the workers. To me, the incident pointed to the extent to which managers try to control even the most mundane aspects of office life. (fieldnotes 8/1/90)

The office restructuring that occurred toward the end of the study was a more serious manifestation of workers' lack of autonomy. Prior to restructuring, the women had private offices, complete with windows and doors. In July 1990, however, the office director decided to move the child protective service workers (social workers who deal with child neglect and abuse) into the private offices and to place the AP workers in semi-private cubicles in the center area of the building.

The workers were unanimously angered by this decision, which was made without their consultation or consent. They had no control over where in the cubicle section they would be placed, and much of the furniture they received was damaged. In short, they were being moved from larger, more comfortable, private offices to smaller, cramped, noisy cubicles that would allow their supervisors to keep an even closer eye on what they were doing. Although management argued that social workers needed the private offices in order to maintain client confidentiality, AP workers were quick to point out that the majority of child protective service workers' interactions with clients took place away from the office and that public assistance clients needed confidentiality as well. The real reason for the move, workers argued, was that they were of lower status than the social workers. Nora Ryan, for instance, claimed that AP workers would not have been treated so poorly if they all had had college degrees. Restructuring was viewed as one more example of workers' low standing in the department, and of the extent to which their bosses controlled, with impunity, every aspect of their work lives.

Bodily Harm

My work gets done but I suffer for it. (Peggy Stewart)

In a survey of 364 AP workers throughout Michigan, Wertkin (1990) explored various dimensions of AP worker job satisfaction. Although not explicitly addressing power and powerlessness, issues related to control over one's work life provided the major focus of the research. A number of "satisfaction items" were rated by the workers in the study. Those with which workers reported more satisfaction than dissatisfaction were salary, safety, office space, job challenge, orientation (introduction to the job), evaluation, administrative support (clerical staff), and job structure. Those with which workers reported more dissatisfaction than satisfaction were reasonable job expectations, input into policy changes, professional treatment, and job prestige. With the exception of office space, about which the workers in my own study were extremely unhappy, Wertkin's portrait matches that constructed by the women of Kenyon County.

The Kenyon County workers expressed dissatisfaction in part by drawing connections between their jobs and their health. Fran Knight's tale of a client hearing illustrates how workers linked their powerlessness vis-à-vis managers and recipients with their physical and mental well-being. Recall that client hearings, attended by a recipient, their AP worker and the worker's supervisor, are organized in order to respond to client complaints.

Why Don't I Count?

One of Fran's clients lodged an official complaint on the grounds that Fran had not given her all the assistance she was entitled to. Fran's supervisor informed her of the situation, indicating that they would eventually have a hearing to deal with the matter. Assuming that she would be given adequate notice of the hearing, Fran continued to see her other clients as scheduled.

One afternoon, however, Fran received a phone call from her supervisor informing her that the hearing was to be held that day. Fran's protest that she had a number of clients already scheduled to come in for appointments made no difference: "they wouldn't move it, nothing at all, right, so I had to move all these clients, cancel 'em, reschedule 'em, whatever." In contrast, she said, "all it would've taken is for that client to call and asked to be rescheduled, for whatever reason, I don't care, because she fell down and scraped her knee, and it would've been rescheduled immediately."

Fran's sense of powerlessness was reinforced when her supervisor failed to support her during the hearing. Her account of events was given little weight, and she felt publicly humiliated. "You wonder," Fran reflected, "why I have ulcers." Not only did she suffer from (two) ulcers for which she took ulcer medication— "I keep waiting for the one to perforate, I know it's getting close"—and pain killers —for "when my ulcer starts to hurt too badly"; she also was on medication for depression. Both the ulcers and depression had developed since Fran began her job as an AP worker. The reason for this, she felt, had to do with the nature of AP work, and with, at least in part, ignorance on the part of supervisors and managers. Indeed, after spending ten years as a computer operator in the central office of the welfare department, Fran's assessment was that there was "a lot of bullshit down there. The problem is that nobody down there knows what's going on. 'Til you're actually out here nobody has the vaguest idea." Paradoxically, those with the least understanding of working conditions had the greatest power, while AP workers were given no voice at all. As Fran put it, "I have nothing, I am worse than nothing." (DSS 6/28/90)

The physical toll of workplace stress was a common conversational topic among the workers. Peggy Stewart, for example, made frequent reference to the connection between her job and her irritable bowel syndrome and migraine headaches. Another worker, Judy Reynolds, attributed her high blood pressure to the job, while Sally Blake often made jokes about the relationship between her bouts of pneumonia, flu, and other respiratory illnesses and job stress. Finally, Lucy Seale, a former AP worker who took a demotion to clerical work because she was no longer willing to tolerate the pressure of the job, had also suffered from irritable bowel syndrome. When I showed the long list of illnesses I had generated in less than a month of fieldwork to Peggy Stewart, she added that many of her co-workers were also taking anti-depressants. The reason for this, she explained, was expectations—those of clients, and those of fellow workers and supervisors. According to Peggy, the problem was

not being able to . . . physically or mentally, any way possible, get everything done . . . . It's like no matter how hard you work and no matter how hard you try you cannot physically do it. It can't be done. And unfortunately, you know, some people can manage and some can't. You know, my work gets done but I suffer for it. (DSS 6/28/90)

Peggy's references to anti-depressants and to the mental strain of AP work point to the psychological difficulties of keeping up with the job. This psychological pressure is tied to the physical demands of AP work, implying that what the institution requires of workers is unreasonable.

Stress leave, associated with the mental repercussions of AP work, was also a feature of the welfare office. During the course of the study, I knew of four workers who were receiving counseling (provided by the department) for problems related to workplace stress. Three months after I concluded the research, Fran Knight's ulcers flared up and she went on leave for over two months. Unfortunately, there are no statistics available on stress-related leaves or on the number of AP workers who make use of counseling services. This reflects, perhaps, an official view of stress-related illnesses as caused by individual rather than structural problems. Workers, however, considered that many of their physical and mental problems were an outgrowth of their work situations, rather than of personal psychological imbalances or family difficulties. Recall Judy Reynolds's comment from the beginning of Chapter 1. She made this comment in exasperation one day when I asked her why she thought AP work made people ill:

Well, just the . . . constant rushing and paper work, and, and when you stop and think of it, this really is the lowly job in DSS, because the clerks (sort of) control what you do, the people above you control what you do . . . you are given all this responsibility and yet you don't really have any rights, I mean . . . you're responsible for this and you're responsible for people eating, and . . . paying their rent, and yet you really have no say in anything that goes on in the department, you have less say than any person in this department. (DSS 8/24/90)

Betwixt and Between

In the conversations explored in this chapter, workers express their sense of powerlessness. From case loads to hearing schedules, from policy changes to decisions in particular cases, they experienced frustration, anger, and sometimes sadness over their lack of control. In general, they constructed themselves as professionals thwarted by the system, as victims of exploitation on the part of both management and recipients. This was the "us" of the women's everyday conversations.

Again, like other street level bureaucrats, the AP workers in the Kenyon County welfare office sat at the boundary of their organization. They had to respond directly to the demands of their clients, and in this respect were in a "helping orientation" towards them, but they were also beholden to the department, which required that they "judge and control clients for bureaucratic purposes" (Lipsky 1980:73). The women thus experienced a tension between the demands of individuals applying to the department for assistance, all of whom wanted help, and needs of the institution, which required that workers deny assistance to some people, and process large numbers of cases by the legal deadline. As Lipsky observes (1980:140), street level bureaucrats are confronted with a contradiction: on the one hand, they are expected to respond to *individuals*; on the other hand, their workloads necessitate that they "process people in terms of routines, stereotypes, and other mechanisms that facilitate work tasks." It is to these facilitating mechanisms that I now turn.

Chapter 7
Good and (Mostly) Bad Clients

She's the one that was scamming all along, and the father ((of the child)) was living with her full-time, employed full-time, and had the daughter on his insurance. (Colleen O'Connell, commenting on her discovery that a client had withheld information on household income)

Now there's a prime example of a working person, twenty-two years old . . . and we aren't gonna be able to do shit for her because she's not permanently disabled. (Diane Kane, commenting on a client who could not get medical insurance through her employer but who earned too much to qualify for Medicaid)

The social construction of the client, involving the client, others relevant to the client, and the public employees with whom they must deal is a significant process of social definition often unrelated to objective factors and therefore open to the influence of prejudice, stereotype, and ignorance as a basis for determinations. (Lipsky 1980:69)

In the last chapter, I explored the various pressures experienced by AP workers in the Kenyon County welfare office. At the most general level, the women shared the constraints of occupational segregation and a household division of labor in which they were assigned primary responsibility for childcare. It was partly as a result of these restrictions that the women found themselves in their current job. Once in the job, they were confronted with large case loads, lack of autonomy and low status, exclusion from official decision-making, and the competing demands of the institution and its clients—all of which took a physical and psychological toll on their well-being.

The women developed a number of coping strategies in response to these burdens. A key area in relation to which they could develop shortcuts to ease work pressure was the assessment of applicants. I have already pointed out that AP workers are in the business of constructing clients out of otherwise significantly more complicated human beings (Lipsky 1980; Prottas 1979). Once they have transformed people into "clients," workers can respond by providing (or not providing) particular services, depending on what kind of client the applicant now is, if indeed they qualify as a client at all. Stereotypes provide a useful short-cut in this process insofar as they simplify the social world: the range of people who should receive assistance is narrowed, and, among that narrow group, the number of people who should receive good service is further limited. Lipsky (1980) states in this regard:

> Thus workers do for some what they are unable to do for all. The street-level bureaucrat salvages *for a portion of the clientele* a conception of his or her performance relatively consistent with ideal conceptions of the job. Thus as the work is experienced there is no dissonance between the job as it should be done and the job as it is done *for a portion of the clientele.* The worker knows in a private sense that he or she is capable of doing the job well and can better defend against the assaults to the ego which the structure of street-level work normally delivers. (1980:151–152; emphasis in original)

The need to manage oversized workloads, however, is not the only thing impinging on workers' constructions of clients. There are also considerations related to the nature of face-to-face interaction. In any encounter, participants' attention is limited, with the result that certain phenomena or attributes are stressed while others are ignored (Erickson and Shultz 1982). Precisely what waxes and wanes in salience is related to both the institutional context of the encounter and to the specific features of the interaction. Both elements may be situated in a larger cultural context—in this case, one characterized by theories of poverty that locate the cause of poverty in defects of personality.

Negative Constructions of Clients

In the Kenyon County welfare office, "bad" clients were assumed to be the norm: engaging in negatively evaluated behavior was part and parcel of being a client. Indeed, workers expected this from all their clients, and expressed surprise when they did not encounter it.

"I think a lot of them know what to say and what to do": The Maneuvering Client

The most frequent claim that workers made about their clients was that they were deceitful and manipulative. In their view, dishonesty was a strategy clients used to intervene in the system. It took various forms, ranging from outright lying to playing by the letter, but not the spirit, of welfare policy. On one occasion, for instance, Sherry Nelson and Valerie Wood discussed two women's attempts to manipulate information in order to increase their benefits. In both cases, the women cohabited with their male partners but maneuvered so that the men's incomes would not be included as part of the household income by the welfare department. One woman claimed that she and her partner ate separately, thus excluding his income from the food stamp budget, and increasing her allotment considerably. As Sherry told the story:

Well I had one little girl that came in—this one always makes me mad, Valerie's heard the story a MIllion times—I had this girl come in . . . not too long ago and her ((cousin is)) a new case worker in Golden County, and she came in, she didn't even know how . . . her cousin answered the appliCAtion, she's living with a boyfriend and pregnant, and she says they don't prepare food together, which I think is a bunch of crAp but . . . you know, I have to take it for what they say. THEN, HE's been living there in this apartment for four years, she's eighteen and just moved in, now they're claiming the rent's three fifty, they're claiming that she pays the full three fifty . . . and that she pays completely for heat and utilities. Now he's been there for four years, now I KNOW that he's been, but, in this case she will get the full amount even though—and he's WORKing, he's got a good job, but we can't count his INcome or ANYthing, I think he was making like . . . sixteen hundred dollars. . . . SILLY, silly things, those are IRRitating sometimes, FRUStrating. (DSS 6/19/90)

Sherry's claim that "Valerie's heard the story a MIllion times," indicates that this kind of manipulation on the part of clients is considered common. Significantly, Valerie had been an AP worker for less than a year at the time. And, indeed, Valerie was able to produce her own story:

oh I hate that . . . that's what this one that I was doing was closed for fraud, she claimed she paid FULL rent, she claimed she paid heat and utilities and the heat and utilities were VENdored in HER name, the WHOLE amount. (DSS 6/19/90)

In both stories, clients are constructed as cunning and deceitful. They know enough about how the system works to manipulate it, and have no scruples about accepting illegitimate benefits. A detailed transcript and analysis of Sherry's and Valerie's concerted construction of their two clients is included as Case #5 in Appendix A.

Because clients were viewed as devious, workers often approached them with more than a modicum of skepticism. On one occasion, for instance, Karrie Holmes had asked an applicant about his assets, to which he replied that he had none. When he later mentioned that he had been living in his car, Karrie jumped in and asked, "a CAR? I thought you said you didn't have a car?" She later told me that she had been "burned" several times, and so was quick to be suspicious (DSS 6/6/90). A week later, Karrie received a rental form from another applicant on which a man's name had been written in and then crossed out.

She immediately called the landlord to inquire whether the man in question had actually vacated the apartment. Because the landlord could not verify the case either way, Karrie decided that things looked questionable and turned down the application on the basis of insufficient information (DSS 6/14/90).

Like Karrie, most of the workers could produce a story of being "burned," or of someone they knew who had been. This contributed to an atmosphere in which an assumption of deceit was in operation, and in which very little evidence was required to interpret a client's actions as manipulative. Moreover, workers often reacted to a client's purported dishonesty as if it were a personal affront, rather than, for example, an attempt to make ends meet. As Fran Knight put it, "I'm empathetic to all my clients 'til they lie to me. Once they lie to me I hate them and I won't give them anything" (DSS 8/10/90). Fran's use of "I" and "me" is noteworthy, and is in keeping with general pronoun usage among the workers. In their own phrasing, *they* were the ones who paid clients' rent, processed their food stamps, and stopped the gas company from turning off their utilities. Given this attitude, one can understand how workers could feel betrayed and cheated by clients who appeared (or were) dishonest.

"LAZY" Clients

In the workers' view, one of the reasons why clients lied and cheated was that they were lazy, wanting to get something for nothing. If it were not for such indolence, many clients would not have gotten on the relief rolls in the first place.

The following describes how Sherry Nelson approached one of her "least favorite" clients, who was due to arrive at the office any minute for an appointment that she had rescheduled twice. The story, told to me and Valerie Wood, exemplifies workers' constructions of clients as lazy.

"Miss Nelson, Miss Nelson, Here's Another Excuse"
Cindy Smith was due to come in for her yearly review appointment, during which eligibility for assistance is redetermined. Rather than keeping her appointment, however, she called Sherry, and, realizing the ramifications of failing to meet her obligation, pleaded, "Miss Nelson, Miss Nelson, my case is going to close, I want a new appointment." Sherry obliged, and set up a second meeting. Again, however, Cindy failed to keep the appointment. She also neglected to telephone Sherry until four days later, when she complained, "Miss Nelson, Miss Nelson, I missed my appointment on THURSday . . . and I just got a CLOSure letter and MY case is going to close." Sherry told her that her case was indeed about to close and that she needed to bring the appropriate papers into the office so they could have their meeting. "Well can't I mail the stuff in?" asked Cindy. Sherry's reply

was clear: "Cindy, you don't WORK . . . you are COMing IN, you HAVE to come in for this appointment . . . we only ask you to do it once a YEAR." Cindy acquiesced, and a third appointment was scheduled. Sherry warned Cindy that, "if you're not here at nine o'clock I'm not gonna see you . . . and I will NOT have an appointment."

Sherry meant what she said. Recently, for instance, another client, Barrie Teton, had also missed and then rescheduled two appointments. Sherry was flexible enough to schedule a third meeting, but she told Barrie that she expected her to "be prompt." Barrie, however, did not want to meet at the appointed time of 1:30, but at 2:30, and so failed to arrive at the welfare office until shortly after 2:30. In response, Sherry decided to punish her by leaving her in the waiting room for a while: "So I made her wait 'till 3:30, and then she came in, she said, 'MISS NELSON would you like to remind me what time my appointment was?' I said, 'Yeah I would, your appointment was at ONE-thirty and you wasted an HOUR of MY time . . . so I wasted an hour of YOURS.'" In Sherry's view, clients like Barrie and Cindy were simply "LAZY, lazy, lazy, lazy, lazy." (DSS 6/18/90)

A transcript and analysis of this story, which was part of a conversation I had with Sherry and Valerie Wood early one morning, is included as Case #6 in Appendix A. In this conversation, Sherry and Valerie characterize as lazy anyone who misses an appointment, regardless of the reason. In their view, employment is the only viable excuse for canceling meetings; it is the only activity that constitutes "work." Even school—let alone mothering—doesn't count in this case. Valerie made this clear in her talk about a client who was attending community college:

I HAD, one ((appointment)) scheduled for like the fourth, she ((the client)) called me and said, "well I have to change it because bla bla bla, and this and that," so I changed it, to last week, and I said, "I really do NOT like to see my appointments this late, you know, if you don't get all your papers in, you know, and this and that, your case is gonna CLOSE." So . . . she said, "Well, I have exams next week, and well . . . can I come on Monday?" I just thought, "oh boy." (DSS 6/18/90)

Sherry and Valerie refer to these clients in a pejorative tone of voice, sometimes resembling that of a stern parent speaking to a naughty child. Indeed, when they imitate their clients, their voices take on the tone of spoiled, whiny children. Again, laziness is the reason why clients fail to fulfill their obligations, whether it takes the form of missing appointments, not completing paper work, not being employed, or—the focus of the next section—not showering before going into the welfare office. Indeed, after her appointment with Cindy Smith, Sherry commented that if she could take a shower before seeing her clients every day, her clients should be able to take showers before seeing her, rather than just tumbling out of bed and rolling into the welfare office any old time.

Clients as Unclean

I remember putting rubber bands around my pant legs when I went to this one place . . . because I didn't want any rats running up my pants. (Debbie Brown)

Although workers did not refer to slovenliness on the part of their clients as often as dishonesty or laziness, they found it particularly repugnant. It was also the subject of derisive jokes. One morning, for instance, I accompanied Karrie Holmes and Valerie Wood on a visit to Myra Goodwin's home; Myra, it will be recalled, lived in a trailer with 30 cats. Not only did both workers change into old clothes for the visit, but Karrie brought along a can of spray disinfectant. She displayed the can to the other workers as we were leaving the building and on our return; the workers responded with jokes about the "cat lady." Although Karrie and Valerie repeatedly referred to the strong odor around Myra's trailer—indeed, Valerie refused to enter the trailer on the excuse that she couldn't stomach the stench—Karrie never actually used the spray. Fran Knight, however, did make occasional use of the disinfectant she kept in her desk drawer, spraying it around the chairs polluted by clients she considered dirty.

Uncleanliness often co-occurred with other traits, as pointed out in the above discussion of laziness. In the following, Nora Ryan tells me about a couple who had come in for a conference with her and her supervisor. In this case, uncleanliness concurs with stupidity.

Too bad you . . . weren't here yesterday when we had a . . . pre-hearing conference. Empty, absolutely empty. Vacuum. I mean . . . they're both barely able, they smell, they had a very strong odor, and what they were complaining (about) had nothing to do with policy. (DSS 6/14/90)

Clients who appeared disheveled or unbathed, or who emitted an odor, were thus constructed by workers to be inherently lazy, stupid, or otherwise inadequate. The possibility that they might not have the resources to bathe properly or appear neat and tidy was not entertained. Nor was it possible that intelligent, competent people might choose to appear unkempt for political or lifestyle reasons.

The Social Construction of Clients' Characters: Two Examples

The following cases display the processes involved in constructing particular types of clients. In both cases, the constructions are central to workers' decisions to intervene (or not) in specific ways: that is, they are part of workers' officially unsanctioned production of policy.

A General Case: Clients as Criminals

One morning, Judy Reynolds, Becky Wright, Sherry Nelson, and I had a conversation about a local stabbing that had involved clients. In this conversation (see Case #7, Appendix A for detailed transcript and analysis), the women moved back and forth between clients and criminals, often conflating the two.

As Becky described the stabbing, "I thought they were probably down on the street, and he was just calling him names and then they, they said he stabbed him right in the heart with a kitchen knife." As it turned out, the man who had been murdered was one of Judy's clients. He had been released from jail only one month ago, when Judy had added him on to his wife's AFDC case. In addition, the apartment in front of which the stabbing occurred belonged to one of Sherry's clients. When I asked whether the person who had committed the murder was also a client, Sherry and Judy responded, in unison, "oh, probably." Or, as Sherry put it, "the one who did the MUrdering probably just got out of jail and (is on SOme case load SOmeplace)."

The women expressed no sympathy for any of the people involved in the stabbing. Becky, whose son Ben had had an alteration with the murdered man, reported that, "the county cop told Ben to go down to the funeral home and spit on 'em ((laughs)), 'cause Ben said he was looking forward to kicking his ASS and, and now (he's dead so he can't)." Judy shared Becky's disdain. Without clarifying whether she is referring to the murdered man's status as client or criminal, she states:

As I SAY, they will all eliminate each other soon or LAter so just let 'em keep going TO it . . . . he is JUST, he's just the SCUZ of the EARTH, and I mean, and there's no loss to ANYthing, not to ANYbody . . . . I know it sounds really cold hearted, but you know THAT'S just like all those drug gangs. (DSS 8/3/90)

Becky's response to Judy was to argue that such people should simply be done away with: " . . . too bad they ((the police)) don't know when they have these parties, then they could just BOMB the houses, you know ((laughs)), (and just wipe out all the houses)." Judy agrees: "if INNO-CENT people didn't get killed. . . . I don't want INnocent people getting killed, but if they just got, I mean, WHY BOTHER with the tax money for trying to STOP 'em? ((laughs)) Let them do it . . . they just kill each OTHER." Sherry then went on to describe her ideal prison, in which the worst criminals would be locked up with no guards, and provided with food, water, and weapons. The criminals would no doubt kill each other off, and the prison could then be plowed over and a garden planted in its place. Although Judy comments on my possible reaction to this conver-

sation ("boy, Catherine is going to wonder . . ."), both she and Becky go
along with Sherry's description ("let 'em kill, kill each other," "like Lord
of the Flies"). Shortly afterward, when Ester Dove, a supervisor, walks in,
Becky and Judy explain to her what we have been talking about:

B: we're discussing variables in clients
J: we're discussing if all these clients just eliminated each other what a wonder-
      ful world we'd have, but then we'd have to look for another JOB
      (DSS 8/3/90)

Throughout their discussion, the women make little distinction between
clients and criminals. Clients and criminals are indeed often the same
people, and Sherry's story about encouraging incarcerated criminals to
murder each other could be applied to clients as well as to convicted
killers. Indeed, Judy refers specifically to the "wonderful world we'd
have" if "all these clients just eliminated each other." The movement
from client to criminal and then back again is thus smooth and unmarked. Moreover, in her vehemence, Judy later declares that she will
take steps against the murdered man's wife: "and I didn't know he
worked, so now I'm gonna charge his little wife and two children with a
FRAUD." The wife, tainted by her husband, is now also a criminal. As
pointed out above, however, Judy felt compelled to comment on what I
might be thinking of what they were saying. Both she and Ester again
addressed my presence later in the conversation. In addition, after Becky
told Ester that the murdered man had previously been involved in an
assault on her son, and that her son and a local police officer had joked
about going to the funeral home to spit on the corpse, Judy and Ester
explained to me that joking was one of their coping mechanisms.

     This conversation, then, is at the extreme of worker's negative con-
structions of clients. Nevertheless, it provides one example of workers
jointly constructing the people with whom they interacted on a daily basis. In this particular context, the categories "client" and "criminal"
overlap, and the behavior of several people is generalized to encompass
an entire group. In the following case, rather than extrapolating from a
particular case in order to make a generalization about all (or a large
segment of) clients, the worker extrapolates from various pieces of evidence to construct one particular client as a child abuser.

A Specific Case: Client as Child Abuser

The construction discussed above involves a male world of criminality
and violence as against the norm of orderliness. When the workers
turned their attention to families and women, the negative attributes

they invoked related to women's (lack of) moral fitness, or, as in the next example, to women's neglect or abuse of children, in contrast with the norm of good mothering.

Harriet Eaton had been having trouble with her client Lana Tucker, an overweight African American who wanted funds to move to a new apartment. The traits of overweight and African American identity seemed to work against Lana in this case, symbolizing for Harriet irresponsibility, shiftiness, sloppiness, and laziness. The trouble started, according to Harriet, when Lana was evasive about her current living arrangements and lied about having paid rent at her previous address. Harriet and Lana had several telephone conversations concerning these matters, during which hostilities were exchanged (Harriet accused Lana of lying, Lana expressed feelings of persecution). The trouble reached a peak when Harriet discovered a recording on her message machine that sounded to her like Lana telling someone to hit and kick one of her twin babies. Apparently Lana had been unaware that the machine had started recording. Harriet was extremely upset by the incident and felt obliged to write a referral to the child protective services unit.

The following talk all occurred on the same day, during the course of which Harriet, myself, Lana, Sherry Nelson, and finally Mike Smith, a social worker, were engaged in constructing or contesting Lana's identity as a child abuser.

I met Harriet in the coffee lounge first thing in the morning. She was visibly agitated as she poured herself a cup of coffee and told me about the distressing recording on her answering maching:

> . . . it was in the afternoon, and I, I was gonna play ((a previous phone message from Lana)) back, you know, to be sure I had the right phone number, and when I played it BACK on my machine there was ANOTHER instance of her being on, apparently she had tried to call and my—'cause I asked her about it when I did get a hold of her, I said, "did you try to call TWICE?" and she said, "yes, they put me through but your machine didn't give any message." Well, all there was was her and the, you know, I could hear a child crying in the background, and SHE was saying "HIT 'EM! KICK 'EM! KICK 'EM! HIT 'EM!" Yes, and so, you know, later I . . . went to a protective SERVICE worker, to Mike Smith, and asked him to come listen to the tape. Think I could FIND it? I must have accidentally ERASED it, so . . . I talked to him though and, and I told him that. You know, he just kinda GLOSSED over it—"well the woman's under a lot of pressure"—and, and "we don't know that it was an adult doing it," you know, that she was talking to. I said, adult or CHILD, what kinda—what mother TELLS somebody to kick and hit, because this child was really really CRYING in the background, and when I DID talk to her, I said, uh, "Lana, did you try to call me earlier?" and she—that's when she said yes she had waited for . . . the tape, and I asked her what was going on and she didn't say, so, I, you know, I want to write OUT my protective service referral this morning. (DSS 6/19/90)

Harriet begins to make her case by establishing that it was indeed Lana's voice on the answering machine: as she points out twice, Lana admits to having called her. Harriet then describes what it was that she heard on the tape: a crying child and Lana's voice saying "HIT 'EM! KICK 'EM!" Harriet proceeds to describe how the social worker, Mike Smith, had failed to take the situation as seriously as she would have liked. A key feature of Harriet's construction of Lana as a child abuser comes out when she asserts, "what mother TELLS somebody to kick and hit." Harriet invokes the category of "mother," complete with the attributes of caring and protectiveness, as something which Lana falls short of. By the end of her report, the child is not just "crying in the background," but is "really really CRYING in the background." Lana's refusal to tell her what was going on when asked about the message provides Harriet with additional justification for her child protective services referral.

Back in her office, Harriet again attempted to retrieve the message on her answering machine. She was unable to do so, although all the other messages she had received several days prior to and since were intact. She then repeated her claim that she must have accidentally erased Lana's message, and reiterated the distressing nature of what she had heard:

I don't see . . . I guess I ERASED it accidentally, you know, and . . . he ((protective services worker)) didn't sound all that interested in, hearing it either but I, I just thought it'd give him a better idea because it was, it was an AWFUL sound and it was not a chi—it didn't sound like a child crying because they're upset or because they're, ANGRY at something, it sounded like a child that was being hurt, and then to have her standing there saying "HIT 'EM! KICK 'EM! HIT 'EM!" (DSS 6/19/90)

Harriet is now even more specific concerning the nature of the crying she heard. Whereas initially she described a child who was "crying," and, later, who was "really really CRYING" (i.e., seriously crying, as opposed to crying over something trivial), here the crying sounds are like those of a child "that was being hurt." Harriet again expresses shock at a mother who could encourage someone to hit her child ("and then to have her standing there saying 'HIT 'EM! KICK 'EM! HIT 'EM!' "). She is clearly distressed—"it was an AWFUL sound"—and is suffering genuine anguish over what she interprets as a child being beaten.

Shortly after providing me with a description of the telephone message, Harriet presented further support for her interpretation of Lana's comments on the answering machine by citing the fact that Lana had lost custody of a child before. Although this had occurred seven years previously, when Lana was 16 years old, and for reasons unknown to Harriet, she nevertheless concluded, "so she's been abusive in the past."

Harriet's conviction that Lana was a child abuser, well-established by this point, is manifested in the following interaction she had with Lana later the same morning, during which she tries to convince Lana to speak with the social worker. In so doing she encounters Lana's resistance, thereby, in her view, uncovering even more proof of Lana's guilt.

1	H:	okay, and I, um, you ARE, I DID want you to talk to another gentle-
2		man in the office this morning
3	L:	who?
4	H:	okay his name is Mike
5	L:	who IS he?
6	H:	okay, he IS with protective services
7	L:	I'm not talking to 'em
8	H:	okay, the reason I—the reason I DID it is because of that phone mes-
9		sage yesterday
10	L:	WHAT phone message?
11	H:	okay, when I played my tape
12	L:	oh, 'cause a something you heard in the background
13	H:	mm huh, right
14	L:	oh I'm not TALKing to him, I will NOT talk to him and you can't make
15		me, I REFUSE to talk to him, I will not talk to him
16	H:	okay, WHY would you refuse to talk to him Lana?
17	L:	because I REFUSE to talk to him, I will not talk to ANY protective
18		services worker, I have one child already gone and they will NOT get
19		the twins
20	H:	okay well they would have no REASON to take the twins
21	L:	I don't wanna TALK to him
22	H:	okay, I guess TALKing to him would probably—
23	L:	talking to him won't do any good, I will NOT talk to protective services,
24		I will not
25	H:	mm kay, he'll assume that there's something to HIDE then probably
26	L:	let him assume whatever he WANTS to assume, they have to FIND me
27		first if they wanna to talk to me I will NOT talk to him, all he's going
28		to do is say "what did you—" what DIFFerence does it make what you
29		heard in the background of a conversation?
30	H:	okay, well I guess he'd wanna KNOW what was happening
31	L:	WHY is it his business "what is happening"? WHY is it his business
32		"what is happening"? You know TV, you know, some of the kids were
33		watching wrestling, people HAVE VCRs
34	H:	mm huh
35	L:	people LIKE wrestling, people LIKE boxing, people LIKE sports, but
36		NO, everybody assumes 'cause you have kids and they hear somein'
37		about kick and hit that somebody's abusing children, I WISH I could
38		go inside people's minds, and really find out where they're coming
39		from
40	H:	I GUESS the reason I thought it was because it sounded like your
41		VOICE
42	L:	it WAS my voice

```
43  H:   saying the "kick 'em" the "hit 'em"
44  L:   oh, I LIKE boxing, and I like wrestling I have, you know, friends
45       who have VCRs who watch, who tape you know, WWF DOES tape
46       their matches, I get very in to it
47  H:   well, I just thought I should explain to you WHY I did it, WHY I, made
48       the referral    (DSS 6/19/90)
```

Nothing that occurs during their meeting convinces Harriet that she should withdraw her protective services referral. In fact, Harriet and Lana are at loggerheads, with neither willing to entertain the other's point of view. When Harriet mentions that she would like Lana to talk to "another gentleman in the office" (lines 1–2), Lana is immediately suspicious, and as soon as Harriet admits that he is a social worker, Lana cuts in to declare her refusal to speak with him (line 7). Lana reaffirms her position an additional 10 times by line 26, indicating her anxiety (she had, after all, had a child taken away from her before), and her need to pre-empt a protective services investigation. Lana is already aware of Harriet's "evidence," as she indicates at line 12 when she states, prior to any explanation on Harriet's part, "'cause a something you heard in the background." In response to her anxiety about losing her children, Harriet assures Lana that protective services "would have no REASON to take the twins" (line 20), which is untrue since child removal is a clear option in cases of child neglect or abuse, the situation Harriet in fact suspected. At the same time, however, she construes Lana's refusal to talk to Mike as an attempt to hide something (line 24). This puts Lana in a difficult position, to which she responds by directly confronting Harriet. Although Lana had questioned Harriet's evidence earlier (line 12), the line of questioning she begins at line 27 is more forceful: "what DIFFerence does it make what you heard in the background of a conversation?" and "WHY is it his business 'what is happening?' " Not only does she in effect accuse Harriet of being unreasonable, Lana also recounts her version of what it was that Harriet overheard. Harriet, however, has no response, despite her indication at line 29 that an explanation from Lana was what was being sought. Instead, she summarily closes the topic.

Returning then to the official purpose of their meeting—funds for an apartment—Harriet gathered Lana's paperwork and left to go to the photocopying machine. While Harriet was gone, Lana asked me if I was planning on becoming an AP worker. When I responded in the negative and told her that I was trying to find out, among other things, what it was like to be on AFDC, Lana replied that, "it's horrible . . . and they treat you like dirt." At this point, Harriet returned, finished Lana's paper work, and concluded their meeting by saying, "I know you don't believe this, but I really do wish you the best." She then sent Lana to the reception area to wait for a bus pass to Madrid. It was at this time that Mike

Smith approached Lana and insisted that she accompany him to his office. Prior to the following segment, Sherry Nelson, another worker, had been describing to Harriet and me the interaction between Lana and Mike; Harriet then reports to Sherry what Lana had claimed about the answering machine message:

```
 1   H:   she just, you know, said that it, er, it was part of the TV in the back-
 2        ground and so forth that I heard, which is a bull, you know
 3   S:   bunch a bull?
 4   H:   "I like, I like boxing"
 5   S:   that's what she said?
 6   H:   yeah, so
 7   S:   you shoulda said, "you should like boxing, that's fine, but not on your
 8        KIDS"
 9   H:   well, she's trying to—
10   S:   you can't SAY that
11   H:   she was saying "hit 'em, kick 'em, hit 'em, kick 'em" because of the
12        boxing thing, but (you know) the little kid was
13   S:   bull
14   H:   crying in the background, but, so, you know, I'm glad she . . .
15   H:   didn't just get up and take OFF    (DSS 6/19/90)
```

Sherry is clearly a co-participant in the construction of Lana as a child abuser. After clarifying Harriet's use of the word "bull" (Harriet rarely used such words and thus tended to use them inappropriately) and listening to Harriet's version of Lana's story, Sherry suggests what Harriet might have said to Lana ("you should like boxing, that's fine, but not on your KIDS"; lines 7–8). While Sherry's self-correction at line 10—"you can't SAY that"—indicates a behind-the-scenes discourse that workers know they cannot employ in face-to-face interactions with clients, she is clearly in agreement with Harriet's evaluation of the situation. She shows her support for this assessment not only at lines 7–8, but also at line 13, when she gives her view of Lana's story: "bull."

Later in the morning Harriet spoke with Mike about his interview with Lana. Mike claimed that he found no evidence on which to base an investigation, and that all he could do was offer Lana voluntary access to counseling services. He did, however, state that she was "an accident waiting to happen." He then went on to characterize Lana's approach to the system:

```
 1   M:   you know, I'm saying that she's pretty savvy to the system, she KNOWS
 2        what she needs to say, and, uh, you know, I have no MEANS of DE-
 3        TERmining at this point if, you know, what she's telling me is what she
 4        feels I need to hear, or what, what, if she—
 5   H:   MY main concern was, that those children, the sound I heard yesterday
 6        was ((coughing in background))
```

```
 7  M:  and her RESPONSE to that—
 8  H:  and you checked 'em over and you don't see any bruises, then, you
 9      know, you, you are the one responsible for, for THAT
10  M:  that's correct, that's correct
11  H:  but I . . . cannot get that SOUND in the background of that child
12      (out of my head)
13  M:  I understand that it DISTRUBES you
14  H:  ((coughs)) I wish I WISH I could get that tape again because it would
15      disturb you also because that child was crying HYSTERICALLY
16  M:  well I'm not . . . I'm not SAYing you know, I'm not saying, I'm not saying
17      it's not DISTURBING, okay, what I—
18  H:  but you don't really FEEL that there was any abuse going on, at that
19      point
20  M:  even if I FEEL there was some abuse going on, okay, I DON'T have
21      the RIGHT, the legal RIGHT to interVENE in a circumstance where
22      I cannot support a finding
23  H:  right, but if you looked a child over and you don't, you just did not
24      see any bruises at all
25  M:  right, right
26  H:  okay um    (DSS 6/19/90)
```

Mike's characterization of Lana as someone who is "pretty savvy to the system" and who "KNOWS what she needs to say" (lines 1–2) does little to reassure Harriet. Harriet was unhappy with this outcome; she had wanted a full investigation. As far as she was concerned—and she seeks reassurance three times, at lines 8, 18, 23–24—Mike had provided no evidence to contradict her assessment. Confused about the ability of an investigator to discern abuse on an African American child (at one point, she wondered out loud if bruises would be visible on dark skin), only a thorough examination would have satisfied her. A cursory look was insufficient.

In the end, a lack of what Harriet considered concrete evidence indicating that Lana was *not* beating her children, Sherry's active support of Harriet's views, and the lack of challenge on my part and on the part of Mike Smith, all contributed to the construction of Lana as a child abuser. In keeping with the assumption that clients were bad in nature, Lana's guilt was clear to Harriet from the outset. All that remained was to intervene.

Positive Constructions: The Good Client and the Non-Client

Good clients were not unheard of in the Kenyon County welfare office, however. Such clients had to pass two tests. First, they had to fail to display the negative traits workers typically associated with recipients of public assistance—specifically, with the "undeserving" poor. As was the case with Lana, clients were usually guilty until proven innocent, and only a demonstrated absence of bad behaviors could dispel the assumed presence of negative attributes. Second, good clients should behave in ways that were positively evaluated in and of themselves, regardless whether or not one was a welfare recipient; for example, they should work hard and be pleasant. Such clients were the "deserving" poor, sometimes referred to as the "working poor."

The clients most frequently constructed as "good" were those who were "trying to make something" of themselves, specifically, those who were pursuing education or other job training. Such individuals were not getting a "free ride" on public assistance, but were "working" so that they could improve their financial circumstances and, by extension, those of their children. This was in marked contrast to the manipulation and laziness workers so often perceived in their clients, indicating instead the positive character traits of persistence, commitment, and, above all, adherence to the work ethic. Accordingly, workers entertained the hope that such clients would not be receiving public assistance "forever," and were therefore different from "career" clients. In this regard, Valerie Wood described a mother of three who was working toward a college degree as one of her favorite clients, because she seemed to be going somewhere, rather than sitting around doing nothing (DSS 6/20/90). On another occasion, Edith Saunders expressed frustration over not being able to provide medical care for a client who was no longer employed but who was under 65 years old and thus ineligible for Medicare. In her complaint, Edith pointed out that the woman in question had been employed steadily for 26 years (DSS 7/5/90). Age complemented evidence of hard work in this instance to place the client squarely in the deserving category.

One of Nora Ryan's clients, Shelly Barr, was the epitome of the model client. First of all, Shelly was meticulous in her adherence to departmental procedures—her forms were always properly filled out, and she provided Nora with timely notification of any changes in her situation. Nora was so impressed with Shelly that at the end of one interview she told her, "I've enjoyed working with you . . . you've been very cooperative." After Shelly left the office, Nora turned to me and said "she's very, very good . . . she reports good, things like that," and "she got a good head on her shoulders" (DSS 6/29/90). As with clients who were pursuing an education, Shelly stood out from the crowd. Second, not only did she fail to display negative traits typically associated with welfare recipients; she also exhibited characteristics that were positive in and of themselves, such as being "nice" and "friendly." Accordingly, Nora kept pictures of Shelly's babies in her wallet. At the time of my study, Shelly was pregnant with her third child; and although she was transferring to another welfare office, she promised Nora that she would bring the baby to the Webster office after it was born. "That made me feel good," Nora told me later (DSS 6/29/90). Shelly's worthiness also compelled Nora to go out of her way to help her. At the end of one of their meetings, for instance, Nora made a tour of the office to see if she could find a ride home for Shelly so that she could avoid a long wait for the bus. Karrie Holmes's efforts on behalf of Myra Goodwin, the elderly woman who took care of stray cats, provides another good example of this. Others advocated for Myra as well: on one cold winter evening, for instance, Harriet invited Myra to spend the night at her house because she felt that Myra would not be able to keep warm in her mobile home.

Clients who displayed self-motivation, then, and who thus promised to eventually extract themselves from the welfare rolls, gave the workers pleasure, and contributed to their (occasional) sense of accomplishment, as Nora indicated when she told me, "I do look forward to going to work, though . . . I really do care about people—some more than others, because I think some try to help themselves more than others" (DSS 8/10/90). Nora also got fulfillment from helping those people who "will never be able to take care of themselves" (DSS 8/10/90)— truly inept people who were deserving by virtue of their incompetence. Myra Goodwin was perhaps in this category.

In addition to the good clients, on one occasion Peggy Stewart interviewed an applicant, Sara Ramsay, who she felt "didn't belong" on welfare—who was, in a sense, a non-client:

Too Dignified to be a Client
Sara Ramsay was a strikingly attractive single woman in her mid-twenties. One day, she came into the Webster office to apply for assistance with her housing costs. The worker to whom she was assigned, Peggy Stewart, helped her complete her application form, informing her that she might qualify for food stamps as well as General Assistance (a program supporting single poor adults). At one point, Sara asked Peggy if they had met before, and after exchanging notes on their respective histories they discovered that Sara had dated Peggy's younger brother some years back. Their conversation became friendly and familiar.

As the interview progressed, however, Sara became increasingly uncomfortable with the extent to which her privacy would invaded if she pursued her application. For instance, she would have to provide the department with various papers verifying her identity, income, living arrangements and so on, some of which required signatures of employers and landlords. Sara pointed out that she only wanted temporary assistance, since she would soon receive her beautician license and be able to get a job that would provide her with enough money to support herself. She felt that the invasion of privacy was unacceptable and decided to withdraw her application.

When Peggy later told the story of her meeting with Sara to Anne Jensen, Anne immediately suspected that Sara withdrew her application because "she was hiding something." Peggy countered this assessment, claiming instead that Sara, who she characterized as a "real pretty girl," "((is)) gonna make it," and that she "didn't belong here." (DSS 7/6/90)

In claiming that Sara was not "client material," Peggy constructed Sara as too competent to be on welfare. By implication, welfare recipients in general are constructed as by nature incompetent, and perhaps, in this case, physically unattractive. Again, as with many positive constructions of clients, the construction of Sara as non-client was a construction in opposition to the norm. It was, in fact, the only instance of a non-client construction that I encountered during my months at the welfare office.

Workers at the Boundary: The "Deserving" Versus the "Undeserving"

For the class parade to be a full success it seems there must be one class that highlights in its evil all the virtues of the others. (Kornblum 1991:202)

While workers did not employ such global categories in their talk, the distinctions they made in their constructions of clients reflected a general distinction between the "good" and the "bad," the "deserving" and the "undeserving." In doing their job of constructing clients to whom they and the institution could respond in one fashion or another, the women produced and policed this positive/negative distinction, and articulated it with actual policy production.

At the broadest level, there were certain evaluative criteria, such as age, race/ethnicity, and gender, that seemingly applied to every client, and that could be mobilized in the work of maintaining the boundary between the deserving and the undeserving. With regard to gender, for instance, a man caring for five children would be favored over a woman in the same situation, whose morality and reproductive responsibility would no doubt be questioned. With regard to age, falling into the category of "elderly" was almost always beneficial to clients, assuring the sympathy of the worker, if not her positive character evaluation. Consider the following story Colleen O'Connell told me about one of her elderly clients who was having to bear the costs of a Medicaid program that required her to pay, up front, a monthly medication bill of $1,600:

She . . . has a real problem with ((Medicaid)) because she's got a heart transplant and . . . ((Medicaid)) doesn't work for her because she has . . . 1,600 dollars worth of medication every month, beginning of every month. Her spend down is like 213 dollars and that's not bad, but she has to pay for all the medicine at once and she has to drive down to ((a hospital 60 miles away)) to pick it up, and so she has to pay for all the medication, and then be reimbursed . . . . 1,600 dollars is a lot of money . . . and I would like some way to make her eligible since she's going to be every month, you know, have her pay us 213 dollars you know, for her spend down, and just constantly have her eligible and just have her, have a pay amount deducted. Well, you can't do it that way. (DSS 6/14/90)

In other words, Colleen would like to set up an arrangement whereby her client would only have to pay $213 each month, rather than having to pay $1,600 and wait for a reimbursement of $1,387. Age and illness combine in this instance to produce the opposite of the norm; namely, an innocent and deserving woman who is being victimized by the system.

Clients' various attributes, however, were not always weighed equally, and their salience could wane in a particular case if something else waxed more important. This is particularly clear with regard to ethnicity and race. For instance, an African American woman in her early twenties, with two children and pregnant with a third, who had never been married, whose children had separate fathers, and who had never held paid employment, would, on an abstract level, be placed by the workers in this study in the category of "undeserving." On the other hand, if she came in looking as if she had just showered and was "positively" engaged with her children (i.e., was not yelling at them to "shut your mouth and sit down," but rather coaxed them in middle-class fashion, "here, Johnny, here's a toy for you, now do you think you could sit there nice and quiet for mommy and the nice lady?"), the negative weight of her race, youth, "questionable" moral standing, and poor work history could be minimized. This was the case with Shelly Barr, Nora Ryan's favorite client (see pp. 112–113). Age, gender, and ethnicity, then,—or, simply, difference—did not determine a worker's evaluation of a client, but rather provided resources that could be mobilized in making an evaluation. The evaluation remained a negotiated phenomenon (Erickson 1984; Hymes 1981). AP workers therefore did not indiscriminately apply ready-made stereotypes to applicants, but rather actively engaged in interpreting their actions. In the course of these interpretations, they variously drew on, invoked, modified, and occasionally dismissed received views of gender, age, race/ethnicity and public assistance.

At the end of the day, however, most clients were "bad." The views of poverty prevalent in U.S. society provide a significant resource for workers to draw on in their constructions of clients. In this larger context, poverty is stigmatized, and public relief is viewed in terms of "costs to society, not benefits" (Lipsky 1980:181). On the one hand, workers' negative constructions of clients resist the welfare bureaucracy insofar as they are unsanctioned, and are part and parcel of their attempts to decrease, rather than fulfill, their work obligations. On the other hand, these constructions accommodate the idea that most people are to blame for their own poverty. In other words, while street-level bureaucrats' "responses to work stresses arise out of the work situation . . . their content or direction are colored by prevailing cultural assumptions" (181).

This does not mean, however, that workers' positive constructions of clients contested prevailing cultural assumptions. On the contrary, and despite the workers' good intentions, their positive constructions of clients reproduced the distinction between the deserving and the undeserving. First, no one who was seen to have an unpleasant demeanor, or who failed to pay homage to the work ethic, was considered deserving. The content of these categories as they are constituted in the wider society was thus upheld. Second, the ratio of deserving to undeserving was as one would expect: again, most poor are seen as poor through their own fault. Thus in the Kenyon County welfare office the vast majority of clients were constructed as undeserving.

Just as recipients engaged in concerted constructions of workers as "them," so workers jointly constructed the "them" of clients. In doing so, workers by implication constructed themselves as different from the majority of their clients. I explore variations on the "us" of the workers and their production of policy in the next chapter.

Chapter 8
Further Productions: Attitudes and Policy

All of the workers in the Kenyon County welfare office had difficulties with management, work loads, and clients. They all participated in constructing deserving and (mostly) undeserving clients. There were, however, two distinct worker cultures in the office which workers distinguished as "Pollyannas" and "Blues Boulevard." These two cultures represented opposing approaches to what all workers saw, for one reason or another, as an unsatisfactory and disempowered situation. From the perspective of upper management, the Pollyannas and Blues Boulevard reflected "positive" and "negative" attitudes, the one being productive, the other unproductive and self-defeating. The key difference between the groups was that, while the Pollyannas tried to look on the bright side of things, the members of Blues Boulevard were more inclined to voice discontent rather than acquiescence or resignation. Each group looked with scorn on their opposite, the members of which, it was felt, suffered, on the one hand, from a delusional cheerfulness, and, on the other, from pessimism and irresponsibility. Only two workers, Gilda White and Debbie Brown, remained unaligned.

The Pollyannas

The Pollyanna culture had eight members: Harriet Eaton, Karrie Holmes, Sherry Nelson, Valerie Wood, Nora Ryan, Edith Saunders, Emma Nichols, and Colleen O'Connell. Unlike the members of Blues Boulevard, the Pollyannas did not consider themselves a group; indeed, the label "Pollyanna" was not self-chosen but rather was externally imposed by the Blues Boulevard workers. The Pollyannas did claim, however, that they were individuals with "positive" attitudes, who did their best to keep up with what everybody recognized as a "formidable" workload (Emma Nichols's term, appropriated from the office director), and who took responsibility for office atmosphere and morale.

The main features of the Pollyanna culture were an acceptance of workplace hierarchy and a focus on personality rather than external circumstances. The following commentary by Sherry Nelson, the unacknowledged leader of the Pollyannas, exemplifies both features. Sherry had been describing the attitude differences between the "negative" and "positive" workers, when I asked her to speculate on what would happen if the workers from the two groups were seated together in cubicles after the office restructuring (which they were). The following is her response:

I figure it this way, I know Harriet is very upset, and a lot of 'em are, but as far as I'm concerned, the problem is that ((protective)) services is whining and . . . they're gonna get those offices, and I could really make myself get upset and work myself up over this, thinking it's very unfair and I don't like it and it's miserable and everything, and I've sat in cubicles and they're terribly loud . . . so I could get myself worked up over this, I could be really upset about it, if I wanted to, but then I have to ask myself, is it gonna do any good, is making myself worry and sick and bitching about it and everything, taking all the time it takes to discuss it and everything, is that going to do any good? Or are they still gonna put us in cubicles? And what I basically come to conclude is that basically they'll put us in cubicles no matter what we say or do, and . . . even writing a proposal, it . . . would be a good attempt but it's not gonna stop them from putting . . . us in cubicles so . . . I can either make myself sick by worrying about something that's going to happen anyway or I can just accept it and say, they're gonna do it and there's nothing I can do about it and . . . it's just the way it is and, shit happens, and we don't like everything that happens to us, nobody said this job would be fair. (DSS 6/29/90)

Sherry has no illusions about the office hierarchy. She points to workers' lack of control a number of times: "they're going to do it," "there's nothing I can do about it," "it's just the way it is," and "nobody said this job would be fair." Clearly, management makes unilateral decisions and implements them regardless of worker sentiment ("basically they'll put us in cubicles no matter what we say or do"). Sherry accordingly sees no reason to get herself all "worked up over this." Any expenditure of energy in this regard—even writing a proposal suggesting alternatives, let alone "worrying about something that's going to happen anyway"— would be wasted effort. Her emphasis, rather, is on facing and accepting reality, albeit a reality in which workers have no control.

The following story, in which Sherry recalls a confrontation she had with Blues Boulevard workers in the computer room, underscores the idea that AP workers are responsible for their own experiences—that if they are bitter it is because they have chosen to be so.

One day I was in the ((computer room))—this was when they were real negative and they were just on and on and on and on and on, about the county and about this and that . . . and I was tired of it and I was having a hard day anyway and . . . last thing I wanted to hear (was) them bitching and, I don't know, I was tearing out the paper . . . and somebody walked into the room and I said, "hi, how are ya?" and . . . they all looked at me as if . . . I'd done something wrong and they said, "how can you be so happy in this miserable place?" and I said, "you, if you're miserable, you make yourself that way," and I said, "if you are miserable your whole life is miserable, you're miserable everywhere," and I said, "and I'm not gonna sit here and listen to you make me miserable and sound as shitty attitude as you sound", and I said, "I have a family, I have people who love me, I have a job, I get paid every other week," and I said, "I get, I make fairly good money," and I said . . . "I'm sick of it," I said, "so just shut up, if I want to say, hi, or sound cheery even if things (are) miserable in here that is my way of bringing myself up, it's easy to sound down, it is harder to sound happy," and I said, "so if you wanna sound miserable, do it on your Saturday." (DSS 6/29/90)

Resigned to her powerlessness, Sherry has no intention of worsening the situation by cultivating a bad attitude—which is exactly, in her view, what the "negative" workers do. They "make themselves" miserable. Instead, people should be thankful for what they have in life and make the best of whatever circumstances they find themselves in. Moreover, if the Blues Boulevard workers want to complain about work, they should do it on their own time rather than poison the office environment for everyone else. Although not ecstatic about AP workers' lowly position in the department, then, Sherry felt compelled to count her blessings: "I have a family, I have people who love me, I have a job, I get paid every other week."

The Pollyanna focus on personal responsibility was also manifested in how the workers used their free time. During morning and afternoon breaks, and sometimes at lunch-time as well, the women went for walks through the surrounding neighborhoods and recorded the miles covered on a wall chart in the hallway. These walks, they felt, would improve their mental and physical health. This was in contrast to the Blues Boulevard approach to break-time, which consisted of sitting outside, smoking, joking, and complaining about work in language rarely used by the Pollyannas.

Therefore, while unhappy with the organization of their workplace and disappointed that their opinions were given little weight by management, the Pollyannas removed responsibility for a "miserable" atmosphere from their bosses. Instead, they placed it on the shoulders of the workers, who could decide, as individuals, to have a good or bad attitude. They thus accepted full responsibility for their own happiness while acknowledging a lack of control over the structure of their work lives. In one respect the Pollyanna view of the world resembles the bad-people-exist-but-I'm-not-one-of-them approach taken by recipients: in interacting with management, Pollyannas could always point the finger at the members of Blues Boulevard, and blame them for problems with, for instance, office atmosphere. As such, the Pollyanna culture provides an example of accommodation to the hierarchical relationship between workers and management, and to less than optimal working conditions.

It is not surprising, then, that these "positive" workers were admired by the office director and served as a model of what AP workers should be. Indeed, workers from the two groups were seated next to each other in the office move, in the hopes that the Pollyannas could soften the virulent "negatives." In addition, when I began my research at the Kenyon County office, the two women assigned to assist and oversee me were Pollyannas. In a sense, the Pollyannas were the AP equivalent of the deserving poor, displaying the positive traits of the "working poor" while highlighting the self-destructiveness of the undeserving, who, in the Kenyon County welfare office, lived on Blues Boulevard.

The View from Blues Boulevard

The workers on Blues Boulevard made no effort to remain cheerful in the face of their "formidable" workloads. Instead, the seven women— Peggy Stewart, Judy Reynolds, Fran Knight, Sally Blake, Becky Wright, Anne Jensen, and Diane Kane—bitterly complained about work conditions. From their point of view, the Pollyannas were overly genial optimists who played into the hands of management. Instead, the women who proudly named themselves Blues Boulevard situated themselves in opposition to a management bent on the exploitation of its workers, rather than in alliance with them in a shared endeavor.

The kind of talk Blues Boulevard members produced was markedly different from that of the Pollyannas. With regard to the office move, for instance, Blues Boulevard workers went beyond expressions of betrayal to discuss more practical forms of subversion. To give an example, after a staff meeting about the types of cubicles workers would have (shoulder-height versus ceiling-height walls), Anne Jensen, Diane Kane, and Judy Reynolds debated recommending that all their clients request official hearings on the grounds that they could no longer be provided a guarantee of confidentiality. While significantly increasing AP workloads, this kind of response on the part of clients could force management to reconsider the restructuring. The women also contemplated moving clients' chairs so that they would protrude into the walkways between the cubicles; this would make the point that cubicles were not large enough to accommodate interviewing needs. On other occasions, Blues Boulevard workers talked about advising their clients to protest against particular policies to state legislators, and about the use of symbolism, such as office displays of toilet plungers to signify the "shit" workers had to wade through. Finally, the women frequently made derisive comments about supervisors and other managers.

Fran Knight's, Sally Blake's, and Peggy Stewart's approaches to "telephone hour" (the hour in the morning during which workers were required to be available for consultation with clients over the phone) epitomize the Blues Boulevard attitude and illustrate contrasting forms of resistance. Fran, who did not like being told what to do, had a straightforward response: "well, some of us do ((have telephone hour)), some of us ditty bop in an out any time they feel like it ((laughs)) . . . I'm not gonna be LOCKED to my desk for an hour simply because my boss says I have to be" (DSS 8/3/90). Sally claimed to practice a more subtle form of defiance. Speaking in a high-pitched, high-speed, and sarcastic tone, she reported that:

I stay at my desk during phone time because that's what I'm ordered to do and when people call me and they need me to run to the computer and check on something I SAY, I say I'm not allOWed to, I'm only, I can only answer the phone between eleven and twelve (o'clock) those are the rules. (DSS 8/3/90)

When challenged by Fran, who calls her a "suck-ass" for following the rules, Sally points out that, on the contrary, her strategy works to keep "OTHER people from trying to call." Sally's approach is thus to play by the rules to such an extent that productivity and efficiency are undermined. In so doing, she appropriates one aspect of management discourse in order to resist another. Her quick speech and sarcastic tones, moreover, indicate that her professed respect for the telephone hour rule is not meant to be taken literally. As an added bonus, her strategy provides a tool for managing client demands.

Peggy provides yet another approach to telephone hour:

man when I got 'em on the phone I find out what the problem is and I tell 'em right THEN, I don't wanna call them back, I do it RIGHT then, I don't like calling people back. (DSS 8/3/90)

Peggy appears to be speaking literally, and seems less interested in issues of accommodation and resistance to management than in doing things in a manner that is comfortable for her. She takes care of each problem as it arises not because she wants to defy her supervisor but because that is her preferred way of working. Perhaps this is a form of defiance, however, insofar as she does not care if her preferences suit the needs of management; indeed, in claiming to attend to her clients on the spot, she implies that she leaves her desk during phone hour to work in the computer room.

A transcript of the telephone hour conversation, which illustrates each woman's own strategy as well as their responses to each other's strategies, in included as Case #8 in Appendix A.

Given their relatively powerless position, it is not surprising that most of the strategies of resistance the Blues Boulevard women chose to discuss were indirect ones, rather than ones in which they would confront the system head-on (Scott 1990). None of the responses to telephone hour, for instance, are highly visible or dramatic. They illustrate, however, resistant perspectives, and resistant ways of speaking. And if called to task by their supervisors or clients, the women would no doubt be able to produce legitimate justifications for their behavior. Sally, for instance, is only following the rules, while Peggy is just trying to take proper care of her clients. Fran is the one exception. Given her preference for confrontation, she might challenge her supervisor over something like phone hour. On the other hand, she did comply when management requested that she not wear a T-shirt emblazoned with the words BAD ATTITUDE given to her by several of her co-workers.

The contrast with the Pollyanna approach is striking. If Blues Boulevard workers were angry, it was not so much because they chose to be, as Sherry Nelson would argue, but because management gave them good reason to be. Blues Boulevard workers were not willing to accept their place at the bottom of the hierarchy, and they did not take pride in struggling to meet their bosses' demands. From their perspective, the problem was not an internal one calling for attitude adjustments, but an external one requiring structural change. Resistance, accordingly, was directed at office rules and regulations, and at management and Pollyanna views concerning appropriate worker attitudes. The women were unwilling, as individuals, to pay the price for what they saw as an inequitable, exploitative system.

This emphasis on external phenomena, rather than on internal states of mind, resembles that produced in welfare rights meetings. Again there was nothing wrong with the women's personalities. It was the system that was to blame. Blues Boulevard workers, however, did not apply their understanding of their own situation to that of their clients. They were no more and no less likely than Pollyannas to blame recipients for their own misfortunes.

Why the Difference?

At one level, the division between Pollyanna and Blues Boulevard workers parallels the good/bad, deserving/undeserving distinction they applied to recipients; and, as in that distinction, the two groups stand in a mutually defining relationship to each other. What, however, might help explain this division? In her work on the relations among women in the welfare bureaucracy, Withorn (1984) claims that divisions among welfare workers are common. She includes in her list of contributing factors workloads, client demands, and conflicting views of workers' roles. The first two factors are shared across the Pollyanna and Blues Boulevard divides in the Kenyon County office: workloads did not differ from one group to the next, and clients were assigned to workers on a revolving basis. In considering Withorn's third possibility I questioned what the genesis of conflicting views of worker's roles might be. There are no significant differences in the average age of the two groups of women, or in the average numbers of years in which they have been AP workers. Therefore I cannot argue, for instance, that the Pollyannas were as a rule younger women who had less experience in the welfare bureaucracy, while Blues Boulevard workers were soured by too many years of service.

The only difference I found between the two groups related to their supervisors. The seventeen workers were divided among three supervisors, Edna Lewis, Ester Dove, and Cynthia Mead. With the exception of one neutral worker, all the women under Cynthia's supervision were Pollyannas. The reverse held for Edna, who supervised one neutral worker and five members of Blues Boulevard. Finally, Ester's unit consisted of three Pollyannas and two Blues Boulevard participants. Not only was Ester's unit the only mixed one (not counting the neutrals); the most vehement Blues Boulevard workers (Fran, Sally, Peggy, and Anne) and Pollyannas (Sherry, Valerie, and Colleen) were under Edna's and Cynthia's supervision respectively. The core of each group thus had different supervisors. Nor did the workers self-select into their units; rather, they were assigned to supervisors on the basis of management need and regardless of whatever wishes they may have had.

Given my focus in this study on worker and recipient views and relationships, all I can offer at this point is conjecture. In reality I spent very little time with supervisors. What I do know is that Edna, the supervisor of the most notorious "negative" workers, had a reputation for intrusion and sarcasm that was shared only minimally by Ester and not at all by Cynthia. Also, while the women complained about all their supervisors, Edna was considered the most reticent about confronting upper management on behalf of AP workers. In other words, it is possible that supervisory units behaved as sub-cultures, in which supervisors strongly influenced the tone and content of talk. Had I continued this study, I would have turned my attention to the worker-supervisor relationship. I have no doubt that insight into the nature of this relationship would add to, if not modify, the interpretation of workers' worlds that I have presented here.

Accommodation, Resistance, and the (Co)Production of Policy

The decisions of street-level bureaucrats, the routines they establish, and the devices they invent to cope with uncertainties and work pressures, effectively become the public policies they carry out . . . . [P]ublic policy is not best understood as made in legislatures or top-floor suites of high-ranking administrators, because in important ways it is actually made in the crowded offices and daily encounters of street-level workers. (Lipsky 1980:xii)

One day, Fran Knight, Sally Blake, AP supervisor Edna Lewis, and I were debating whether I would make a good AP worker (they believed I would; I argued I would not). As part of this debate, we discussed some of the characteristics of an effective worker:

```
 1   E:   the only thing you have to be is intelligent, fast, organized and, a me-
 2        dium line between empathy and hate
 3   C:   ((laughs)) a medium line between empathy and hate
 4   F:   you gotta add the ARROGANCE too, this job isn't any fun without a
 5        little touch of arrogance
 6   C:   ((laughs))
 7   E:   you have to know when to be empathetic and when to, get out your
 8        whip
 9   F:   I already know THAT, see? I'm, I'm empathetic to all my clients 'til
10        they LIE to me, once they LIE to me I HATE them and I won't give
11        them ANYthing ((laughs))
12   E:   WHOA ((laughs))
13   S:   ((sarcastic tone)) not REVENGE (oh yeah)
14   F:   yes it IS ((laughs))
15   E:   ((sarcastic tone)) you're supposed to do a TRAINING process with
16        them ((regular tone)) make them overVERIFY but still give them what
17        they're entitled to
18   F:   oh they get it EVENTUALLY
19   E:   okay, don't say you won't give it to 'em, just say that they have to JUMP
20        MORE ROPES to get it, that's OKAY
21   F:   unfortunately they just have to . . . WAIT a while    (DSS 8/10/90)
```

Workers, then, not only constructed their clients' characters and images of both themselves and management, but they had, within limits, practical power over their clients. For the most part, this power took the form of control of information and time. As Fran, Sally, and Edna indicate, workers did not only implement policy—which is what they were hired to do—they also produced it in their specific, day-to-day decisions about which clients would have access to what and when. When Edna states that "you have to know when to be empathetic and when to, get out your whip" (line 7), she is referring to *workers'* decision-making, not to departmental policy concerning eligibility or fraud.

This exchange points to one of the places where policy is produced, namely, in peer interactions. In their conversations with each other, workers (and in this case a supervisor as well) produce interpretations and classifications that provide a basis for the practical decisions they make when they meet with clients face-to-face. These behind-the-scenes conversations provide informal training for workers on how to make sense of and handle the various situations they encounter in their work.

What is being produced in the above exchange is a policy on waiting. Waiting—a ubiquitous feature of recipients' relationships with the welfare system, and one that they often complained about—took a number of forms: sitting in the waiting room, waiting for workers to provide information, waiting for applications to be processed, waiting for AFDC checks or food stamps to arrive in the mail. In this instance, the workers' talk concerns the time it takes to review applications. Officially, applications for AFDC must be processed within 45 days. When Fran says, "oh, they get it EVENTUALLY" (line 18), she means that she will delay processing an application from a client who she believes has lied to her until the end of the 45-day period. This policy was not uncommon:

While I was in Becky Wright's office discussing one of her clients, Sherry Nelson came in to ask her what to do about an applicant, Marie Watson, who was waiting in her office—Sherry was not sure what program to process her for. While asking for advice, Sherry told us a little about Marie: her first child was living with Marie's mother in another state, and she was one month pregnant with her second child. The reason her first child was with Marie's mother was that protective services had removed the child on grounds of abuse. When Sherry asked who had done the abuse, Marie claimed that other people living in her house had done it, but that her daughter was taken away from her because she had been there while the abuse was going on. Although it was not clear to me exactly what this meant, to Sherry and Becky it indicated that Marie had been physically present (watching) while her daughter was being abused. Sherry made a comment that "we" (the welfare department?) should simply open up Marie's belly and remove the baby from her womb. Becky suggested that Sherry should at least make her wait the 45 days before processing her application. (fieldnotes 8/8/90)

This policy of manipulating official processing periods applied not only to clients constructed as liars or child abusers, but also to those constructed as pests: workers reported putting clients' applications at the bottom of the pile if they called too many times to inquire as to their status.

In the above examples, the workers are more or less operating within the confines of official policy. Becky does not suggest, for instance, that Sherry ignore legal time limits. Adherence to official policy is also upheld in the conversation I had with Fran, Sally, and Edna. Indeed, Fran is forced to clarify the meaning of her claim, "I won't give them ANYthing" (lines 10–11): Edna, Fran's supervisor, points out that she must "still give them what they're entitled to" (lines 16–17), and cautions her against saying "you won't give it to 'em" (line 19). In response, Fran explains that "they get it EVENTUALLY, unfortunately they just have to . . . WAIT a while (lines 18–21). Once Fran's meaning is clear, Edna agrees. She has no problem with the idea of making clients "JUMP MORE ROPES to get it" (lines 19–20), which is what she has in mind when she suggests making clients "overVERIFY" (line 16; oververifying entails requiring clients to produce more evidence than necessary about, say, their employment status). Waiting and oververifying are constructed as legitimate responses to inappropriate behavior, in this case, lying. Within the confines of official policy, then, there is considerable latitude. And in using this latitude, workers in effect produce the policy of the department to the benefit or detriment of individual clients (or groups of clients, such as "liars").

Other policies as well were open to manipulation and thus reformulated on a case-by-case basis. As was made evident in the case of Myra Goodwin's application for funds to repair her roof (see pp. 91–93), decisions had to be made regarding whether or not Emergency Needs applications would be processed at all. This was also the case with fraud referrals. Recall the stabbing incident discussed in Chapter 7: Judy Reynolds was so disgusted by her murdered client that, since it turned out that he had been employed without notifying the department, she decided to charge his wife with welfare fraud. Her decision to make a fraud referral implies that she could have decided not to. Indeed, about a week later Harriet Eaton decided against investigating an overpay on a particular case because she was reluctant to place any additional burdens on the family in question. In both cases, the clients in question had received more money from the department than they were entitled to, but in one case the policy was to try to reclaim the money while in the other it was to let bygones be bygones. Finally, specific benefits (other than food stamps and AFDC) were provided to some applicants and not to others. These were the benefits that not all clients knew about, such as transitional day care, a new program that contributed to recipients' childcare costs for up to one year after they stopped receiving AFDC. At the end of the exchange about lying discussed above, Fran Knight added, "I won't offer them extra"—the "extra" here referring to information regarding other programs or supplemental benefits. Clearly, the withholding or providing of information on a selective basis could have a considerable impact on applicants' financial well-being. Those clients who did not arrive at the welfare office already informed of the various programs for which they might apply might then not receive assistance to which they were legally entitled.

In this sense, specific policies and programs were resources that workers drew on in handling individual cases. This is similar to the point I made about the relative salience of attributes such as race and age (see pp. 114–115). The policies are there, but they take on different meanings and uses in different contexts. The implementation of policy is thus its production.

In addition to intentional policy decisions, the workers engaged in more subtle activities that produced particular kinds of relationships between themselves and clients. This had implications both for clients' access to knowledge and workers' control over the "gate" to welfare benefits. An excerpt from the beginning of a meeting between Diane Kane and an applicant, Sandy Hutchins, provides an example of this with regard to workers' control of agendas and knowledge. Note that length of pauses, in seconds, is indicated in parentheses.

1	D:	okay, scanned through your app, um, you're pregnant, is that the rea-
2		son why you're applying for Medicaid?
3	S:	mm huh
4	D:	and, (what), I'm looking at Medicaid for you, without your husband?
5	S:	right
6	D:	okay ((leafs through application)) (6) applying for food stamps ((leafs
7		through application)) (5) okay, if you're eligible for food stamps, do
8		you want somebody else to be able to pick them up for you?
9	S:	no
10	D:	besides you?
11	S:	I can do it
12	D:	okay ((shuffles through some papers)) (2.5) okay, your driver's license,
13		social security cards for you and your husband?
14	S:	I have his numbers
15	D:	do you have his card?
16	S:	no, I don't have his card
17	D:	does he have his card at home?
18	S:	yes
19	D:	okay ((paperwork)) (3)
20	S:	I don't have a social security card, I know the number, that's all
21	D:	guess what? ((laughs)) you're going to go and apply for a social security
22		card then
23	S:	okay
24	D:	((gathers papers, hands them to Sandy)) (7) you can (go ahead and)
25		complete, one through seventeen ((paperwork)) (8) and what I'll do is
26		make a copy of that stuff
27	C:	when you're ready I can do the xeroxing for you
28	D:	okay, sounds good, Brian is your husband correct?
29	S:	yes, Brian is my husband (DSS 7/2/90)

This segment lasts approximately 1.5 minutes. Diane does not tell Sandy why she needs to know if Sandy can pick up her own food stamps (lines 7–10), or why she needs the various forms of identification she requests (lines 12–13). Although it is not a complicated issue to ascertain the motivation behind Diane's questions, the point is that she gives Sandy no indication why she is doing what she is doing. She doesn't explain that the law requires her to verify clients' identities in particular ways or that whether or not Brian is Sandy's husband is significant for her "grant" determination. The interview continues in this vein for another 10.5 minutes, during which Diane asks numerous other questions and stops talking for long periods of time while she writes things down and gathers the necessary forms. Finally, 12 minutes into the interview, Diane begins to explain to Sandy what the various forms she must complete are for and how her application will be processed.

Diane's approach to interviewing applicants, like that of the other workers in the Kenyon County office, is routinized. These routines give workers control of the agenda (they introduce topics, they decide when topics have been exhausted, etc.) and of the knowledge to which the interviewee is given access. While it might be possible to argue that Sandy is also acting strategically, Diane is clearly in control of the meeting. One does not get the impression of equality. In addition, Diane subjects Sandy to yet another form of waiting: in this case, waiting for information on what she has to do and on what benefits she will receive, if any.

Workers took risks, however, when they produced policy. They could be chastised by their supervisors (or by savvy clients) for failing to provide benefits or apply sanctions. Sally Blake, for instance, once told me that she wanted to change the date on a medical form so that a woman could receive Medicaid coverage for a previous injury. Although Sally acknowledged doing this kind of thing in the past, in this particular instance she decided it would be too easily detected. She was fully aware that such an action, if discovered by management, could place her job in jeopardy. So why did workers take the risk? First, in an environment where workers are given little authority, the unsanctioned production of policy is an assertion of autonomy. Second, the production of policy—in other words, workers' routines, shortcuts, and case-by-case decisions—provides a way to manage workloads.

I have already established that Kenyon County AP workloads were substantial, and, from the women's point of view, unreasonable. Since workers cannot accommodate all the demands made of them, they must inevitably devise means to make their situations more manageable (Prottas 1979). Two approaches that the women in the Kenyon County office found useful were discretion in the application of certain policies (e.g., those which are not closely monitored by the department, or which need to be decided on a case-by-case basis), and the unsanctioned categorization of clients. Again, these practices help them to maintain some control and autonomy in a work environment in which they are given few official discretionary powers, and in which they are continually bombarded by more—and often conflicting—demands than they can meet (Prottas 1979). Indeed, it could be argued that, just as the structure of welfare forces recipients to "cheat" in order to survive, so the structure and organization of the welfare bureaucracy forces workers to take short-cuts, many of which are not officially sanctioned. Workers' relationships with their clients, then, must be viewed within the context of workers' relationships with the welfare department.

Situating workers' actions towards clients in this context provides insight into the relationship between workers' exercise of power, and accommodation and resistance. On the one hand, making policy decisions that work against recipients' interests may be a form of resistance to the constraints of AP work. Again, workers feel that they are powerless: they have no say over policy or over the organization and conduct of work in the welfare office. The only place in which they may exercise autonomy is in their interactions with clients, despite the fact that in those interactions as well they are expected to follow departmental procedures. Using power against clients may be a product of the women's need to control their workloads, and to exercise autonomy and discretion wherever and whenever possible.

A similar point may be made about workers' manipulations of policy to benefit their clients. As Prottas (1979) has pointed out, welfare workers have a notion of what constitutes their "proper" role, a notion that includes doing a good job—providing services to clients. Helping clients they believe are deserving of aid is one way of doing a good job, of making sure that the system serves those for whom it was designed. When workers ignore or reformulate policies, however—when Harriet fails to investigate a family that is receiving more aid than it is entitled to, or when Sally contemplates changing dates on medical forms—they are not accommodating the department. Rather, they are contesting and undermining policies that they believe are inappropriate or inhumane in particular cases. These actions nevertheless reproduce the implicit departmental and explicit societal distinction between the deserving and undeserving. They thus serve the department's need (and perhaps that of society at large) to avoid providing "free rides" to the undeserving. They are in one respect resistant, and in another accommodating.

Similarly, while contesting client demands and departmental control in the day-to-day, workers' negative exercise of power over clients may also serve to accommodate the hierarchical nature of the welfare bureaucracy. The welfare system has an interest in making public assistance an unpleasant affair for recipients, and thus AP workers are taught, in both subtle and direct ways, to be suspicious of clients. Such de facto and de jure policies operate as disincentives to clients, both potential and actual. Workers' own constructions—based on interactions with clients, on the stereotypes they bring with them to their work, and on the views of the welfare department as expressed in policy and training—seem to reinforce negative constructions of clients. Another way to view workers' production of policy, then, is to consider it as both reflection and reinforcement of the welfare system's hierarchical nature. This is in keeping with Scott's claim (1986) that negative actions directed at subordinates (as opposed to superordinates) constitute accommodation rather than resistance; and Wineman's claim (1984) that oppressed people often have access to and engage in some form of oppression against others.

In sum, workers' production of policy, whether helping or harming their clients, may be interpreted in terms of both accommodation and resistance: resistance to the mundane, day-to-day details of the workplace, and accommodation to the hierarchical organization of the welfare bureaucracy. Workers' co-production of policy in their talk with each other, and in their meetings with clients, is at least partly an outgrowth of the official division between policy formation and implementation. This demarcation divested workers of authority, while simultaneously providing them with some space within which they could exercise considerable de facto power and autonomy. Workers' production of policy at the ground level also contributed to maintaining the hierarchical relationship between workers, as gatekeepers to welfare benefits, and recipients, as clients of the system. In the next chapter, I explore this relationship between workers and clients in more detail.

Chapter 9
Trapped as They Are

It'd be REALLY INTERESTING to, to find out when you get all through with this, if a profile of an AP worker and a profile of a CLIENT are VERY very much ALIKE . . . like a whole, all OVER, overwhelming sense of POWERlessness, and we in a sense are AS TRAPPED as they are. (Anne Jensen 6/28/90)

When Anne made the above comment she was expressing comembership. Specifically, workers and recipients are the same insofar as both are trapped in the welfare system, and both suffer from an "overwhelming sense of powerlessness." These feelings of entrapment and powerlessness were of course shared by recipients, who frequently referred to the dilemmas of being "stuck on welfare." Such sentiments, moreover, express the economic reality of both groups' dependence on the welfare system.

As I have already discussed, the two groups of women did not share high levels of educational achievement, and none of them came from well-off families. Indeed, one of the workers grew up in an AFDC family, and another had a sister who was currently receiving AFDC. It is perhaps not surprising, then, that a comparison of the women's employment histories shows that the kinds of jobs that recipients had or were currently holding are strikingly similar to those that workers had held prior to becoming AP workers (see Table 1). Most of these jobs were low paid, low status, and defined as "women's" work. Jobs that did not overlap were also often similar in terms of pay and status (e.g., janitor, bakery worker, dry cleaning worker, farm laborer, etc.). The difference between the two groups is that, in the category of jobs not shared, workers held more "professional" jobs in bookkeeping, teaching, management, and the like; and, that workers did not report engaging in illegal work activities such as prostitution or check stealing. Nevertheless, the vast majority of workers had been clerical workers prior to becoming AP workers (see Appendix B, Table B2); and recipients, as well as workers, listed several "professional" jobs, such as math tutor (junior college level), lab tech-

TABLE 1: Workers' and Recipients' Employment Histories

Jobs held in common by AP workers and recipients

Restaurant worker (cook/waitress)
Clerical worker
Domestic worker
Cashier
Bar tender/server
Factory worker
Daycare worker
Nurse
Lab technician
Government reporter/inspector

Jobs not held in common by AP workers and recipients

AP workers	Recipients
Community aide	Carnival worker
Safety officer	Farm laborer
Janitor	Street vendor
Bakery worker	Sewing (alterations)
Dry cleaning worker	Gas station attendant
Data operator	Tutor
Computer operator	Illegal:
Library aide	Check stealing
Bookkeeper	Prostitution
Teacher	
Store manager	

nician, and nurse (see Appendix B, Table B1). Despite the variations, then, and in terms of both income and status, the women's employment backgrounds appear more similar than different. Clearly, both groups of women suffered from the general economic oppression of women in U.S. society: from occupational segregation by gender, in which women are restricted to certain forms of work (Ehrenreich and Piven 1984), and from the attendant low level of women's earnings relative to those of men (Shortridge 1984). In addition, AP work itself, being in the "helping" professions, fits into the category of "women's" work.

Issues of Control:
Shared Relationships to the Welfare System

Anne alludes to more than economics, however, when she refers to an "overwhelming sense of POWERlessness." She is also pointing to the lack of autonomy and control the women experience in their relationships with the Department of Social Services. Recipients, for instance, were routinely told where they could live, what kinds of medical care they could receive, what kinds of relationships they could have with men, and what decisions they could make concerning employment and schooling. Workers, for their part, were divested of control over almost every aspect of their work lives: from knowledge to attire, from the organization of work to the organization of space. Although the department did not have the power to regulate intimate aspects of workers' lives outside the welfare office, workers felt as if the department *did* control their entire lives. Recipients and workers accordingly held some similar views:

1. Both recipients and workers believed that the people in power (legislators in the case of recipients; managers in the case of workers) "had it easy," and were ignorant of what conditions (for poor people and AP workers) really were. Both felt that those making decisions about their lives were incompetent to make such decisions. At a legislative hearing, for instance, Susan Harrison, the president of LIFE, invited a legislator to come to her house and see for himself what living on welfare was like (LIFE 5/8/90). This resembles Edith Saunders's comment that, "I would like to have a week of the people ((management)) coming down here to be on the front lines and maybe they'd understand a little bit more" (DSS 8/24/90).

2. Both groups questioned their "choice" to participate in the welfare system. Recipients argued that applying for public assistance was a matter of financial necessity, and workers claimed that they had little option but to continue working for the welfare department.

3. Both workers and recipients believed that the welfare system undermined their efforts to fulfill the goals the system expected of them. Workers' jobs were organized in such a way as to preclude them from doing a good job; and the structure of public assistance left recipients "stuck" and unable to remove themselves from the welfare rolls. As a result, the system itself generated the negative behavior it so readily condemned in its workers ("bad attitudes") and clients (lying).

4. Both recipients and workers claimed the "overwhelming sense of POWERlessness" to which Anne Jensen referred. They both felt that they had little control over the day-to-day aspects of their lives, and both expressed a desire to be treated like "human beings," that is, respectfully.

While relationships between workers and recipients are typically marred by hostility, then, there is potential, at least in theory, for the two groups of women to develop alliances. As Piven (1984:18) states, "The infrastructure of the welfare state . . . creates the basis for cross-class alliances among women. . . . The welfare state has generated powerful cross-ties between the different groups of women who have stakes in protecting it." Recognition of their shared constraints and views would thus go a long way towards diminishing the antagonism between them. More specifically, construing each other's "negative" attributes as generated by the system itself, rather than as reflective of personality, would reduce hostility and generate understanding. Indeed, one could envision workers and recipients uniting against a welfare bureaucracy that oppresses them both, and, moreover, oppresses them in somewhat similar ways.

We're (Almost) the Same: Taking the Other's View

As I defined it in Chapter 3, comembership entails a recognition and expression of commonality (Erickson 1975; Erickson and Shultz 1982; Shultz 1975), and provides a basis upon which solidarity may be built. This is different from sympathy and understanding. However, in the context of a relationship that is characterized (by both participants and observers) as uncongenial, the ability to understand the other's viewpoint may be a step in the direction of comembership.

I demonstrated in Chapter 5 that recipients expressed fewer positive views of workers than constructions of them as arbitrary or deliberately nasty. On those infrequent occasions during which recipients depicted workers in a positive light, emphasis was placed on their helpfulness. At a LIFE meeting, for instance, one woman touted her worker as both knowledgeable and helpful: "Meg knows her way around every single one of those ((policy)) books . . . they could've cut my ADC off when Eric moved in if they really wanted to, but she (had) a way around that, and she took it" (LIFE 8/19/90). This characterization is significant, however, only insofar as it goes beyond the usual typifications of workers; it is, moreover, the exception that proves the rule. There are only two cases in my data that may be interpreted as examples of understanding or comembership. First, recipients sometimes expressed sympathy for workers' workloads. In these cases, they referred to overburdened workers when explaining workers' errors, or to the women's need to hold on to their jobs at all costs. The second case, of which I have only one example, concerned LIFE's public demonstrations against the welfare department. Three members of LIFE were discussing handing out fliers on LIFE at the welfare office when one of them commented, "who knows, we might get a few people that work for DSS interested, once they know we're not head-hunting" (LIFE 3/11/90). ("Head-hunting" here refers to singling people out for attack.) Nobody picked up on this comment, except to agree that LIFE was not in the business of attacking department employees, and within a minute the women were again speaking of workers in a derogatory tone. The comment, however, could be construed as an example of comembership: the speaker may have been implying that workers and recipients had some shared interests in terms of their relationships with the welfare department.

Clearly, recipients were not by and large sympathetic to or understanding of the constraints on workers, and they rarely situated workers' actions in the larger context of the welfare system (as opposed to blaming the workers' personalities). With the exception of the comment at the LIFE meeting just discussed, expressions of comembership—of recipients and workers as an "us"—were virtually nonexistent.

While workers' expressions of sympathy towards recipients were also rarer than negative evaluations, they were more frequent. In this regard, workers most commonly referred to recipients' desperation, pointing out that they only came to the welfare office when they had exhausted all other resources. This view provided workers with a framework for making sense of behavior that was nevertheless on most occasions interpreted as "pushiness." Workers also expressed sympathy for recipients' problems with medical bills. Such sympathy approached comembership insofar as it was based on a potentially shared problem: anybody can fall ill and suffer severe economic hardship if they have no medical insurance. Finally, some workers mentioned suggesting to recipients that they call their legislators to complain about certain aspects of welfare policy which they considered unfair.

A conversation I had with Colleen O'Connell provides an example of how one worker expressed comembership. Our discussion occurred after Colleen had interviewed a woman who was "falling through the cracks"—who was ineligible for medical coverage because she was not yet 65 years old and had too much income. Colleen began by making a connection between the state of the economy and the size of the welfare rolls:

If we had jobs available that would be a different matter, but we don't. We know when our case loads go up, you know, somebody goes on strike. Webster was hit pretty bad because . . . Sandia Industries went on strike and then . . . they hired the scabs in and so all these people, even though they're still drawing strike pay it's only one hundred a week, you know, and it's just not enough to live on, so we, we got all those people in and . . . most of them are, well, I shouldn't say most, but a lot of them are still on ((welfare)) but some of them are finding jobs. But yeah . . . it's directly linked to the economy, and it's just not getting much better. (DSS 7/5/90)

If jobs were there for the taking and recipients were not taking them, "that would be a different matter" in Colleen's view. Then recipients would be to blame for their own poverty. In reality, however, jobs are scarce. Colleen thus locates the cause of expanding welfare rolls in the economy, rather than in, for example, recipients' character defects: there are not enough jobs to go around, and when workers go on strike, union support is insufficient.

As our conversation continued, Colleen discussed her and her husband's own economic vulnerability, pointing to their dependence on General Motors, a major employer in the area that had recently instituted a number of layoffs. At the time, according to Colleen, General Motors was laying off people who had been employed with the company for fewer than fifteen years. The company was also offering early retirement packages to those who had worked for General Motors for more than fifteen years, in an attempt to further reduce their work force. The packages consisted of lump-sum payments, the amount of which was dependent on years of service. Once an employee accepted the lump-sum payment the company had no further obligation to them regarding, for example, pension. Colleen's husband, Frank, who had twenty-one years of service with General Motors, was constantly receiving offers of early retirement from his bosses. Colleen explained why she and Frank were not interested:

His was a sixty thousand dollar ((payoff)), and then we figured by the time the taxes ((were deducted)) it'd be forty thousand. He can make that in a year, he makes sixty thousand in a year if he works holidays, or he used to . . . when he worked all the overtime. But, it's not worth it to us, what are we gonna do? I mean, that's a year by the time the taxes are taken out, that's just a year wages for us. We can't leave ((General Motors)). You know, it would be nice to have that much money lump sum, but you've got to think of the long term, and you know, a lot of them took it, a lot of them took that buy-out, and a lot of them are back in applying for assistance. (DSS 7/5/90)

Like other workers, Colleen and her husband are unprotected from the vagaries of the labor market. Many of the people who were unfortunate enough to accept General Motors buy-outs were now on public assistance, as were those who went on strike against Sandia Industries. Colleen and her husband have been lucky so far, but at the same time they have little choice other than to remain where they are.

In her talk, Colleen is expressing comembership: her husband and other workers—workers who are now receiving public assistance—are in many ways the same. She sees more similarity than difference between the currently employed (herself and her husband) and this particular category of welfare recipient. Although the $40,000 to which Colleen refers would represent considerable wealth from the point of view of most recipients, the comembership she is expressing does not concern the specifics of financial resources but rather a shared economic vulnerability. Again, however, it is important to note that the recipients with whom Colleen aligns herself fall into the "deserving" category of the poor, insofar as they have been employed and would continue to be so if possible. She thus establishes comembership with only a segment of the welfare population.

Anne Jensen's comment, with which this chapter opened, is the clearest expression of comembership that I encountered. Again, both recipients and workers are trapped and powerless. Significantly, Anne makes no distinctions among types of recipients, but rather aligns workers as a group with recipients as a group. Were such views common to both workers and recipients, the relationship between them—and potentially both groups' relationship with the welfare system—might look very different from those which I present in this book.

Welfare Makes Us Do It: The Institutional Context of Hostility

At first sight, given the similarities in the women's economic backgrounds and in their relationships to the welfare system, the paucity of expressions of comembership is puzzling. The institutional context of their relationship, however, involves a number of factors which seem to override the shared experiences of occupational segregation, family obligation, and powerlessness vis-a-vis the Department of Social Services.

Structural Locations and Personalized Relationships

Recipients of public assistance and AP workers are in structurally antagonistic positions. The recipient's goal is to try to qualify for benefits, and the gatekeeper to these benefits is the AP worker. Most recipients are aware that there is considerable flexibility in the system: workers have 45 days to process applications, there are a variety of assistance programs that can be applied for, and workers always have the option of formally applying for exceptions to the rules.[1] What this means is that part of the business of recipients is to enlist the help of workers.

The business of workers, however, is not only to process applications,

---

1. As Prottas (1979) points out, these factors are probably not common knowledge among all recipients, which is why a worker's decision to either provide or withhold information can have a serious impact on her client's well-being. While recipients may in general be unaware of the various programs available to them, of exceptions, and so on, it is nevertheless the case that most are fully aware of the existence of workers' discretionary powers.

but also to manage out-sized workloads and, significantly, to avoid getting "burned." In this regard, workers bear the considerable burden of discerning honesty and dishonesty on the part of their clients. This burden is increased by departmental training, which often reinforces stereotypes of the poor (Withorn 1984). Harriet Eaton, for instance, told of attending a workshop on interviewing where workers were encouraged to develop skill in "listening between the lines," in order to tell whether a client was telling the truth. The metamessage here is that recipients will be dishonest if they can get away with it, and that workers therefore need to be on their guard. To give another example: during a training course for new AP workers, the group discussed the need to make clients understand that they were expected to contribute to their utility bills when they were enrolled in the Heating or Emergency Assistance programs. One of the trainers quipped, as if to underscore recipients' thick-headedness, "Impressing *anything* on clients is difficult" (DSS 7/17/90). Stereotypes of the poor can also be reinforced unintentionally if they are not addressed or challenged. Consider the following fieldnote entry, again from the training course:

Worker A asked how many times DSS would pay for a battered woman's shelter if she kept on returning to the relationship. Worker B then asked if battered women are put at the top of the list for subsidized housing. When Trainer 1 replied in the affirmative to Worker B's question, B responded (paraphrase): "I have clients who are on the list forever, but then someone (battered) walks in and gets into subsidized housing right away, and I don't think that's fair." Worker C then brought up the topic of food banks, claiming that her clients complain about the food that they get through the banks, to which Worker D responded that clients "shouldn't be so proud."

Although I wasn't able to keep track of all the comments, they were by and large negative. And the trainers were by and large passive. Although on occasion mildly challenging (e.g., [paraphrase] "it's better to put someone up in a hotel for the night than to risk finding them frozen to death under a bridge the next morning"), the usual response of both trainers was to smile stiffly and move on to the next topic. (fieldnotes 7/18/90)

When the trainers—official representatives of the Department of Social Services—did not challenge the new workers' views of clients, they reinforced constructions of recipients as stupid, lazy, and ungrateful. At no time did the training course consider the needs or perceptions of the population ostensibly being served by the programs under discussion; rather, attention was focused on the needs of the department with regard to paper work and public relations.

What transpires between workers and recipients when they meet is thus a manifestation of their positions in the system and of what they have to do in order to survive. Their meeting is also a face-to-face interaction in which the relationship between institution and client is personalized as one between two individuals, one a welfare worker, the other a recipient. As I discussed in Chapter 7, for instance, workers were personally insulted by recipients' attempts to manipulate the system: recipients were lying to *them*, and trying to get extra money from *them*. This negative behavior on the part of recipients was usually attributed to character defects. Even "legitimate" requests from recipients were interpreted in somewhat personal terms; recipients' appeals for money or food were, after all, directed at workers. Workers frequently displayed this interpretation in their talk. Judy Reynolds, for instance, claimed that workers are "responsible for people eating, and . . . paying their rent" (DSS 8/24/90). Sherry Nelson made a similar point when she told a story about an "obnoxious" client: "she ((the client)) said, 'you have never helped me with rent,' and I said, 'what do you mean? *I* never helped you with rent?'" (DSS 6/14/90). Workers spoke in this regard of a need to maintain distance between themselves and their needy clients. As Debbie Brown put it:

you have to be able to detach yourself from a lot of this . . . or you can become very emotionally involved with the people, when they're in trouble, because we are kind of like the last resort, you know, and if you can't help somebody . . . there's nowhere else they can go, more or less. (DSS 8/17/90)

Judy Reynolds and AP supervisor Ester Dove made a somewhat similar point when explaining their callous approach to the stabbing incident discussed in Chapter 7:

J: this job makes you cold in the heart, Catherine, it makes you a HARD person
C: ((laughs))
E: right, it is—you gotta laugh at it or you, you go nuts   (DSS 8/3/90)

There is a tone of responsibility in Debbie's comment, as if she has to struggle against feeling personally responsible for the individuals whose applications she processes. Although such a stance is not immediately evident in Judy's and Ester's comments, they nevertheless reflect a need to be distant, a callousness developed of necessity. Consider the following entry from my fieldnotes:

Today I introduced myself to Edna Lewis, one of the AP supervisors. She asked me to shut off my tape recorder and then began discussing the troubles that AP workers have. She talked of the disappointment of not being able to really help people because the money provided through the various programs is insufficient. She also spoke of the frustrations involved in having to deal with policies that provide money for those who don't need it (her example was of paying for hotel rooms for adolescents who are "homeless" because they don't want to abide by their parents' rules), while bypassing those who do need it (her example was of a man with five children who just lost his wife in a car accident). According to Edna, many workers suffer from "burn-out," the signs of which include ulcers, migraines, taking illegal drugs, and hostility towards clients. (fieldnotes 6/11/90)

Workers, in other words, face sorrow and desperation on a daily basis; and although they are responsible for responding to this sorrow and desperation, they have little control over the mechanisms or sufficiency of the department's programs. The hostility to which Edna refers—like Debbie's detachment, Judy's cold-heartedness, or Ester's need to laugh—may be a manifestation of this contradiction between responsibility and control. This in turn may work against the establishment of alliances between workers and their clients.

Sometimes workers' personalization of their relationships with their clients was less direct, as was the case in a discusson of how AP salaries and welfare benefit levels should be connected. The participants in the conversation, a transcript of which is included as Case #9 in Appendix A, were Peggy Stewart, Fran Knight, Debbie Brown, and myself. We had been talking about the union's resistance to the way in which the welfare department categorized AP workers (which in turn determined salary levels), when Debbie asked how many AP workers there were in the state altogether. Peggy and Fran speculated that the number was between eight and ten thousand. Debbie's reponse was as follows:

When you multiply that by fifty thousand dollars a month for ((laughs)) each person ((laughs)) that we give away, I figure I give away fifty thousand dollars a month. We send out a quarter of a million in food stamps from this county a month. (DSS 8/3/90)

In other words, each worker is responsible for approximately $50,000 in benefits a month. Perhaps in response to my surprise at such a high amount, Peggy confirmed Debbie's numbers by stating that she had a million dollars worth of food stamps on her case load in a previous county. Fran then suggested that the amount of money each AP worker "gives away" could add up to considerably more than what was covered in the worker's regular case loads if Emergency Needs funds were also included. The point of the women's talk was that AP workers are responsible for an inordinate amount of money and thus should be appropriately compensated. What they were doing in their conversation, then, was relating what "they" give away in terms of welfare support with their own remuneration, which they see as insufficient and bordering on exploitation.

Recipients, too, personalized their relationship with the welfare system, often portraying the outcomes of their interactions with the welfare department as due to their relationships with their workers. Indeed, as Prottas (1979:128) points out, "for the client, the bureaucrat's behavior is the behavior of the agency." Although they on occasion interpreted workers' actions in the context of workloads or welfare policy, most often, like workers, they viewed the others' actions in terms of personality characteristics. I provided some examples of this in Chapter 3: "it ((what you get)) depends on who your case worker is," and "discrimination against personality ((on the part of workers)), that's a major problem" (LIFE 4/29/90). In the following narrative, Leslie Goldenberg refers to her relationship with her worker in attempting to explain an unexpected change in her food stamp benefit. Leslie had called me at home several days prior to an MWRO meeting to present her problem, and I had suggested that she attend the meeting in order to get more knowledgeable advice. This is how Leslie presented her problem to the group:

I've been living in . . . Hamilton ((apartment complex)) for almost three years—no it's been about two and a half years—and my food stamps were down to fifty-five dollars 'cause my rent's seventy-four, and I get child support most of the time, usually it's fifty dollars, but it—my food stamps would be fifty-five, and it just didn't ever seem right, and then about four or five months ago, she ((Leslie's AP worker)) upped it to eighty-nine, and I was getting fifty dollar child support checks regularly at this time, then all the SUDDEN for this mo—MONTH, I get a hundred and ONE, I've never received a hundred and one, since I've lived there . . . that's the highest I've ever received, 'cause most a the time I lived there I got fifty-five dollars, a month, and all the sudden out of the clear blue sky, it went up . . . and so I was like, there's something wrong. WE ((Leslie and her AP worker)) don't get along, we don't argue, but . . . when I first met her I told her I wanted to go to school full time, she asked me why, and I told her so I could have her seat, so I could sit where she's sitting, and she just looked at me like I had lost every little bit of sense I HAD ((laughs)), and so, we—from that day on we never got along, 'cause I'm very, I speak my mind, and if I find something OUT that she's wrong about I tell her about it, and then I speak to her supervisor, and SO we don't—but if something needs to be raised, she'll never raise it unless I call her, if something needs to be dropped, it's dropped IMMEDIATELY, so . . . we just, you know, so I don't think there's something right. (MWRO 3/7/90)

Leslie's construction of a personal relationship with the welfare department is apparent when she states that "she"—her worker, not the welfare department—increased her food stamp allotment. Leslie's interpretation of this unexpected change in terms of her relationship with her worker is evident in her movement from a description of the changes in her food stamp allotment to a description of the antagonism between her and her worker. When Leslie told her worker that she wanted to attend school full time "so I could have her seat, so I could sit where she's sitting," her worker "looked at me like I had lost every little bit of sense I HAD"—as if Leslie intended, literally, to usurp *her* position, or at least to be on equal footing. Their encounters had been unpleasant ever since. Accordingly, Leslie is suspicious of her worker's actions: as she explains, her worker is quick to decrease benefits but slow to increase them. Leslie concludes that "I don't think there's something right." She cannot fathom why her food stamp benefit would increase. Policy changes are not within the realm of possibility, as all alterations in benefits are reduced to the whim of the individual worker. Workers' suspicion of their clients was thus reciprocated.

Creating Distance: A Case Example

The following example illustrates some of the various co-occurring factors that contribute to a lack of comembership between recipients and workers. The case displays workers' construction of a client and their coproduction of policy, a client's (unsuccessful) efforts to manipulate the system, and antagonism, rather than comembership between a particular worker and her client. I am somewhat hampered in my presentation of this case, in that I lack data on how the client interpreted her interaction with the worker. The incident nevertheless provides insight into the generation of conflict in recipient-worker interactions.

Leila Harding and her partner, Mark Miller, were recipients of General Assistance (GA), a program for poor adults without children. Several issues prompted Leila to set up an appointment with Becky Wright, her AP worker. First, Leila claimed that Mark had not received his most recent GA check; second, she did not understand why her GA "grant" had decreased; and, finally, she and Mark were on the verge of being evicted from their apartment for failure to pay rent and thus wanted to apply for Emergency Needs funds. In addition to her client's concerns, however, Becky had her own agenda: to find out if Leila was earning money on the side.

The two women first discussed Mark's check. In order to verify whether the check had been mailed, Becky and I left to consult the computer records, leaving Leila in Becky's office. We had the following exchange when Becky discovered that the check had indeed been sent:

1 C: so he DID get his checks?
2 B: YEAH he got his checks, it would be rare if he didn't. I don't know if
3   these people are stupid
4 C: say what?
5 B: I don't know whether these people are real ignorant, if they're STUPID,
6   or if they just preTEND to be
7 C: what do YOU think?
8 B: I think they pretend to be, I think that they're VERY intelligent, I really
       do   (DSS 7/2/90)

Becky's claim, then, is that Leila is feigning ignorance and confusion in order to receive another check. Leila is intelligently using displays of stupidity in her attempt to fool Becky, and through her, the welfare system.

Back in Becky's office, Leila accepts the computer verification of Mark's check, and the two women move on to discuss the threatened eviction. Leila claims that their landlord has given them only a few more days to meet their rental obligations. Becky asks Leila if she received her most recent GA check (for $111.50), implying that she should have used some of the money for rent. Although Leila did receive the check, she is not sure how much of it goes to the landlord—she thinks it's $68. With a loud sigh, indicating that this is not the first time she has explained this, Becky responds by correcting Leila—she is to give $84, not $68, to the landlord. In addition, since Leila and Mark have already received Emergency Needs funds once this year they are not eligible for additional funds unless they actually receive an eviction notice, which they have not—again, they were supposed to pay rent from their regular checks. Becky then points out that the reason why Leila's "grant" decreased was that she quit her job. Leila expresses confusion throughout. First, she doesn't understand why her benefits were cut as she did not quit her job but was fired. Becky explains that "a job quit and firing are the same thing for General Assistance, they consider it all a voluntary thing," adding, however, that "I don't think that's necessarily fair." Second, Leila is confused about the amount of her current check. She claims that Becky told her the amount of the check would be "$223 and now it's only $111." Becky points out that two checks for $111.50 amount to $223 a month. It is precisely this display of confusion over basic policies which have already been explained that leads Becky to question Leila's intelligence. Sometimes she claims that Leila is intelligent but feigning ignorance (as indicated above), and other times she constructs her as truly "slow."

Having responded to Leila's inquiries, Becky takes the opportunity to address her main concern: the accusation by Mrs. Hanson (Leila's landlord) that Leila has another job she has not reported to the department. Becky tags her question on to the end of a statement about department mailing schedules.

1	B:	they're beHIND and they, there's nothing basically I can do HERE
2		about it. 'KAY now I have a question for YOU: are you WORKing?
3	L:	no
4	B:	okay, Mrs. Hanson says you ARE. She says you have a part-time job at
5		Madrid Pet Center
6	L:	uh uh
7	B:	okay ((B fumbles and drops something)) I pulled Mark's case and you
8		WERE working at Mad- Pet—Madrid Pet Center but that doesn't matter
9		because if you're not working there you're not working there, but she
10		claims you're working right now, a part-time job

11   L: no I'm not
12   B: okay and you're SURE of that
13   L: uh huh
14   B: okay, ANYway, because we have to pursue it REGARDLESS if you say
15   there isn't or IS, if somebody calls in and says this person is working and
16   it's not the Madrid Pet Center, it wouldn't matter where it WAS . . . so be
17   it that I have to check it OUT no matter what   (DSS 7/2/90)

What Becky has done here is provide Leila with evidence that Leila has been withholding information (the landlord's accusation plus the documentation provided in Mark's application form—which Leila had not provided in her own application). She gives Leila four opportunities to confess (lines 2, 4–5, 8–10, 12). Becky also indicates that she will pursue the accusation, with the implication that if Leila is employed her status as a General Assistance client will change (lines 14–17). With an almost friendly "but we won't worry about it for now," Becky drops the topic, leaving Leila to make the next move.

The women's talk up to this point lends itself well to the kind of analysis Goffman presents in *Expression Games* (1969):

Just as it can be assumed that it is in the interests of the observer [Becky] to acquire information from a subject [Leila], so it is in the interests of the subject to appreciate that this is occurring and to control and manage the information the observer obtains; for in this way the subject can influence in his [sic] own favor responses to a situation which includes himself. Further it can be assumed that the subject can achieve this end by means of a special capacity—the capacity to inhibit and fabricate expression. (1969:10)

It is probable, then, that Leila knows there is something at stake in this interaction. It is also possible that her displays of confusion are deliberate, as Becky sometimes suspects. At any rate, what is crucial here is Becky's conviction that Leila is putting on a performance with regard to her employment status. When Becky asks, seemingly out of nowhere, whether Leila is working, she is making an "uncovering" move; she is attempting "to crack, pierce, penetrate, and otherwise get behind the apparent fact in order to uncover the real ones" (Goffman 1969:17–18). Simultaneously, however, she practices "seduction": "The observer's object . . . is to manoeuver a definition of the situation such that the subject is led to believe that the observer is to be treated as something of a teammate, to whom strategic information (among other things) can be voluntarily trusted" (1969:37). Becky does this in two ways: first, by stating that she disagrees with the GA policy of reducing benefits when a client is fired ("I don't think that's necessarily fair"), and second, after she has asked Leila about her employment status, by adding "but we won't worry about it for now" (this, however, can also be read as a move designed to make Leila uncomfortable and to make her sit with her discomfort for a while, a practice common in police interrogations [1969: 34]). Becky's second, and crucial, seductive move occurs in the following exchange, when she gives Leila yet another opportunity to admit to her job, and, when she does not, colludes with her in discussing a "hypothetical" work situation. Just as this is a strategic move on Becky's part, it is a strategic error on Leila's.

```
 1   B:   Do you have any other questions before I let you go?
 2   L:   um, what type of difference would it, would it make if I, you know, if I
 3        DID get a part time job?
 4   B:   then that, that depends on how much you were making. You can make
 5        UP to about, let me think, if you're working about twenty hours a week,
 6        at, four-fifty an hour, you would be okay, you would NOT—it would
 7        affect your GRANT greatly, but it would not close your case, and that
 8        would still give you General Assistance, Medicaid and food stamps, and
 9        it would give you SOME money, it just wouldn't give you much
10   L:   So, when, the, the money wouldn't go towards the RENT then
11   B:   There PRObably would not be enough in your grant (to pay that) to be
12        honest with you . . . They DO give you a whole bunch of DISregards
13        when you're earning, but, usually if you're working part time it usually
14        cuts your grant at LEAST in half
15   L:   uh huh
16   B:   so it would probably be less than a hundred dollars in total
17   L:   'cause I was THINKIN' about, 'cause I DID work there and I'm thinkin'
18        about going BACK
19   B:   uh huh
20   L:   ( ) just to get this bill situation turned ar—
21   B:   caught UP
22   L:   yeah    (DSS 7/2/90)
```

Throughout the discussion, both women act as if the situation were hypothetical rather than real. Leila for instance, guesses that if she *were* to work, it would be part time (lines 2–3), and the two women calculate the impact of Leila's earning based on a hypothetical pay rate of $4.50/hour (lines 5–7). In keeping with the imaginary nature of the discussion, no mention is made of deceit, or of the potential policy implications of such deceit, namely, fraud referral. Again, bringing up the topic at all is a strategic error on Leila's part, particularly her reference to the fact that she did indeed work at the Madrid Pet Center at one point and was considering returning (lines 17–18). Her efforts may provide, on the one hand, an example of a failed "counter-uncovering move"—an effort to go along with the observer enough to fool them (Goffman 1969:19–20), or, simply, an "unwitting move," one "whereby the subject acts mindlessly relative to impression management" (17).

After Leila has left the office, Becky confirms her conviction that "I think she's working, I think she's been working right along." Becky also predicts that Leila will not confess immediately but will wait a month or so before revealing her employment situation in order to save some money. In projecting this move, Becky constructs Leila as intelligent and manipulative, a construction bolstered by the landlord's view of Leila and Mark:

This landlord can't STAND these people but she's BENT OVER BACKwards to meet them half way, and she honestly cannot STAND them, because she thinks they are SCUM. She said . . . there are welfare clients, that are in need of assistance, and good people, and then there are welfare scum, and she said these are two welfare scums, trying to feed off the system, two able-bodied people, that COULD work, trying to scam the system. And so when she TOLD me, she told me CAsually that this girl had a JOB, she said "between the GA and her job she didn't give me one BIT," she didn—yeah that's how she MENtioned it, and I, and THIS girl had not even PAID this landlord, see, she just automatically expects we'll patch it UP, like she came beeboppin' in like this was some emergency today, this is no emergency, I can't do a damn thing for her, and to be honest and tell you the truth I wouldn't, right now. We've caught her rent up once and if she's got a JOB there is NO reason why that girl should NOT be catching that rent up, and I'm putting her case into negative action, it'll will close for . . . failure to report a JOB, and I don't think, I think she was working the whole TIME, I don't think she GOT this job while she was on assistance, I think back when Mark came in and applied she's had that job ever SINCE. (DSS 7/2/90)

Using the landlord's voice, Becky distinguishes between the deserving poor—those "that are in need of assistance, and good people"—and "welfare scum," in this case, "two able-bodied people, that COULD work, trying to scam the system." Not only is Leila lazy; she is also arrogant: she "automatically" expects the department to take care of any problems she might have. The fact that Leila is actually employed (which Becky verified by calling the Madrid Pet Center) is forgotten.

Becky's construction of Leila, and her personalization of Leila's interactions with both herself and the landlord—again, the manipulation is a personal one rather than one of a system—provided the basis for a conversation she had with Diane Kane, in which she got support for her decision to pursue a fraud referral. Their conversation clearly illustrated worker's coproduction of policy. Specifically, Becky could do one of two things: she could send a form to Madrid Pet Center to verify Leila's employment and then use that to compute changes in Leila's General Assistance benefit; or she could pursue a fraud referral, in which case Leila would not only lose her benefit but be required to pay back the money she had received fraudulently. The first option would be the more benevolent, but it is not the action that Becky chooses to pursue, given her assessment of Leila's character and intentions. She had already indicated this to me when she stated that she would not help Leila even if she could. This position is solidified in Becky's discussion with Diane, in which Diane suggests that a fraud referral is the proper course of action. The decision to put the case in negative action, however, is based on certain assessments; namely, that Leila lied about her job, and, moreover, that she lied from the start and continued to lie, even when confronted face-to-face by Becky. A transcript and analysis of this conversation is presented in Appendix A as Case#10. What Becky and Diane's talk illustrates is that workers do not implement policy automatically. While the department expects workers to make fraud referrals in these kind of situations, Becky and Diane's decision-making indicates that the choice *could* have been made to leave Leila's case open.

Again, as I argued in Chapter 8, worker's decisions to invoke or ignore policy amount to their production of policy. In this example, the (co)production of policy is occurring at more than one level. First, Becky produces policy in her talk with me and then with her coworker Diane. Becky and Leila are also coproducing policy in *their* interaction, despite the fact that they are not meeting as equals. While the outcome is clearly in Becky's hands, each participant makes moves intended to influence the other's next move. I can only conjecture how Becky would have responded if Leila had immediately "confessed." What is evident is that Leila's moves had an impact on the policy outcome of the interview, and that the distinction between deserving and undeserving was a key feature of the resultant policy decision. Clearly, the possibilities of comembership were limited. Regardless of her intention (fulfilling financial obligations, trying to live the easy life), Leila tried to deceive Becky about her employment status. This offended Becky and reduced her sympathy for Leila's financial circumstances.

In sum, the relationship between institution and client was a personal one—recipients and workers were, after all, frequently engaged in face-to-face interaction. In recipients' view, workers were not simply blind instruments of policy, but gatekeepers who chose, for their own idiosyncratic reasons, to help or hinder their clients. I believe I have shown this to be the case, but for systemic rather than idiosyncratic reasons. Likewise, in the workers' view, recipients approached not the system, but themselves, whether the approach was one of appeal based on "real" need, or one of manipulation based on "laziness".

This personalization of the recipient-worker relationship was, moreover, couched in primarily negative—or at least distancing—terms. Recipients' and workers' different positions, both in the world at large and in the welfare bureaucracy in particular, were made evident in their face-to-face interactions; thus recipients' appeals based on desperation contrasted with the workers' position of relative economic comfort and their power over recipients as gatekeepers to the welfare system. In this context, recipients' efforts to manipulate the system in order to survive were transformed into attempts to "use" individual workers. And processing applications for the welfare department became, for workers, an exercise in which *they* provided individual recipients with food stamps or AFDC checks—or, as in the case of Leila, meted out justice. In this sense, the nature of the encounters between workers and recipients accentuated differences between the two groups of women.

The story of Becky and Leila illustrates not only the structural inequality between worker and recipient, but also two additional factors that may contribute to worker-client hostility. The first is professionalism, which "serves to reinforce dominant class and race differences and to disallow the politicized and personalized sense of one's work" (Withorn 1984: 41). In other words, workers, as professionals, inhabit a particular role and fulfill particular functions on behalf of the Department of Social Services. These roles and functions do not officially include interacting as caring human beings responding to the needs of the destitute. Thus Becky does not entertain the possibility that Leila may be lying in an attempt to get what she needs in order to survive. Second, standard bureaucratic procedures do little to decrease conflict (Withorn 1984). Typically, such procedures engender routinization and the abstraction from whole human beings of specific traits or pieces of information. In this case, Leila was reduced to the traits of "manipulative" and "deceitful," and the only information of interest to Becky concerned Leila's employment status.

Structural Locations and Gender Relations

The nature of the welfare bureaucracy is not the only factor relevant to worker-recipient relationships. Gender is also crucial. As Withorn (1984) points out, the fact that the people with authority are women may be frustrating to recipients who assume that people in power are men and that women should be allies. Similarly, workers may be threatened by women who choose paths (such as single motherhood and dependence on the state) different from those that are traditionally acceptable for women in U.S. society. On the other hand, the welfare system is "centrally defined by women's roles and women's issues" (1984:46) and, as such, provides opportunities for the formation of solidarity among recipients and workers. An adequate understanding of division and alliance between the two groups of women therefore depends on an understanding of ideologies concerning women's proper role and the appropriate embodiment and expression of power.

More frequent than workers' recognition of a shared economic vulnerability and oppression by the welfare system was their recognition of the mutual concerns of motherhood. Workers who had experienced it sometimes discussed pregnancy with their pregnant clients, as Nora Ryan did when she gave women advice on how to deal with morning sickness. "Member-adds"—meetings that occurred for the purpose of adding newborns to recipients' cases—were usually pleasant and marked by chit-chat about baby matters, particularly when the newborn was present. It was in reference to women's role as mothers that Debbie Brown spoke of the need to arrange welfare policy so that women could stay at home with their young children. She herself had been a single mother, and was well aware of the dual burden shouldered by women who are responsible for both child care and the financial support of their families.

More often than not, however, pregnancy and motherhood provided grounds for expressions of difference rather than comembership. Karrie Holmes for example, drew on her experience of single motherhood to accentuate the differences, rather than the similarities, between herself and her clients. Deserted by her husband two months after their child was born, Karrie was forced to move in with her parents and find employment. Since she had managed to both be a single mother and hold a job, she saw no reason why all single mothers could not work. In other cases, pregnancy provided evidence of, at worst, promiscuity, and at best, irresponsibility. For instance, Peggy Stewart once expressed resentment towards an applicant who had two children and was pregnant with a third. While, in Peggy's view, the woman in question did not have to worry about support for her children—it would be provided for by the state—Peggy herself could not afford to have a third child. She felt that she had to be "responsible," while her client did not. On another occasion, Sherry Nelson gave a client a form to fill out in order to verify that the father of her child was not living with her. When the client said that the father probably was unaware of his status as a father—that it was just a "one night thing"—Sherry made a haughty face, paused, said "oh" in a condescending tone, and reached into her desk drawer for a different set of forms.

Issues related to gender, then,—and to pregnancy and motherhood in particular—were central to workers' expressions of comembership with or difference from recipients. This was not the case with recipients, who, as I have already indicated, seldom expressed comembership with workers on any grounds.

The Impact of Welfare: Bad but for Different Reasons

The distance between workers and recipients was also displayed in their contrasting views of similar issues. A key area of conflict concerned the impact of public assistance on recipients' lives. For instance, while workers and recipients agreed that welfare engendered poor habits, they differed in their explanations of this phenomenon. For their part, recipients believed that it was the insufficient support provided by the welfare department that engendered the development of negatively valued behaviours, such as irresponsible spending habits and lying. Martha Hill made this clear:

You don't know what you're going to get . . . next month, until you get this (check) in the mail . . . . It is incredibly difficult, and it brings, I think, impulse buying: spend money while it's in your hand, even if it's for things that you need but you really can't afford to buy. (Martha Hill 8/8/90)

In contrast, workers often contended that public assistance programs were too easy on recipients, fostering poor work and spending habits:

I see that we're actually keeping them from accomplishing anything in their life . . . because it's too easy for them . . . everything now is just handed to them . . . there's nothing there to encourage them to go out and get a job, nothing . . . I mean, I've had many clients that say, well, what's the sense of working? I can't make this kind of money working . . . and there's something wrong with that . . . it's drastically wrong. (Judy Reynolds 8/24/90)

Edna Lewis, a supervisor who had formerly been an AP worker, echoed this sentiment:

At first, you really believe you'll help these people get off welfare and lead a productive life, and that's not true—all you are doing is helping them to become more helpless and more dependent. ((Referring to her experiences as a single mother:)) I worked daytimes for the State, nighttimes for a bar, and I worked weekends . . . so I know they can do it, but we . . . make them not want to do it because all they have to do is watch their soaps and go to their fricking mail box. (DSS 8/10/90)

Similarly, while recipients felt that the system was structured in a way that prevented them from severing their ties to the welfare department, some workers felt, as indicated above, that public assistance provided recipients with few incentives to remove themselves from the relief rolls.

Interestingly, this set of contrasting views mirrors left and right political positions in debates concerning welfare reform. Piven and Cloward (1987), for instance, point out that proponents of the right during the Reagan administration claimed that welfare *caused* the disintegration of moral behavior (with regard to reproductive behaviour, work habits, and family composition). This seems to be the stance of some of the workers. According to Piven and Cloward (1987), whose views represent left-wing assessments of public assistance, the perspective of recipients is more accurate:

It is not receiving benefits that is damaging to recipients, but rather the fact that benefits are so low as to ensure physical misery and an outcast social status. Even these benefits are given only under close surveillance . . . and are conditioned on modern rituals of degradation such as publicized "hot lines" encouraging relatives, friends, and neighbors to report information on welfare recipients—all of which surely have disabling and demoralizing effects. (1987:37)

In other words, current welfare programs are "so punitive and stigmatizing that they [recipients] do indeed come over time to produce some of the demoralizing effects attributed to the fact of social provision itself" (1987:34).

Paradoxically, then, workers and recipients agreed that public assistance promotes dependency and undermines incentive. Their reasons for this differed, however, and had implications for how they viewed policy. On the one hand, workers claimed that welfare was "too easy" on recipients; accordingly, they felt that cuts in public assistance were warranted. Recipients, in contrast, did not think that cuts would increase their motivation to work. On the contrary, given that meager "grant" levels made their lives too difficult, only increased funding would liberate them to work toward a future free of public support.

The distinction between contract and charity, a major one in the discourse of welfare (Fraser and Gordon 1992), may help to contextualize this conflict. The distinction is closely linked with that between the deserving and the undeserving, insofar as participants in contract exchanges are deserving while recipients of charity are not. In the contract mode of exchange—the model for which is the exchange of labor for wages—equal parties exchange equivalents. Charity, the opposite of contract, is not recognized as an exchange, but rather as a gift given without return.

Historically, noncontractual exchange and obligation have gradually been restricted to the domestic or private sphere, becoming defined as "female" and as charity. Contractual exchange, on the other hand, occurring in the public, male sphere, has become the more prevalent, and accepted, mode of interaction between individuals and parties. As Fraser and Gordon (1992) state:

. . . the hegemony of the contract helped to generate a specifically modern conception of "charity" as its complementary other. Charity came to appear a pure, unilateral gift, on which the recipient had no claim and for which the donor had no obligation. Thus, whereas contract connoted equal exchange, mutual benefits, self-interest, rationality, and masculinity, charity took on contrasting connotations of inequality, unilateral gift-giving, altruism, sentiment, and, at times, femininity. The contrast, moreover, assumed the guise of a stable, conceptually exhaustive dichotomy: all extra-familial relations had to be either contractual or charitable; there appeared to be no other possibilities. (1992:59)

One consequence of this is particularly relevant to the women involved in the welfare system. All interactions fit into one mode or the other, with charity always being "less" than contract. Accordingly, "charity" lowers the status of the recipient while enhancing that of the giver. Despite the rhetoric of contract and exchange in workfare programs, public assistance is still seen as charity, especially, in this case, from the point of view of workers. In the relationship between workers and recipients, then, recipients lose status.

Marriage, Misogyny, and Class

The greatest division of interests between women in the west today is perhaps between women who work or who are married to men who work, and women whose labour is not required in paid employment or women who are caring for dependants, and who are thus forced to depend on the state for their subsistence—the unemployed, single mothers, and old age pensioners. (Ramazanoglu 1989:105–69)

One of the big differences between the two groups of women concerned their relationships with men. Most of the welfare recipients (8, 67 percent) were divorced; and they were all, at one time or another, single mothers. In contrast, the majority of workers were currently married (13, 77 percent); only six (36 percent) had been divorced, and only four (24 percent) had been or were single mothers. As a group, then, AP workers were more protected from poverty, not only because of their currently well-paid jobs, but also because of their relationships with income-generating men. Such relationships are a major contributor to class differences among women, especially given that changes in the economy over the past two decades have increased families' needs for two incomes (Currie, Dunn, and Fogarty 1990). "In the emerging class structure, marriage is becoming a major axis of stratification because it structures access to a second income. The married female as 'secondary' wage earner lifts a former working-class or middle-class family into comparative affluence, while the loss or lack of access to a male income can force women and their children into poverty" (Stacey 1990:341). "Marital instability," then, "continually refuels a large, cheap female labor pool that underwrites the feminization both of the postindustrial proletariat and of poverty" (351). I have already (in Chapter 3) established that relationships with wage-earning men were highly relevant to recipients' initial contact with the welfare system: divorce, or having a child without the financial support of the child's father, were the most common events precipitating women's applications for relief. Recipients' ongoing connections with the welfare department also often waxed and waned in accordance with their relationships with income-generating men.

While this relationship between men and welfare was not as clear with workers, those workers who had been single mothers all mentioned the economic pressures they had experienced as a result of this situation. This is in keeping with the economic vulnerabilities suffered by single mothers throughout the United States; as Ehrenreich and Piven (1984: 163) have pointed out, "forty percent of divorced fathers contribute nothing [for child support], and those who do contribute pay on the average less than $2,100 a year." The financial troubles experienced by divorced mothers, then, crosscut class to a certain extent. In addition, the majority of both workers and recipients mentioned children as a key element of their involvement with the welfare system: support for their children was a major factor in women's decisions to apply for AFDC, and the wish to fulfill their roles as mothers (whether that meant earning high wages, or being physically close-by in order to provide care) influenced workers' decisions to either seek or remain in AP work. Interestingly enough, this emphasis on childcare concerns resembles many recipients' explanations of their initial involvement with the welfare system and of their subsequent inability to sever these ties.

In sum, all the women in this study were subject to constraints imposed by their limited educational credentials and by occupational segregation. Also, marriage/cohabitation and motherhood played key roles in the women's lives and in their relationships to the welfare system. The difference between the two groups was that fewer of the AP workers had experienced single motherhood, one of the greatest contributing factors to poverty among women in the United States. Through their marriages to men who could generate good incomes, and their own abilities to acquire work in the Department of Social Services, the workers were able to place themselves in a different class position from their clients.

It is perhaps in this regard that Withorn (1984) refers to "woman-hating," a misogynist ideology of distrust that fosters distance between women. One form of this "woman-hating" relates to workers' judgments of recipients' life choices. In a society with particular views concerning what is realistic and appropriate for women to do, many workers who are both employed and responsible for care-taking in their families may feel angry or threatened by recipients who "choose" welfare (ibid.:40). Similarly, recipients' need to assume "client" roles in their relationships with other women conflicts with societal views of men as authority figures, and with a view of women as allies (1984:42). As Withorn puts it (43), "the need for women clients to get what they want from the system over which women workers have little power makes the underlying similarities fade away."

Discussion

According to Wineman (1984:160), one of the key mechanisms for generating and maintaining of divisions among oppressed groups is "the tendency of people who are oppressed in some ways to compensate for their degradation by seeking other ways in which to exercise superior status and power." This is especially the case in a "competitive society which teaches people to believe that coming out 'ahead' or 'on top' is the primary measure for personal value" (1984:183). One way that workers may compensate for their low position in the welfare hierarchy, then, is in turn to oppress the clients over whom they have a modicum of power.[2] The practice of such oppression clearly works to enhance distance, rather than the recognition of commonalities.

The key dimensions along which workers and recipients might have expressed comembership were gender—in terms of both role and economic vulnerability—and oppression by the welfare system. As I outlined above, mutual role concerns were explicitly recognized by workers but not by recipients. Even in the case of workers, however, these concerns were a resource that was drawn on more often to augment than to diminish differences between themselves and their clients. Economic backgrounds also contributed more to the maintenance of division than to the establishment of comembership, and may even have served to override the recognition of commonalities based on gender roles. The fundamental similarities in the economic experiences of recipients and workers were overshadowed, perhaps, by current differences—differences which, given workers' employment backgrounds and cuts in the work force currently being considered by Michigan's governor, may be more precarious than workers would like.

Discussing stereotypes of the poor, Leacock (1971) states that

It appears . . . that the closer a person's experience has been to that of his [sic] poorer brethren, the more strenuously he may argue that it takes will and ability to get ahead, and that the poor are poor out of laziness, stupidity, or lack of ambition. He thereby not only vindicates his own gains, and assuages, perhaps a lingering guilt that he does not wish to cast behind a helping hand, but he also reassures himself. It is important to him that his position should follow from an intrinsically greater worthiness; this helps protect him from the threat of social vagaries like the rise and fall of unemployment, the greater insecurity that comes with age . . . the unpredictability of technological displacements, or the occurrence of serious accident or illness. (1971:17–18)

2. Interestingly, Wineman's claim (1984) that oppressed people oppress others sheds light on recipients' constructions of negative characterizations of other, less deserving, recipients, and of LIFE's call for punitive policies toward men. See Chapter 4.

Economic similarities, then, may paradoxically have helped maintain distance, rather than promote alliances between recipients and workers.

In addition, workers' power to help their clients has the same source as their power to oppress them—which was by far the more likely occurrence. Workers are allowed little autonomy by the welfare department, and it is primarily in their interactions with clients that they have the opportunity to exercise the few officially sanctioned discretionary powers at their disposal (e.g., formally seeking exceptions to general policy), and the unsanctioned discretionary powers that they claim for themselves (e.g., classifying clients as "deserving" or "undeserving" and accordingly going or not going out of their way to help them) (Prottas 1979).

In sum, I have scant evidence that workers and recipients either legitimated each other's view, or developed comembership. Recipients expressed significantly more antagonism than understanding towards workers, and almost never expressed comembership. In contrast, workers were more likely to express understanding of or sympathy for recipients' perspectives or circumstances, and they did, on occasion, express comembership with recipients on the basis of shared economic vulnerabilities and motherhood. Even workers' expressions of comembership, however, were rare when viewed in the context of the data as a whole.[3] Again, the power inequalities between the two groups of women may provide some insight. With regard to workers' recognitions of commonality, it may be the case, simply, that they can afford it better than recipients can. Being in a position of greater power, workers have more latitude than recipients, who are (or at least perceive themselves to be) beholden to their workers for their food and shelter. Recipients' feelings of dependence and powerlessness in their relationships with workers do not endear the workers to them, and may account for their inability, or unwillingness, to recognize comembership.

This lack of comembership among recipients and workers both reflects and contributes to maintaining the hierarchical relationship between them. To establish comembership would be an act of subversion, with potentially revolutionary implications for the welfare system. Workers, for instance, could collude with recipients to garner whatever benefits possible. If all workers followed Sally Blake's desire to change the dates on applications so that recipients would qualify for more benefits, or if, like Harriet Eaton, they "didn't have time" to process fraud refer-

3. Although some of the data I have used here derive from actual encounters between workers and recipients, the bulk of the data derive from workers or recipients interacting among themselves. Clearly, analyses of actual recipient-worker interactions would be the next step in an investigation of comembership.

rals, they would be working against the interests of the welfare department, and for recipients. (As I discussed in Chapter 8, while workers did take actions that worked to the benefit of their clients, these actions were occasional, and reproduced the deserving/undeserving distinction.) At a more abstract level, recognition on the part of workers and recipients that they share a certain economic oppression could have potential implications for thought and activity outside of the welfare department. While the potential for comembership was there, however, it remained unrealized, perhaps for some of the reasons outlined above. "If there is a single distinctive genius to the American political/economic/social system, it has been its ability to create and sustain deep divisions among oppressed people" (Wineman 1984:159).

Chapter 10
Conclusions

At the end of the day, nothing much changed. The hierarchical relationship between workers and recipients, and between each group of women and the welfare bureaucracy, remains intact. The counter-hegemonic discourses produced by the women in this study have not overturned the more powerful discourses of the New Right. It has not been my goal in this book to argue that women are not oppressed by the welfare system, that their agency means that they are responsible for their own victimization, or that they are powerful enough, in their practice of constructing meaning, identity, and policy, to significantly influence the current climate of relief in the United States, at least in the short term. However, while what they accomplished in their talk had no discernible impact on the structure and organization of the welfare system, the women actively produced constructions that in many cases countered dominant views. At the most, these oppositional views might provide the basis for future changes in the welfare system, or even in the larger society within which the welfare system is embedded. At the least, they indicate that the structures and views associated with the welfare system are not smoothly reproduced. The women who participated in this study were thus not only victims of forces more powerful than they, but also active agents engaged in exercising whatever power they had to create meaning in their worlds and, hopefully, eventually to change them for the better. Clearly, recipients and workers are not simple carriers of cultural material. They are, rather, involved in creating, invoking, modifying, or challenging cultural meanings and structures for their own purposes at hand. Even when stereotypes are reproduced—for example, when workers discuss their "lazy" clients—they are being locally produced for specific local reasons and in response to locally perceived phenomena.

The accommodation and resistance of MWRO and LIFE members and of the AP workers in the Kenyon County welfare office were firmly grounded in the specific nature of their participation in the welfare system and American culture. At the ground level, the women's resistance stemmed from an everyday self-interest (Scott 1986) with regard to both material and identity-related issues. Both groups were aware of how they were oppressed by the welfare bureaucracy, and they resisted these oppressions specifically. In the process, they also contested some of the larger gender and class structures characteristic of U.S. society. Although the women I worked with did not often refer to the oppression they were resisting in terms of gender or class, issues relating to class and gender were part and parcel of what the women were confronting and were, as I have shown in previous chapters, invoked in various ways. There is a connection, then, between the women's economic marginalization in U.S. society and their experiences with public assistance: the latter is inextricably tied to the former, and resistance to the one is part of resistance to the other.

The women's acquiescence was also based on material realities, specifically, their financial dependence on the welfare system. For both groups of women, open confrontation with the system could have jeopardized their incomes, a risk that neither group entertained taking during the course of this study. Workers and recipients also considered individual confrontation to be more dangerous than confrontation en masse. Thus workers contemplated presenting a petition from *all* the workers to management in order to protest the office restructuring. This would indicate the scope of worker dissatisfaction while protecting individuals. Likewise, welfare rights groups focused on group activities as opposed to individual protests. Even when recipients filed for hearings (an action that placed departmental focus on individuals), both MWRO and LIFE stressed the importance of having several group members accompany plaintiffs through the hearing process.

Recipients and workers had to contend not only with material limitations, but also with cultural constraints on resistance, specifically, the constraints of dominant discourses and of what is considered appropriate behavior for members of various classes, age groups, ethnicities, genders, and so on. Violent rebellion, for instance, was not an option considered by the women in this study; it would not only be materially and physically risky, but also socially inappropriate, especially for women. In this regard, MWRO and LIFE members had a particular aversion to any behavior that could be interpreted as "aggressive," which they equated with "feminist."

The limits to resistance do not simply deter it, however, but rather serve to channel it in particular directions (Scott 1990). Thus the ubiquity of "hidden" forms of dissent among the women in this study: for instance, recipients' failure to report extra income or other adults living in the household, the derogatory remarks shared in MWRO and LIFE meetings, and the appropriation of dominant discourses to build arguments against the inequities of the welfare system; and workers' behind-the-scenes jokes, their similar appropriations of the dominant discourse, and their participation in various small-scale resistances to office regulations that could not easily be detected as such by management.

There is one major respect, however, in which the women in this study were not only unable to resist, but acted to reproduce the system which oppresses them, and that is in their failure to establish comembership. Both workers and recipients devoted considerable energy to constructing views of themselves as well-meaning and hard-working victims of a system over which they had little control. This work entailed constructing views of "them" as well as of "us." As I have shown in Chapters 3–9, the views of "them" constructed by the women were more often negative than positive. These negative characterizations, however, are bound up with the hierarchical arrangements from which both groups suffer, and thus, while understandable, they are unfortunate. In failing to recognize and act on their shared oppressions as subjects of the welfare system—perhaps the greatest act of resistance they could engage in—the women perpetuate the welfare hierarchy and their places in it.

This hostility between workers and recipients may have been accentuated by the fact that this study was conducted in the aftermath of the Reagan era and at a time when, in Michigan, numerous cuts in both welfare grants and the numbers of welfare workers were being considered and in some cases instituted. Although I believe that the negative views the women held of each other go beyond a reflection of economic times, there is some evidence that in more expansive economic and political times, relationships between workers and recipients—or at least their intentions for their relationships with each other—have been less hostile than they currently seem to be (Hertz 1981; Piven and Cloward 1971; see also Withorn 1984). The larger social context, then, as well as the specific organization of the welfare bureaucracy, must be kept in mind when interpreting recipient-worker hostility. This of course points to the difficult nature of the relationship between accommodation and resistance. It is probably most useful to view the two as points on the same continuum, and to keep in mind the larger social and cultural formations within which they are embedded, as well as their immediate contexts of production.

So where to now? In one respect, nothing short of revolution will do. If, as I have argued, the welfare system is embedded in a society that holds particular views of poverty and gender—views which often do not serve the interests of women—then whole patterns of thought and practice need to be changed before the realities of workers' and recipients' lives improve. Perhaps recognition of comembership, if it could be achieved, would provide part of the foundation for this kind of massive change. In the short run, we may have to settle for incremental change. While the good that can be generated through incremental reform is limited by the constraints of the larger culture, there is always the possibility of creating small changes which can make a big difference.

Workers' production of policy might be a good place to start. In Chapters 7 and 8 I described how workers produce policy in their interactions with each other, and in meetings with their clients. In producing policy, workers are claiming autonomy. Their production of policy, however, is unsanctioned by a bureaucracy that positions them as the executors rather than the producers of policy. The kind of policy they produce, moreover, by and large has a negative impact on recipients. It is control-oriented, rather than service-oriented:

Control approaches are those which enhance and legitimise the power of the executive levels of the state over the front-line state workers . . . direct providers of publicly funded services, and members of the public for whom these services are intended. Service-delivery approaches are those which enhance and legitimise the capacity of those front-line workers, direct service providers and members of the public to influence the range, extent and types of publicly funded services. When control approaches are uppermost, senior-level public servants are required to act as the instruments of executive control, and to filter, restrain, and keep off policy agendas the demands from front-line workers, service providers and members of the public for better and more extended services. When service-delivery approaches are accorded legitimacy, senior-level public servants are asked to assume a role of facilitating these demands so that they may inform efforts to improve public services. (Yeatman 1990:38)

I would argue that the control-oriented nature of workers' production of policy is related not only to a wider culture in which poverty is stigmatized, but also to the fact that workers' production of policy is illegitimate, and to the low status workers hold in the welfare bureaucracy. It is of course conjecture to claim that workers' production of policy would become more service-oriented if they were viewed as legitimate producers of policy—if there were feedback loops fostering productive communication between workers and managers with regard to official policy decision-making. What is clear is that a lack of recognition of workers as policy producers contributes to the control-oriented nature of their policy. Legitimate spaces for workers to produce policy would no doubt work to their benefit, as well as possibly to the benefit of their clients.

Departmental training might be another area in which small changes could be made. Training in "listening between the lines," for example, could be balanced by training in empathy. Workloads, also, could be reduced to reasonable levels.

Welfare "grants" provide another potential target of progressive change. Raising benefit levels so that they reflect the actual cost of living would result in a small revolution in recipients' lives. The establishment of a national minimum income—one of the goals underlying the establishment of the National Welfare Rights Organization in the 1960s (Piven and Cloward 1977)—would be even more ambitious. All of this, of course, would entail recognizing the benefits, as opposed to the costs, of caring for people (Lipsky 1980). It is not difficult to imagine, then, how small revolutions could eventually, perhaps inevitably, lead to confrontation with the big structures—with, for instance, the ideologies informing policy, and with stereotypes. Perhaps, as Zillah Eisenstein (1981) argues with respect to liberal feminism, there is a radical future to incremental change.

In the end, however, I must return to the women's talk. Struggles over various forms of oppression are also "struggles over cultural meanings, values, and goals" (Ong 1991:281). In their endeavors to create oppositional views of themselves and their situations, the women in this study *were* successful. As do cultural beings anywhere, they went about the business of creating meaning. And as women participating in "the everyday struggle to survive and to change power relations in [their] society" (Morgen and Bookman 1988:8), they were engaged in politics. Although they clearly accommodated and reproduced certain ideas that may be detrimental to their interests, they nevertheless exercised considerable power in the construction of their own meanings and identities. The women were thus actively engaged in counter-hegemonic projects— in the construction of views of themselves and the system that were in opposition to dominant views. As such, they may, by participating in the creation or maintenance of cultures of resistance (Ong 1991), be contributing to future possibilities for structural change.

There ain't nothing wrong with me because I'm poor. That don't make me a bad person. (Susan Harrison, welfare recipient)

I am a human, the bottom line is I am a human. (Sally Blake, welfare worker)

Appendix A: Transcripts

As I indicated in Chapter 1, part of the careful exploration of talk entails attending not only to content but also to process, some of which may be represented in transcripts by the use of symbols to indicate phenomena such as overlaps, or fast or slow speech. The symbols that I use in the following transcripts, adapted from Mishler (1986) and Moerman (1988), are as follows:

[	Overlapping speech.
,	Pause, as between phrases or sentences.
(number)	Longer silences, timed in seconds.
=	Connects two utterances produced with noticeably less transition time between them than usual.
—	Cut off. Indicates that the preceding sound is stopped abruptly.
:	Indicates that the preceding sound is elongated.
CAPS	Indicates emphatic delivery.
#	Bounds words/passages spoken very quickly.
*	Bounds words/passages spoken softly and slowly.
( )	Bounds uncertain/undecipherable words/passages.
(( ))	Bounds transcriber's comments or nonverbal vocalizations.
?	Question intonation.
+	Indicates pounding on table for added emphasis.

Case #1

In the following exchange, Dara DeLuca, who had never received public assistance, invokes the category of the "undeserving" poor—in this case, those who abuse the welfare system because they are too lazy to look after themselves. In response, Susan Harrison concedes that such people exist, but claims that they represent only a small proportion of welfare recipients. The participants are Dara, Susan, and Meg Irwin; three other people are present but do not participate in the talk.

```
 1   D:   I understand the people that have kids, and that
 2        can't get a job, yes I understand, but I (don't)
 3        understand people that CAN get a job and that are
 4        on WELfare
 5   S:                    yep
 6   D:                       you know
 7   S:                              well that's what
 8                                [
 9   D:                                and that, you know,
10                                        [
11   S:                                    we're
12        HERE for
13   D:              I go,you you LOOK AROUND and you see these
14        people driving these nice cars and you know damn
15        WELL they're on welfare because of the way they
16        LIVE
17   ?:       *yeah*
18                      (2)
19   D:              you know damn WELL, or they've
20        TALKED about it with you, so how the hell'd you get
21        this nice CAR if you're such a, you know, on
22        WELfare, who are YOU screwing ((laughs)) you
23        KNOW=
24   S:         =that's IT, that's it
25   D:                        and I don't agree with
26        that, hell NO, I don't ((laughs))
27   S:                          I don't EIther,
28        but see that's, THAT'S just a FEW out of the
29   D:   oh yeah
30   S:         you know
31                        (1)
32   M:                    the, they're gettin' away
33        with—
34        [
35   S:   there IS gonna be, there's fifty percent wo:rking,
36        working welfare moms, there's twenty-five percent I
37        think that would LIKE to work but they don't have
38        no HOpe and then we've got the twenty-five percent
39        that just don't GIVE a damn
40                              yep
41   S:                          go out there and
42        do it FOR me# you know type shit
43                      [
44   D:              yeah bullSHIT, huh    (LIFE 5/6/90)
```

The most noteworthy feature of this segment is how long it takes for anyone to challenge Dara. Susan responds to Dara's comments at lines 7 and 11–12 by indicating that challenging stereotypes is one of LIFE's goals, but she fails to contest the image Dara is creating—an image that draws on stereotypes of both welfare abuse and promiscuity—until line 28, even though there was a clear opportunity to do so at line 18. Indeed, since no one else starts speaking at the pause at line 18, Dara continues her turn, more or less reiterating her point about "welfare cheats." Nor did any of the other four people present offer a challenge (Meg's bid at lines 32–33 is unsuccessful, and provides insufficient basis for speculation).

When she finally does challenge Dara, Susan argues that the ones who "don't give a damn"—the undeserving—comprise only one quarter of all recipients. Half of welfare recipients are employed, and are, moreover, also mothers ("working welfare moms"). Along with recipients who want to but cannot work (the 25 percent who "don't have no hope") these recipients are deserving, and should not be penalized for the shortcomings of the 25 percent who "don't give a damn." No one contests the figures Susan uses to bolster her claim that "bad" people are in the minority.

Case #2

In the following transcript segment, Susan Harrison and Meg Irwin draw on the idealized model of the nuclear family in their testimony at a legislative hearing on the welfare budget. Specifically, they endeavor to make the point that women are not on the relief rolls because they want to be, but as a result of unfortunate circumstances. (The transcript begins at mid-turn.)

```
 1   S:    because something happens in their life, not
 2         because you wanna be, you have your kids #you meet
 3         your husband you get married you have your kids or
 4         whatever#, you got the KIDS what'd ya wanna DO?
 5                        [
 6                        ((audience laughter, various
 7         comments))
 8   S:    just, you know? it's, it's not like you're TRYing
 9         to have kids to stay on welfare, it's not like that
10   M:    no, no, no
11   S:              bu:t
12   M:                  you GOT your percentage of some
13         welfare people (1) (that) that
14                                  [
15   S:                             that ARE lazy
16   M:                                    ARE lazy,
17         okay?
18   Sen:      yeah
```

19	M:	(but that's not your maJORity)
20		[
21	S:	but that's not the maJORity (LIFE 5/8/90)

There are two interesting features of this segment. First, Susan, who is trying to convince her audience that women are not to blame for being on public assistance, starts off on the wrong footing when she says, "you have your kids" (line 2). She quickly catches herself, however, and repairs her presentation by contextualizing *how* one acquires children; speaking very quickly now, she recreates the scenario: you meet a man, get married, and *then* have children—you don't have children out of wedlock, and, as she points out at lines 8–9, you don't have children just to stay on welfare. The audience laughter and commentary at lines 6–7 is a response to this blunder.

The second interesting feature of this segment is the implicit connection made between using reproductive capacities to stay on welfare and laziness. Having babies to stay on welfare is—despite the work involved in raising children—a lazy survival strategy. Note how Susan and Meg draw on the bad-people-exist-but-I'm-not-one-of-them argument in making their case. This is not an easy position to argue because they have to admit that some people on welfare do fit the stereotype. Meg pauses for a moment at line 13, as if hesitant. Susan then steps in to help her, and then they both state that some people on welfare "ARE lazy." Meg raises her intonation slightly at line 17, as if to say, "okay, we admit that some people are lazy . . . now—." Although this is not the first time that a speaker has raised her intonation in this way (see lines 4 and 8), it is the first time that one of the Senators responds. In this case, he says, "yeah," in apparent agreement with the stereotype that Meg and Susan have just invoked. Having admitted to the existence of lazy people is only the first part of the bad-people-exist-but-I'm-not-one-of-them argument, however, and Susan and Meg immediately go on to present the second part of the argument, namely, that "that's not your maJORity" (lines 19–21). The overlap between lines 19 and 21 perhaps indicates that Susan and Meg feel a pressing need to get this piece of the argument out on the table, thus distancing themselves from the stereotype.

Case #3

In this exchange, women at an MWRO meeting produce negative constructions of wealthy, male politicians. The exchange opens with a reference to the negative stereotypes of recipients often invoked by legislators, from which the women move on to construct their own stereo-

types of the politicians. Participants are Louise Black, Donna Dey, Rita
Moore, Gayle Adkins, Sandra Barrett, Harry Watson, and myself.

```
 1   L:   Senator Jones is the one who wanted to totally
 2        eliminate General Assistance four years ago, (I
 3        mean) he comes up with some re::al BAD proposals,
 4        and if you, and if you SAY stuff to him, you know,
 5        he will CHALLenge you, if you sa:y,
 6   D:                                      (          )
 7   L:   I've been trying to get a +JOB, I can't get a +JOB,
 8        I deserve enough money to +LIVE, my kids are
 9        +HUNGRY, kids are +STARVING, we, you know we need
10        to do better for 'em, he will SAY to you, well why
11        don't you do something about it? why don't you get
12        off your lazy butt? he will aTTACK, Henley, Henley
13        won't do as much, but they ARE an aggressive kind
14        of GROUP, they will—you'll be aMAZED at the kind
15        of things they will SAY, I mean they will come out
16        with ALL of the myths that you think that only
17        ignorant people have about welfare, these people
18        will come OUT with, you know, so, so it's not
19                                        [
20   D:                                   attack 'em back
21   L:   YEAH, well, TALK
22                     [
23   ?:               ((laughs))
24   D:                         how much do they take—
25   L:   even when—huh?
26   D:                    how much will they take if you
27        attack him right back?
28   G:                  (              you plan) what you're
29        gonna say
30   L:            well, well you know you just, you only
31        get a couple minutes it's not, if there's too many,
32        I've, I've SEEN them, if there's too many
33        recipients in the room they will just not have the
34        meeting, we had a whole lot a
35                   [
36   D:             (well they must) cause they still get
37                                    [
38   L:                              people (    )
39   D:   paid, don't they?
40   L:               sure, they say well, we have to
41        cancel the meeting for a while here until people
42                                   [
43   H:                              gotta get a
44        drink of water
45   L:                   went back to Central and got outa
46        town and then they had their meeting again, they
47        don't really like it too much—they NEED to hear
```

```
48              it, they need to hear it
49                      [
50   D:             but they, it's not, it's more they DON'T
51         wanna hear 'em, all of 'em are set for THEIR nice
52         fancy housing THEIR nice fancy (gardens), they
53         don't WANNA hear about ANYthing else, that's ONE
54         thing I learned with (    )
55                      [
56   S:             they have their real nice meals three times
57         a day
58   D:             OH YEAH and have everything served to 'em on
59         TOP of it
60   G:                  well if they're saying all the
61                              [
62   L:                          but they but they need
63                                      [
64   G:                                  ignorant myths
65         then they must be
66   D:                      ignorant
67   G:                          ignorant
68   L:                                  they NEED, they
69         need to hear some other stuff though
70   G:                                  mm huh
71   L:   I mean somebody needs to be there and tell 'em
72         about it, or somebody needs to be there and just,
73         even LOOK at 'em, even just SIT there, and TALK
74                      [
75   G:                  what time does that meeting (start?)
76   L:   about it, one thirty to five o'clock, and you can
77         FEEL the difference in the ROOM, when you have
78         reCIpients there, when you have people and you
79         don't look at 'em
80              [
81   ?:       (    )
82   L:                      and say, I bet that suit cost
83         three hundred dollars, you know, I (uh) the FEELing
84                                      [
85   D:                          that would
86         be enough to pay my RENT and my car payment and
87         [                                  [
88   L:   is different                      and you can
89         do—you can, you can have an impact, JUST showing
90         up and WATCHin' 'em, just showing up and WATCHin'
91         'em gets 'em nervous, I've seen Nancy sit there and
92         stare Jones right in the back
93                              ((several laugh))
94   L:   #and this man, he is just kept, TRYING TO MOVE AWAY
95         FROM HER YOU KNOW
96                              ((everyone laughs))
97                      [
98   G:                  alRIGHT
```

```
99    L:                              BECAUSE HE'S TALKIN'
100         ABOUT ALL THESE CUTS AND HE LOOKS AROUND AND SHE'S
101         JUST DEAD LOOKING AT 'EM# his WHOLE HEAD just turns
102         red, *right, he gets real NERvous about it*
103   D:                                           ALL of
104         'em do, you should—
105   R:                        was he the one was hollering
106         about well, why don't they stop having babies?
107                            [
108   C:                       no
109   L:    NO that was a DIFFerent one
110              [
111   C:             that was Bradley
112   L:                              that was, that was
113         Representative Bradley, yeah Jones is the same
114              [
115   ?:    (              )   (MWRO 5/2/90)
```

This entire segment is characterized by tones of outrage and indignation—intense emotions indicated by overlapping speech, raised (and alternately accusatory or sarcastic) voices, and variations in the speed of talk. In the first part of the exchange, Louise establishes that legislators are a menace. In citing "re::al BAD proposals" (line 3) and the "myths that you think that only ignorant people have about welfare" (lines 16–17), Louise makes the claim that legislators are uncouth and uninformed. Her talk at lines 7–10, in which she refers to the desperation of a parent trying to look after her children, highlights the degree to which Senator Jones's questions at lines 10–12 are inappropriate ("well, why don't you do something about it? why don't you get off your lazy butt?"). Louise thereby makes two points: first, that recipients are not lazy, and second, that it is not recipients who are aggressive in demanding fair treatment from the welfare bureaucracy, but, rather, legislators who are aggressive with their "re::al BAD proposals" (meaning proposals for cutting the welfare budget). That Louise has succeeded in establishing her points is made evident by Donna's response at line 20: "attack 'em back." How to go about attacking them back and the co-construction of legislators' characteristics provide the focus for the remainder of the segment.

As indicated at lines 32–34 and 50–53, a key problem for the women is that legislators "don't wanna hear it." The purported reason for this reluctance is that legislators live in their own worlds. Referring back to Louise's claim early in the segment, Gayle and Donna again point to the legislators' "ignorance" (lines 60–67). In addition, politicians are more concerned with their own luxuries than with the plight of the poor. Thus the references to fancy houses and gardens (lines 51–52), nice meals (lines 56–57), and $300 suits (lines 82–83). The impression produced is that legislators are basking in excess: not only do they have their "real nice meals three times a day," but they "have everything served to 'em on TOP of it" (lines 58–59).

However, the women also produce the idea that legislators' hesitance to listen reflects deliberation, not default. Louise's story about how public hearings are canceled when there are too many recipients present (lines 30–34) indicates that legislators are aware of the issues recipients raise—so aware that they take direct steps to avoid addressing them. Moreover, Senator Jones's displays of extreme discomfort when recipients are present (he just "kept, TRYING TO MOVE AWAY FROM HER," lines 94–95, and "his WHOLE HEAD just turns red, *right, he gets real NERvous about it*," lines 101–102) indicates that legislators *know* they are in the wrong. Even "friendly" (Democratic) legislators get uncomfortable when confronted by the realities of recipients' lives, as Donna points out later in the conversation:

You go in there ((to see Representative Wenger)) and you have a complaint, he'll sit right there, and you would've swore somebody put a snake in his pants. All of 'em are like that. They're real itchy to get away from it, they don't wanna hear it. (MWRO 5/2/90)

Despite the politicians' efforts to silence them, the women manage to have a voice. This voice sometimes takes the form of a simple presence, as Louise explains at lines 89–91: "you can have an impact, JUST showing up and WATCHin' 'em, just showing up and WATCHin' 'em gets 'em nervous." The background to the references to Representative Bradley (lines 105–113) provides further illustration of the women's ability to challenge legislators. During the incident referred to, Bradley, an advocate of increased cuts in the welfare budget, pulled his wallet out of his pocket, and, waving it in the air, demanded (paraphrase), "why do these people (meaning women) keep on having babies if they can't afford them? I carry a condom in my wallet. Don't they know how to use birth control?" In the uproar that followed, Susan Harrison and Rita Moore pulled condoms out of *their* pockets and waved them back at Bradley, saying (paraphrase) "we *do* use them, honey, let's see *yours*" (the Representative had not actually pulled out a condom, but only his wallet). The audience responded with fervent applause.

In sum, the exchange clearly demonstrates how the women worked together to criticize politicians' negative stereotypes of recipients. In so doing, they produced their own constructions of politicians as ignorant and uncaring. The women also portray themselves as fundamentally different from what the legislators claim them to be. Constructions of "us" and "them" thus co-occur.

Case #4

The following set of exchanges between Sally Blake, Anne Jensen, and myself, all occurring during the course of one rather informal interview, illustrates workers' sense of being "trapped" in AP work. Prior to this conversation, Sally and Anne were explaining how they were unable to keep up with all their paper work, and therefore unable to treat their clients appropriately and fairly.

```
 1   C:   what keeps you in AP work?
 2   S:                        the security
 3   C:                                   job
 4        security?
 5   S:              yeah, it's real close to the last thing
 6        I'd like to do for a living but, well
 7   C:                             what is the
 8        last thing you'd like? ((laughs))
 9   S:                        I was a motel
10        maid one summer in college ((laughs))
11   A:                              a WIFE
12                                   [
13   C:                              that's like
14        my, that's like my secretary
15             [
16   A:        and a house, a HOUSEkeeper, a HOUSEmaker
17   S:   *I'd do that in a minute right now*    (DSS 8/3/90)
```

In discussing the other kinds of jobs available to them, Sally and Anne refer to low status, low paying "women's" jobs. Sally's statement at line 17—"I'd do that in a minute right now"—indicates that the alternatives of secretary, maid, and housekeeper are no less odious than AP work. Her low monotone, moreover, gives an impression of defeat.

In the next segment, Sally and Anne argue that their educational credentials leave them "trapped" in AP work, despite the fact that, in their view, they have developed as much expertise over the years as anyone with a college degree.

```
 1   S:   I don't have a four year degree either, I have
 2        REAL limited options I have a STUpid two-year
 3        degree which is the same as ((laugh))the other
 4        guys with a diploma
 5   C:                 hey
 6   S:                 or a GED
 7   C:                          PhD in
 8        anthropology is gonna get you about as far
 9                      [
10   S:                 ((laughs))
11                      [
```

```
12  A:                              ((laughs))
13  S:   so my options are (I, you know—)
14  A:                                    I THInk that
15       might be part (1) of everyone's PROblem, is you
16                                              [
17  S:                                      reSENtment
18  A:   are trapped
19  S:                    yeah
20  A:                       we can't go ANYplace and get
21       paid as much as we get paid, out of the benefits
22       and the job security
23  S:                          mm huh
24                             [
25  C:                         uh huh
26  S:                              and quite frankly I
27       think fourteen an-and a half years doing this is
28       the equivalent of a college degree and I'm sorry
29       to say that 'cause the
30                             [
31  C:           it's the equivalent of
32                                     [
33  S:                             amount of TIME=
34  C:                                     =MORE
35  S:   you put in=
36  C:             =than that
37  S:                         the experience I've, I've
38       gleaned from this is more than—
39                                      [
40  A:                             we have to KNOW so much
41       about EVERYthing, a little bit a LAW, a little
42           [
43  S:         mm hmm
44  A:   bit a, you know, how—marketing values an—and
45        EVERYthing
46  C:                uh huh
47  A:              (              )
48                     [
49  S:                 you have to MANage people
50  A:   uh huh
51       [
52  C:   uh huh    (DSS 8/3/90)
```

In making their argument, Sally and Anne claim that AP workers are experts in a variety of fields, including law, marketing, and management. I support this claim with my comment (lines 31–36) that their expertise is worth more than a bachelor's degree. In the hierarchy of the welfare department, however, their knowledge is neither recognized nor rewarded.

In this last exchange, Sally further explains what she means by "trapped." She refers specifically to the issue of "choice," which both women find inappropriate given their limited options.

```
 1  S:   that resENtment is there though like Anne said
 2       before, we're tied here by—sure, it's our choice,
 3       you can, you can say to someone oh it's your
 4       CHOice to be here—
 5  A:                        I can go work at K-mart if I
 6       want to but I don't wanna (    ) DO that
 7       [
 8  S:   yeah                              conSIder
 9       the alTERnatives
10  C:             right
11  S:                        and I USED to have a job
12       that I hated, that paid like half what I was
13       earning when I started this job, so:, if you wanna
14       hate a job you might as well hate it for twice the
15       money and the security
16  C:                    that's a good point
17                                      [
18  S:                              and I have
19       these drea::ms of, you know I I would die to go to
20       school and I SAY it but I don't DO it, 'cause I
21       have these dreams of being in debt, being years
22       without a salary, getting a job that I THINK I
23       want but it's STILL work and it still involves
24       people in one way or the other (    )
25                                      [
26  A:                          and you'll be
27       starting at the bottom of the ladder
28  S:                              yeah, yeah
29  C:   you got it
30  S:           what a rush ((sigh)), and I—I've been
31       poor, I, you know, not by CHOICE ((laugh)) though
32       everything is supposed to be your choice, and I
33       was GOOD at it but I'm not going back to it again    (DSS 8/3/90)
```

It is evident in all three segments that Sally and Anne (and, to a lesser extent, myself) cooperate in producing the perception of being "trapped" in AP work. In the first, we all contribute to the list of undesirable jobs: maid, wife and housemaker, secretary (lines 9–16). Similar contributions can be seen in the second segment: Sally and Anne help each other express the meaning of being "trapped" (lines 14–22), and we all participate in establishing that the women's lack of educational credentials does not adequately reflect their abilities (lines 26–52). Finally, in the last segment, although Sally is the primary speaker, Anne contributes both illustrative and supportive statements. Her phrase, "I can go work at K-mart ((a discount store)) if I want to" (lines 5–6), underscores Sally's claim that the notion of "choice" is insidious. Anne also supports Sally's line of argument later in the conversation when she supplements the problems of beginning a new career with her comment about starting "at the bottom of the ladder" (lines 26–27).

Case #5

This exchange illustrates the process by which workers constructed their clients as dishonest. In this case, Sherry Nelson and Valerie Wood discuss two women's attempts to increase their benefits by excluding a portion of their household incomes, specifically, that generated by the male partners with whom they cohabited. One woman, for instance, claimed that she did not share food with her partner. Her food stamp budget was thus calculated on the basis of her income alone, with the result that she received more food stamps that she otherwise would have.

```
 1   S:   old case workers that, or case worker RElative
 2        cases, I HATE case worker relatives, from other
 3        counties
 4   C:              'cause they, they know the?
 5   S:                            well I had
 6        one little girl that came in, #this one always
 7        makes me mad Valerie's heard the story a MIllion
 8        times#
 9   V:        what?
10   S:              I had this girl come in to, not too
11        long ago and her sister's a new case worker in
12        Golden County, and she came in, she didn't even
13        know how or sys—how her, or her cousin is, or
14        how her cousin answered the appliCAtion, she's
15        living with a boyfriend and pregnant, and she
16        says they don't prepare food together, which I
17        think is a bunch of crAp but I, take it as—you
18                         [
19   C:             mm huh
20   S:   know I have to take it for what they say, THEN,
21        HE's been living there in this apartment for four
22        years, she's eighteen and just moved in, now
23        they're claiming the rent's three fifty, they're
24        claiming that she pays the full three fifty
25   V:   oh I ha:te that
26                    [
27   S:              and THAT—YEAH, and that she pays
28        completely for heat and utilities, now he's been
29        there for four years, now I KNOW that he's been—
30   V:   that's what this one that I was doing was closed
31        for fraud, she claimed she paid FULL rent, she
32        claimed she paid heat and utilities and the heat
```

```
33          and utilities were VENdored in HER name
34   S:                                     YEAH=
35   V:                                         =the
36          WHOLE amount
37   S:                     yeah, so that they can get the full
38          amount o:f, you know they don't have to, we
39          don't,see we, we would mark a household of TWO
40          [
41   C:     hmm
42   S:     if they were split
43   V:                     I'm gonna go find Maureen
44          Richards and tell her
45   C:                     mm huh
46   S:                                 but in this case she
47          will get the full amou:nt
48   C:                          phew
49   S:                              even though—and
50          he's WORKing, he's got a goo:d jo::b
51   C:                                   mm huh
52   S:     but we can't count his INcome or ANYthing, I
53          think he was making like, um, sixteen hundred
54          dollars, he works at a (    ), I wanna see if he
55          (   ) but I can't remember, SILLY, silly things,
56          those are IRRitating sometimes, FRUStrating, but
57                              [
58   C:                     mm huh, mm huh, I imagine
59   S:     I guess every job's got its ups and downs   (DSS 6/19/90)
```

Sherry begins the segment with a generalization about clients who are related to AP workers or who are themselves former workers. She is commenting on a story Valerie just told about a former worker turned client who lost her benefits because of fraud. The point, as Sherry goes on to relate in the story she then produces, is that people who know the system can, and often do, manipulate it. That workers consider this to be common is evidenced at lines 6–7: Sherry prefaces her story with the comment, "this one always makes me mad," indicating that what she is about to recount is a recurring phenomenon rather than a unique event. Her next phrase, "Valerie's heard the story a MIllion times," reinforces this notion, especially since Valerie had been a worker for less than a year at the time. Although Valerie's inquiry at line 9 fails to lend support to Sherry's contention, since it indicates that Valerie has missed the point (or that her attention was elsewhere), by line 25 Valerie does know what the point is, as indicated by her reinforcing comment, "oh I ha:te that." She is then able to contribute her own story, which builds on the case Sherry was reacting to in the opening of the segment. In this case, the story is about two people claiming benefits to cover the same item (rent) (lines 30–44; Maureen is the worker who monitors separations and divorces).

From Sherry's and Valerie's point of view, the women's claims are transparent lies. Sherry's response to one woman's assertion that she and her boyfriend did not prepare food together is that it was "a bunch of crAp" (line 17); only someone familiar with the details of food stamp policy would make such a claim. Valerie also indicates disbelief when she refers to another woman's claim that she "paid FULL rent" (line 31), stressing the word "full" to duplicate the woman's obvious exaggeration. In the telling of her story, Valerie, along with Sherry, indicates that despite having to "take it for what they say" (line 20), she will pursue whatever action she can to counter such manipulative strategies. This exchange, then, may illustrate not only the concerted construction of client behavior, but how a relatively new worker learns to participate in such constructions.

Case #6

This exchange illustrates how workers constructed their clients as lazy. The clients in question fail to meet deadlines, and are, in addition, careless, disrespectful, and whiny. Note how the relationship between workers and clients is construed as one between parent and recalcitrant child. Participants are Sherry Nelson, Valerie Wood, and myself.

```
 1   C:   is it TRUE that you're having a review appointment
 2        this morning?
 3   S:                    ye::ah
 4   V:                          ((laughs))
 5   S:                                    you wanna sit
 6        in on it?
 7   C:               I'd LOVE to
 8   S:                          oh GOOD you'll LIKE this
 9        one this is one of my LEAST fave—well, she's
10        [
11   C:   ((laughs))
12   S:   not my LEAST favorite cli:ent, she's just, LAZY
13        lazy lazy lazy lazy (client) well, I mean it's
14              [
15   C:            ((laughs))
16   S:   like THIS, she, her review appointment wasn't for
17        today
18   C:        uh huh
19   S:                   it was FOR (1.5)((ttt)) u:h, nine
20        o'clock on the SEVenth, but that wasn't the first
21        one
22   V:      that's too EARLY wasn't it?
23   S:                            no that's the
24        SEcond, that's the second one Cindy Smith's first
25        appointment was for the FOURth, at eight-thirty on
```

```
26         the fourth, THEN she called and said, Miss Nelson,
27         Miss Nelson
28         [
29   V:    ((laughs))
30   S:              my case is going to close
31   V:                                     ((laughs))
32   S:    I want a new appointment, I said okay no problem
33   V:    ((laughs))
34   S:              nine o'clock on the seventh
35                        [
36   C:                   on the seventh
37   V:                                        she
38         didn't, did she not show up?
39   S:                             she did not (show)
40         up, and she never called unTIL MONday, when she
41         said, Miss Nelson, Miss Nelson, I missed my
42         appointment on THURSda:y
43                    [
44   V:    ((laughs))
45                    [
46   C:    ((laughs))
47   S:              I said you DID?
48   C:                        you DID? I didn't
49         know tha:t
50   S:              WOW! she said, and I just got a CLOSure
51         letter and MY case is going to clo::se she said,
52         on the ninetEEnth, I said, YOU are corrECT, it
53         will close on the nineteenth
54                 [
55   V:           so you're not gonna (leave it in) negative
56         action are you gonna delete it today?
57   S:                                     I'm not
58         deleting it until she comes in today with those
59         appointment papers (    )
60                             [
61   C:                        'til she's physi:cally here
62   S:    yeah she said, if I, she said well can't I mail
63         the stuff in? I said Cindy you don't WORK, I said
64   V:    what do you DO?=
65   S:                       =you are COMing IN, you HAVE to
66         come in for this appointment it's not, a thing, I
67                                            [
68   C:                        mm huh
69   S:    said we only ask you to do it once a YEAR
70   C:                                    mm huh
71   S:    and she said, well I don't HAVE some of my PApers,
72         I said, those were sent to you on the TWENTY-
73         SECOND of MAY
74   C:                    uh huh uh huh
75   S:                          and I said, so I would
76         like to know what the DEAL is, then she said, but
```

```
77            I will be in there (Miss Nelson) I said if you're
78            not here at nine o'clock I'm not gonna see you and
79            you:: and I will NOT have an appointment and (    )
80                                                             [
81    V:                                                      I
82            have one—I have one that was supposed to come in
83            on (      )
84                 [
85    C:         I think she'll sho:w
86    S:                              I don't KNO:W
87                                   [
88    V:                                     'cause I have, I like
89            to see my reviews, like the first couple days of
90            the mo:nth, or (at least) the first couple days of
91            the next week, and I HAD, one scheduled for like
92            the fou:rth, she called me and said well I have to
93            change it because bla bla bla, and this and that
94            so I changed it, to last week, and I said, I
95            rea:lly do NOT like to see my appointments this
96            late because you know, if you don't get all your
97            papers in, you know, and this and that, your case
98            is gonna CLOSE
99    C:                    mmm
100   V:                            so, um, she said well, I have
101           exams next week, and well uh can I come on Monday?
102           I just thought *oh boy*, so if she doesn't have
103           her papers in toda:y
104   S:                          I know well that's just like
105           Barrie Teton was (dealing with it), SHE had two
106                [
107   V:         (          )
108   S:    appointments in the beginning of the—or on the
109           fourth, and the fifth, and, then on the
110           fourteenth, she called all sca:red, and said, you
111           know, and I said, no problem just come i:n
112   C:                                          mm huh
113   S:    so, I said come in at you know one-thi:rty, but be
114           prompt because my, I don't like afternoon
115           appointments, I said I'll be honest with you I do
116           NOT make afternoon appointments because it breaks
117           up my day too much
118   V:                        mmm
119   S:                              I said—she said well Miss
120           Nelson I have—and (you know) #she doesn't work or
121           anything#, I said ALright, one-thirty but that's
122           the best I can do for you
123   C:                          mm huh
124   S:                                and she said
125           okay (1) so what happens? she didn't wanna come
126           in at one-thirty, she wanted to come in at TWO-
127           thirty, so that's the one that DID, she just be-
```

```
128        bopped in a little after two-thirty, about two-
129        thirty fi:ve
130  C:                  ee:ww
131  S:                         YEAH, so I made her wait till
132        three-thi:rty
133  C:                  ee::ww ((laughs))
134  S:                              and then she came
135        in, she said, #MISS NELSON# would you like to
136        remind me what time my appointment was? I said,
137        yeah I would, your appointment was at ONE-thirty
138        and you wasted an HOUR of MY TIME, because I don't
139        want to get anything out of my desk until you get
140        a chance to—
141           [
142  C:     yup
143  S:       you came in here, and I said then, when I found
144        out you were here at two-thirty, I said #I didn't
145        know if you were coming or NOT, this is the THIRD
146        appointment#
147  C:                  mm huh
148  S:                          I didn't know if you were
149        COMing so I (brought out my stuff) and said you
150           [
151  C:     mm huh
152  S:     wasted an hour of MY: ti:me, so I wasted an hour of YOURS
           (DSS 6/18/90)
```

Sherry expresses cynicism toward the client she is about to see at the beginning of the segment when she says to me, sarcastically, "you'll LIKE this one" (lines 8–9). She then characterizes the client as "LAZY lazy lazy lazy lazy" (lines 12–13), explaining, in the remainder of the conversation, what this means. First, clients who repeatedly reschedule appointments, especially those who are unemployed, are clearly lacking in motivation. During the course of the exchange, Sherry refers to two clients, and Valerie to one, who are lazy in this sense. Significantly, the women are missing their appointments even though they seemingly have no other obligations. The women Sherry refers to are are unemployed: "I said Cindy you don't WORK" (line 63); and "she doesn't work or anything" (lines 120–121). Nowhere is the women's work as mothers acknowledged (indeed, the only way I knew they were mothers is that they were on AFDC); if they are not employed, there is no reason for them to miss their appointments. Valerie underscores this sentiment when she asks, "what do you DO?" (line 64), implying that the women don't do anything; and when she refers to her own client's reason for wanting to reschedule an appointment with the words "bla bla bla" (line 93), even though the client was in the middle of exams at community college. It is as if clients could not possibly have good, substantial reasons for wanting to reschedule appointments.

Throughout the exchange, Valerie and Sherry sarcastically imitate their clients, using whiny tones. They speak in their clients' voices ten times in this exchange (lines 26–27, 41–42, 50–52, 62–63, 71, 77, 92–93, 100–101, 119–120, and 135–136); in six of these instances, they speak in high whiny tones (lines 26–27, 41–42, 50–52, 62–63, 71, and 100–101), and in one instance (lines 135–136), Sherry feigns an angry voice. In Sherry's and Valerie's view, these clients lack credibility and are simply making excuses.

As with workers' reactions to lying, Sherry and Valerie take their clients' indolence personally—especially since AP staff work so hard. When relating her response to the first woman, Sherry feigns mockery and ridicule: "I said you DID? ((miss your appointment))" (line 47)—a tone that I echo at lines 48–49. In other cases, Sherry and Valerie take on stern tones, as if speaking to children (lines 63–69, 72–73, 77–79, 94–98, 113–117, and 135–152). Sherry's story toward the middle of the segment, in which she relates insisting that Cindy Smith deliver papers to the welfare office rather than mail them in, indicates a sort of revenge: Cindy having made some extra work for Sherry, Sherry in turn will make some extra work for her. Sherry does not present this decision as policy-based; rather, it reflects her judgement that, since Cindy is unemployed, she should be able to come to the welfare office (see lines 63–69). Her story at the end of the exchange, of how she made a client who was late wait an hour, further expresses indignation at clients' inability (or unwillingness) to fulfill their obligations.

Case #7

This discussion, about a local stabbing, illustrates how workers constructed the relationship between "clients" and "criminals." Participants are Judy Reynolds, Becky Wright, Sherry Nelson, and myself. The transcript opens with Becky's description of the incident:

```
 1   B:   I thought they were probably down on the stre:et,
 2        and he was just calling him names and then they,
 3        they said he sta:bbed him right in the hea:rt with
 4        a kitchen knife=
 5   J:                      =as I SAY they will all elIminate
 6        each other sooner or LAter so just let 'em keep
 7        going TO it
 8   C:                 oh, you're talking about that—
 9   S:   the stabbing last night
10                       [
11   C:                  MURrder
```

```
12   B:                              yeah
13   C:                                  in Grandville?
14   J:     he was my client
15   C:                       first one in four YEARS or
16          something they said? first one in the COUnty in
17          four years
18   B:                  I thought there had been one SINCE
19          then, you know it don't seem like it's been that
20          lo:ng
21                  (2.5)
22   J:                  I guess they DO—I mean he is JUST,
23          he's just the SCUZ of the EARTH, and I mean and
24          there's no lo:ss to ANYthing, not to ANYbody
25                              [
26   B:                          well, the county cop
27          told Ben ((B's son)) to go down to the funeral
28          home and spit on 'em ((laughs)) 'cause Ben said
29                              [
30   ?:                       (                )
31                              [
32   J:                          he JUST got outa
33          jail in June I just added him to the CASE
34                       [
35   B:                          he was looking
36          forward to kicking his ASS and now (he's dead so
37                              [
38   C:                          oh this guy
39          was on your CASE?
40          [
41   B:   he can't)
42   J:                  who's that?
43   C:                          the guy who
44          commItted the murder? the guy who got—
45                       [
46   S:                  all THREE of 'em are (   )
47                              [
48   J:                          the guy who—
49          the guy who's DEAD, I have to BURY 'em today
50   S:                          the
51          one who did the MUrdering probably, just got out
52          of jail and (is on SOme case load) SOmeplace
53   B:                          mm huh
54   S:   I wouldn't be a BIT surprised
55   J:                      you know, that's
56          just like (            )
57                  [
58   S:          it happened in MY client's apartment,
59          and her client got KIlled
60          [
61   J:   I know it sounds really cold hearted, but you know
62          THAT'S just like all those dru:g gangs (   )
```

```
63                                            [
64  C:                                       WAIT a
65        minute it happened in your client's a—apartment
66                                                [
67  S:                                         apartment
68        (it was her client)
69        [
70  C:  it was YOUR client that got killed now does
71       ANYone, is the guy who KIlled anybody's client?
72  S:  oh probably
73           [
74  J:       probably
75  S:                  we just haven't, yeah
76  J:                                 they tend to
77       run with other clients, um, but that's like those
78       drug gangs=
79  B:               =too bad they don't know when they have
80       these parties, then they could just BOMB the
81       houses
82  J:          yeah ((laughs))
83  B:                      you know ((laughs)) (and
84       just wipe out all the houses)
85       [
86  C:  that's a little extREME ((laughs))
87  J:                        but, you know,
88       like the DRUG gangs, if if INNOCENT people didn't
89       get killed
90  B:           yeah
91  J:               you know I, I don't want
92       INnocent people getting killed, but if they
93                     [
94  B:               yeah
95  J:  just got, I mean WHY BOTHER with the tax mo:ney
96       for trying to STOP 'em? ((laughs))
97  B:                           yeah
98  J:                              LET them do
99       it—a, they just kill each OTHER ((laughs))   (DSS 8/3/90)
```

In this exchange, Judy, Sherry, and Becky move from discussing a particular group of clients to discussing all welfare clients as particular types of people. The workers are excited and agitated, as indicated by the frequency of overlapping speech, and by a lack of pauses either between or within turns at talk (the only such pause occurs at line 21).

Early in the segment, Judy suggests that "they will all elIminate each other sooner or LAter so just let 'em keep going TO it" (lines 5–7). The "they" in this phrase refers specifically to people like those who were involved in the murder; but perhaps it also refers to clients in general. Evidence for the equation of criminals and clients is provided at line 46, when Sherry suggests that it is reasonable to assume that all three of the men involved in the stabbing were recipients of public assistance, despite the fact that the workers are only sure about two of the men. At lines 50–52, Sherry again suggests that the murderer is also a client; and at lines 72–74, after I ask if the person who committed the murder was a client of one of the workers in the Kenyon County office specifically, Sherry and Judy respond in unison, "probably." The workers seem to be claiming that many clients are criminals—or at least that many criminals are also on public assistance. As Judy points out, clients "tend to run with other clients . . . like those drug gangs" (lines 76–78)—as if the two groups have similar character traits, and as if they should both be destroyed, like vermin (lines 79–81).

Case #8

The following exchange is typical of Blues Boulevard talk. As part of a larger discussion of time constraints in the office, Fran Knight, Sally Blake, and Peggy Stewart debate approaches to "telephone hour," the hour in the morning during which workers were required to remain at their desks in order to consult with clients over the phone.

```
 1   C:   plus you have phone hour
 2   F:                              well, some of us do, some
 3        of us ditty bop in and out any time they feel like
 4        it ((laughs))
 5   C:                   get that T-shirt on Fran
 6   F:                                    I know it
 7        (     )
 8        [
 9   S:   #I stay at my desk during phone time because that's
10        what I'm ordered to do and when people call me and
11        they need me to run to the computer and check on
12                                              [
13   F:                                      that's
14        'cause you're a sucker
15            [
16   S:       something      I SAY, I say I'm not
17                             ˋ[
18   F:                        ((laughs))
19   S:   allOWed to# I'm only, I can only answer the phone
20        between eleven and twelve (o'clock) those are the
21                                      [
22   F:                            that's 'cause you're a
23        suck-ass
24        [
25   S:   rules    NO:: because that keeps OTHER people
26            [
```

```
27  F:                      suck right UP to 'em, do EVERYthing
28       they tell you to
29       [
30  S:   from trying to call
31  P:                      man when I got 'em on the
32       phone I find out what the problem is and I tell
33       [
34  F:   ((laughs))
35  P:   'em right THEN, I don't wanna call them back, I do
36       it RIGHT then, I don't like calling people back
37  S:   I don't EITHER, but I tell 'em I'm, I'm not allowed
38       to leave my desk (between eleven and twelve)
39                         [
40  F:                      I'm not gonna be LOCKED to my
41       desk for an hour simply because my boss says I have
42       to be    (DSS 8/3/90)
```

This exchange illustrates contrasting approaches to resistance. Fran does not like being told what to do, and so "ditty bop((s)) in and out" during phone hour (lines 2–4). Preferring confrontation to subterfuge, she finds Sally's more subtle form of defiance contemptible; in fact, she calls Sally a "suck ass" (lines 22–23) for supposedly complying with management. Sally, however, who plays by the rules to such an extent that productivity and efficiency are undermined, deploys one aspect of management discourse against another. Her sarcastic tone and speeded up speech (lines 9–30) indicate that she is not speaking literally. In addition, following the rules protects Sally from having to respond to a barrage of client requests (lines 25–30). Peggy, on the other hand, is most concerned with managing her workload as she sees fit. It just so happens that the "telephone hour" rule suits her needs (lines 31–36). Her approach may thus be construed as defiant, insofar as management's needs are irrelevant. Indeed, in claiming to attend to her clients on the spot, she implies that she leaves her desk during phone hour to work on the computers, which are located elsewhere.

Case #9

In this transcript, workers make connections between welfare benefit levels and AP salaries. In constructing themselves as responsible for large amounts of money and therefore deserving of higher salaries, they are countering a departmental categorization of AP workers that provides the basis for maintaining the status quo. Participants are Ann Jensen, Fran Knight, Debbie Brown, and myself.

```
1  A:   'cause they're FIGHTin' the deci:sion, that we
2       were one of the, um, didn't agree with their
3       little ca:tegorizing procedure
4  C:                              uh huh
```

```
 5   A:                                    and I don't
 6        see how they COULD (3) but the (thing is) (3) but
 7        if they rated us too HIGH they'd have to PAY us
 8        see?
 9   C:        right
10   A:             so they, I'm su:re they just
11        deLIberately scored us in the category they
12        WANted us in
13   F:                    of COURSE
14   A:                         because then they couldn't
15        affo:rd to give THIS many people (right) that
16        kind of a raise
17   C:               uh huh
18   A:                       but it's in court right Fran?
19   F:   well, it's for the com—comparable worth (2) law
20        suit=
21   D:   =how many AP workers are there state wide?
22        got any idea?
23   A:             ten thousand?
24   D:                      is there THAT many?
25   F:   I thought it was somen' like eight five eight
26        seven
27   A:         somen' like that, a lo:t
28   D:                        that IS a lot
29   C:   uh huh
30   D:           when you multiply that by fifty thousand
31        dollars a month for ((laughs)) each pe:rson
32        ((laughs)) that we give away (1) I figure I give
33        away fifty thousand dollars a month
34   C:                                 yeah?
35   A:                                 at
36        LEAst
37        [
38   D:   we send out a quarter of a million in foo:d
39        stamps
40   C:        from THIS office?
41   D:                   from thi:s county a
42        month
43        [
44   C:   a MONTH?
45   D:           yes
46   C:            are you KIdding?
47   D:                     no, I asked
48        accounting about that
49            [
50   C:   whoa::
51        [
52   A:        when I did FOOD STAMPS I had a million
53        DOllars worth of food stamps in my (socks) at a
54        time, in Mable County
55            [
```

```
56   F:          that's that's something that you should do
57        too:, is talk to people in accOUnting
58   A:                              (            )
59   F:   and find out what kind of emergency needs do they
60        process for us
61   C:              uh huh
62   F:                    what kind of EP checks
63        they process
64   C:              uh huh
65   F:                     how much food stamps, all
66        the other stuff
67   C:                phew, wow
68                [
69   D:                    yeah, I'd ask accounting
70        (what was the total we give away in a MONTH)
71                [
72   F:                    THAT would give you a little black
73        and white stuff to add to your report, your, your
74        thesis    (DSS 8/3/90)
```

During the first part of the exchange, Ann, Fran, and Debbie are discussing the struggle between the department and the union over workers'
pay raises. At lines 21–22, Debbie asks if anyone knows how many workers there are state wide. Her reason for asking this is made clear at lines
30–33, when she points to the ratio of workers to dollars given out in
public relief. She herself claims that "I give away fifty thousand dollars a
month" (lines 32–33). The remainder of the exchange is taken up with
the issue of assistance levels: Ann claims that she was distributing
$1,000,000 in food stamps a month in the county in which she had pre-
viously worked (lines 52–54); and Fran encourages me to get figures
on how much money workers distribute via the various programs each
month (lines 56–74) (putting the figures in my report would help to
bolster workers' claims that they are responsible for an inordinate
amount of money and thus should be appropriately compensated). In
this exchange, then, the women relate the amount of relief they oversee
to their own pay. When compared in this way, workers' monetary rewards
are woefully inadequate.

Case #10

In the following segment, Becky Wright and Diane Kane make a decision
regarding how Becky should handle Leila Harding's case. The decision,
between two potential policiy avenues, will have a major impact on Leila's financial situation. It is based to a large extent on the women's evaluation of Leila's character and intent, in particular, whether she deliberately deceived the department regarding her employment status.

```
 1   D:   so, did she finally out and out SAY she was or
 2        not
 3   C:        uh uh, but the, Becky called the place and
 4        they said she was
 5   D:                        oh rea::lly
 6   B:                              she didn't even write
 7        it down in the 1171, but the guy that she li:ves
 8        with had written it in HIS 1171 MONths ago, and so
 9        (I figured—)
10   D:                    that she was WORking
11   B:                              so I figured if
12        she didn't put it in HER book that maybe
13   D:                                  oohh
14   B:   (            )
15        [
16   C:   how many HOURS she was working though there
17   D:   so you gonna send a 38?
18                      [
19   C:                    ((yawns loudly))
20   B:                              well, I don't
21        know whether I'm gonna to send a 38, or send a 38
22        and a 176
23            [
24   C:      'scuse me
25   D:              (   )
26              [
27   C:                  what's a 17—wait, a 738 and (   )
28   B:   a 38 is a verification of employment
29   C:                              okay
30   B:   and a 176
31          [
32   C:      176 is a negative ACtion
33   B:                          I'm gonna put her in
34        negative action, I can do that, can't I
35   D:                                okay, for
36        what, for
37          [
38   B:      for failure to report
39          [
40   D:      what reason yeah
41   B:                        she's been wo:rking
42        all aLONG
43        [
44   D:      but are you asking her now though to verify
45        the income?
46   B:                  uh uh
47   D:                    I think NOW you've gotta
48   B:                              do I
49        have to give her ten days to verify income, I may
50        to have to do a FRAUD referral (   )
```

```
51                                              [
52   D:                                         okay so she told
53        you out and out this morning that she's not
54        working, right
55   B:                    uh huh
56   D:                                oh okay so I guess I'd just
57        put it in negative action    (DSS 7/2/90)
```

Becky begins by explaining to Diane that Leila had not listed the job at Madrid Pet Center in her 1171, or application for assistance, but that her boyfriend has put it in *his* application (lines 6–8). She thereby establishes Leila's action as intentional dishonesty as opposed to an innocent error of omission. When Diane responds by asking Becky if she's going to officially verify Leila's job (form 38), Becky responds by wondering if she should just verify employment, or verify employment and pursue a negative action (fraud referral, form 176) (lines 20–22). The rest of the discussion centres on this decision. In the end, both workers agree to the negative action. While the department expects workers to make fraud referrals in these kind of situations, this conversation indicates that workers do not implement policy automatically. Again, worker's decisions to invoke or ignore policy amount to their production of policy.

Appendix B

The following tables provide background information on the recipients and workers I interviewed for the project, with a focus on the women's economic and domestic relationships, that is, their relationships with paid labor and significant others, such as men and children. These data allow us to see patterns within each group as well as the similarities and differences between them.

TABLE B1: Recipients Interviewed*

Name	Age	Education	Marital status	No. of children	Years on AFDC	Reason for starting AFDC	Paid employment
Susan Harrison	33	High school diploma; several college courses	Divorced 3 times; living with fiancé	4	17 years on and off	Husband out of work	Factory worker, water resources centre worker, day care manager, prostitute
Louise Black	38	Two Associate's Degrees	Divorced	1	4 years on and off	Divorce	Math Tutor
Mary McDonald	late 20s	High school diploma; several college courses	Divorced	2	10 years on and off	Had child	Cashier, bar maid
Jody Dixon	42	High school diploma	Divorced	2	9 years steady	Divorce	None
Jane Thomas	32	GED	Divorced; living with fiancé	4	10 years, on and off	Divorce	Nurse's aide, waitress, security guard, janitor
Pat Graham	48	High school diploma; college classes	Divorced twice	3	25 years, on and off	Husband in jail	Domestic worker, cook, waitress, street vendor, carnival worker, gas station attendant, clothes alterations; other sources of income: pan handling, stealing checks.

Name	Age	Education	Marital Status	Children	Work History	Crisis	Jobs
Katie Devon	19	11th grade	Living with fiancé	1 (pregnant with second)	2 years steady	Kicked out of parents' home	Cashier
Dee Cook	25	High school diploma; 3 years college	Single	1	10 years steady	Had child	Unknown, but minimum wage
Tara Hope	29	Working on high school diploma	Single	2	6 years steady	Had child	Cashier, waitress
Maggie Fletcher	39	M.A.	Divorced	1	3 years steady	Divorce, illness	Nurse
Martha Hill	36	High school diploma; in nursing program	Divorced	5	9 years, on and off	Divorce	Animal groomer, factory worker (car parts), domestic worker
Janet Burns	24	B.A.	Single	1	18 months steady	Had child	Secretary, waitress, lab technician, tree farm laborer, horse urine collector (Dept of Agriculture)

*Susan, Louise, Martha, Janet, and Pat were also core members of welfare rights groups

TABLE B2: Kenyon County Assistance Payments Workers Interviewed

Name	Age	Education	Marital status	No. of children	Years in AP work	Reason for starting AP work	Previous paid employment
Peggy Stewart	32	Two years college	Married	2	5.5	Salary, benefits, job security	Clerical worker
Judy Reynolds	51	High school diploma	Married (one divorce)	3	18	Salary, benefits, job security	Clerical worker
Gilda White	44	High school diploma; six months technical-vocational school	Divorced	None	1	Salary, benefits, job security	Fast food server, government crop reporter, tax worker
Emma Nichols	42	B.A.	Married	2	17	Salary, benefits, job security	Data coding operator
Harriet Eaton	59	High school diploma	Married	3	18	Desire to help the needy	Data coding operator
Fran Knight	42	B.A.	Married	3	6	Salary, benefits, job security	Computer operator, nurse, electronics technician

Name	Age	Education	Marital Status	Children			
Sally Blake	42	Associate's degree (two years college)	Married	2 step-children	15	Salary, benefits, job security	Clerical worker, cafeteria worker, library aide, domestic worker
Diane Kane	35	Two years college	Married	3	14	Salary, benefits, job security	Clerical worker
Edith Saunders	43	One year community college	Married (one divorce)	None	16	Salary, benefits, job security	Clerical worker
Colleen O'Connell	38	B.A.	Married	2	15	Salary, benefits, job security	None
Becky Wright	34	High school diploma	Single	3	14.5	Salary, benefits, job security	Bakery worker, clerical worker
Karrie Holmes	40	Two years secretarial school	Married (one divorce)	2	17	Salary, benefits, job security	Waitress, clerical worker
Sherry Nelson	25	Three years college	Married	None	2	Salary, benefits, job security	Bookkeeper

(*Continued*)

TABLE B2: *Continued*

Name	Age	Education	Marital status	No. of children	Years in AP work	Reason for starting AP work	Previous paid employment
Valerie Wood	26	Three years college	Married	None	1.5	Salary, benefits, job security	Preschool teacher, store manager, receptionist
Nora Ryan	50s	High school diploma	Married (one divorce)	2	16	Desire to help the needy	Cashier, factory worker, dry cleaning worker, community aid
Anne Jensen	40	Two years college	Single	None	5	Salary, benefits, packages, job security	Clerical worker
Debbie Brown	48	High school diploma; six months community college	Living w/ partner (3 divorces)	5	15	Salary, benefits, packages, job security	Safety officer, janitor, clerical worker, day care worker, cook, waitress, bartender, factory worker

Bibliography

Abramovitz, Mimi
1988a *Regulating the Lives of Women: Social Welfare Policy from Colonial Times to the Present.* Boston: South End Press.
1988b Welfare, Work, and Women: How "Welfare Reform" Is Turning Back the Clock. *Christianity and Crisis* 48(12):292–97.
Berger, Peter L. and Thomas Luckmann
1966 *The Social Construction of Reality: A Treatise in the Sociology of Knowledge.* Garden City, NY: Doubleday.
Blumer, Herbert
1969 *Symbolic Interactionism: Perspective and Method.* Englewood Cliffs, NJ: Prentice-Hall.
Bookman, Ann and Sandra Morgen, eds.
1988 *Women and the Politics of Empowerment.* Philadelphia: Temple University Press.
Bourdieu, Pierre
1977 *Outline of a Theory of Practice.* Cambridge: Cambridge University Press.
1990 *In Other Words: Essays Towards a Reflexive Sociology.* Stanford, CA: Stanford University Press.
Briggs, Charles L.
1986 *Learning How to Ask: A Sociolinguistic Appraisal of the Role of the Interview in Social Science Research.* Cambridge: Cambridge University Press.
Clifford, James
1986 On Ethnographic Allegory. In James Clifford and George Marcus, eds., *Writing Culture: Twentieth-Century Ethnography, Literature, and Art.* Cambridge, MA: Harvard University Press.
Cloward, Richard A. and Frances Fox Piven
1979 Hidden Protest: The Channeling of Female Innovation and Resistance. *Signs* 1(4):651–69.
Collier, Jane F. and Sylvia J. Yanagisako
1989 Theory in Anthropology Since Feminist Practice. *Critique of Anthropology* 9(2):27–37.
Currie, Elliott, Robert Dunn, and David Fogarty
1990 The Fading Dream: Economic Crisis and the New Inequality. In Karen V. Hansen and Ilene J. Philipson, eds., *Women, Class, and the Feminist Imagination: A Socialist-Feminist Reader.* Philadelphia: Temple University Press.

Dill, Bonnie Thornton
1988   "Making Your Job Good Yourself": Domestic Service and the Construction of Personal Dignity. In Ann Bookman and Sandra Morgen, eds., *Women and the Politics of Empowerment*. Philadelphia: Temple University Press.
Ehrenreich, Barbara and Frances Fox Piven
1984   The Feminization of Poverty: When the "Family-Wage System" Breaks Down. *Dissent* 31(2):162–70.
Eisenstein, Zillah
1981   *The Radical Future of Liberal Feminism*. New York: Longman.
Erickson, Frederick
1975   Gatekeeping and the Melting Pot: Interaction in Counseling Encounters. *Harvard Educational Review* 45(1):44–70.
1979   On Standards of Descriptive Validity in Studies of Classroom Activity. Occasional Paper No. 16, Institute for Research on Teaching. East Lansing: Michigan State University.
1984   School Literacy, Reasoning and Civility: An Anthropologist's Perspective. *Review of Educational Research* 54(4):525–46.
1986   Qualitative Research on Teaching. In M.C. Wittrock, ed., *Handbook of Research on Teaching*. 3rd ed. New York: Macmillan.
1992   Ethnographic Microanalysis of Interaction. In M.D. LeCompte, W.L. Millroy, and J. Preissle, eds., *The Handbook of Qualitative Research in Education*. San Diego: Academic Press.
Erickson, Frederick and Gerald Mohatt
1982   Cultural Organization of Participation Structures in Two Classrooms of Indian Students. In George Spindler, ed., *Doing the Ethnography of Schooling: Educational Anthropology in Action*. New York: Holt, Rinehart and Winston.
Erickson, Frederick and Jeffrey Shultz
1982   *The Counselor as Gatekeeper: Social Interaction in Interviews*. New York: Academic Press.
Fairclough, Norman
1992   *Discourse and Social Change*. Cambridge: Polity Press.
Faith, Karlene
1994   Resistance: Lessons from Foucault and Feminism. In H. Lorraine Radtke and Henderikus J. Stam, eds., *Power/Gender: Social Relations in Theory and Practice*. London: Sage.
Folbre, Nancy
1988   Whither Families? Towards a Socialist-Feminist Family Policy. *Socialist Review* 18(4):57–75.
Foucault, Michel
1979   *Discipline and Punish*, trans. Alan Sheridan. New York: Vintage.
Fox, Richard G.
1991   Introduction: Working in the Present. In Richard G. Fox, ed., *Recapturing Anthropology: Working in the Present*. Santa Fe, NM: School of American Research.
Fraser, Nancy
1989   *Unruly Practices: Power, Discourse and Gender in Contemporary Social Theory*. Minneapolis: University of Minnesota Press.
1993   Clintonism, Welfare, and the Antisocial Wage: The Emergence of Neoliberal Political Imaginary. *Rethinking Marxism* 6(1):9–23.

Fraser, Nancy and Linda Gordon
1992   Contract Versus Charity: Why Is There no Social Citizenship in the United States? *Socialist Review* 22:45–67.
1994   A Genealogy of *Dependency*: Tracing a Keyword in the U.S. Welfare State. *Signs: Journal of Women in Culture and Society* 19(2):309–36.
Freire, Paulo
1970   *Pedagogy of the Oppressed,* trans. Myra Bergman Ramos. New York: Continuum.
Gans, Herbert J.
1992   The War Against the Poor. *Dissent* (fall):461–65.
Garfinkel, Harold
1956   Conditions of Successful Degradation Ceremonies. *American Journal of Sociology* 61(5):420–24.
1967   *Studies in Ethnomethodology.* New York: Prentice-Hall.
Giddens, Anthony
1984   *The Constitution of Society.* Berkeley: University of California Press.
Gilder, George
1981   *Wealth and Poverty.* New York: Basic Books.
Goffman, Erving
1963   *Stigma: Notes on the Management of Spoiled Identity.* Englewood Cliffs, NJ: Prentice-Hall.
1969   *Strategic Interaction.* Philadelphia: University of Pennsylvania Press.
Gordon, Linda
1988   What Does Welfare Regulate? *Social Research* 55(4):609–30.
1990   The New Feminist Scholarship on the Welfare State. In Linda Gordon, ed., *Women, the State, and Welfare.* Madison: University of Wisconsin Press.
Gramsci, Antonio
1971   *Selections from the Prison Notebooks.* New York: International Publishers.
Handler, Joel F. and Yeheskel Hasenfeld
1991   *The Moral Construction of Poverty: Welfare Reform in America.* Newbury Park, CA: Sage.
Hartman, Heidi
1987   Changes in Women's Economic and Family Roles. In L. Beneria and C. R. Stimpson, eds., *Women, Households, and the Economy.* New Brunswick, NJ: Rutgers University Press.
Hertz, Susan Harrison H.
1977   The Politics of the Welfare Mothers Movement: A Case Study. *Signs : Journal of Women in Culture and Society* 2(3):600–11.
1981   *The Welfare Mothers Movement: A Decade of Change for Poor Women?* Lanham, MD: University Press of America.
hooks, bell
1990   *Yearning: Race, Gender, and Cultural Politics.* Boston: South End Press.
Hymes, Dell
1981   Ethnographic Monitoring. In H. T. Trueba, G. P. Guthrie, and K. H. Au, eds., *Culture and the Bilingual Classroom: Studies in Classroom Ethnography.* Rowley, MA: Newbury.
Katz, Michael B.
1986   *In the Shadow of the Poor House: A Social History of Welfare in America.* New York: Basic Books.
1990   *The Undeserving Poor: From the War on Poverty to the War on Welfare.* New York: Pantheon.

Kessler-Harris, Alice
1982   *Out to Work: A History of Wage Earning Women in the United States.* New York: Oxford.
Kornblum, William
1991   Who is the Underclass? *Dissent* (spring): 202–11.
Leacock, Eleanor Burke
1971   Introduction. In Eleanor Burke Leacock, ed., *The Culture of Poverty: A Critique.* New York: Simon and Schuster.
Lipsky, Michael
1980   *Street-Level Bureaucracy: Dilemmas of the Individual in Public Services.* New York: Russell Sage Foundation.
McDermott, R.P., K. Gospondinoff, and J. Aron
1978   Criteria for an Ethnographically Adequate Description of Concerted Activities and their Contexts. *Semiotica* 24 (3/4): 245–75.
McDermott, R.P. and D.R. Roth
1978   The Social Organization of Behavior: Interactional Approaches. *Annual Review of Anthropology* 7: 321–45.
Mead, Lawrence M.
1986   *Beyond Entitlement: The Social Obligations of Citizenship.* New York: Free Press.
Mehan, Hugh
1979   *Learning Lessons: Social Organization in the Classroom.* Cambridge, MA: Harvard University Press.
Meucci, Sandra
1992   The Moral Context of Welfare Mothers: A Study of US Welfare Reform in the 1980s. *Critical Social Policy* 12: 52–74.
Michigan Department of Social Services
1989   *Outreach.* Lansing: Office of Communications.
1990   Michigan Department of Social Services Biennial Report, Lansing.
1991   Michigan Department of Social Services Information Packet, Lansing.
1993   Michigan Department of Social Services Information Packet, Lansing.
Mills, C. Wright
1959   *The Sociological Imagination.* London: Oxford University Press.
Mink, Gwendolyn
1990   The Lady and the Tramp: Gender, Race, and the Origins of the American Welfare State. In Linda Gordon, ed., *Women, the State, and Welfare.* Madison: University of Wisconsin Press.
Mishler, Elliot G.
1984   *The Discourse of Medicine: Dialectics of Medical Interviews.* Norwood, NJ: Ablex.
1986   *Research Interviewing: Context and Narrative.* Cambridge, MA: Harvard University Press.
Moerman, Michael
1988   *Talking Culture: Ethnography and Conversation Analysis.* Philadelphia: University of Pennsylvania Press.
Moore, Henrietta L.
1988   *Feminism and Anthropology.* Minneapolis: University of Minnesota Press.
Morgen, Sandra and Ann Bookman
1988   Rethinking Women and Politics: An Introductory Essay. In Ann Bookman and Sandra Morgen, eds., *Women and the Politics of Empowerment.* Philadelphia: Temple University Press, pp. 3–32.

Moynihan, Daniel P.
1973   *The Politics of a Guaranteed Income: The Nixon Administration and the Family Assistance Plan.* New York: Random House.
Murray, Charles
1984   *Losing Ground: American Social Policy, 1950–80.* New York: Basic Books.
National Health Policy Forum
1992   Welfare Reform in the 1990s: Coercion or Catalyst for Change? Issue Brief 6080. Washington, DC: George Washington University.
Nelson, Barbara J.
1984   Women's Poverty and Women's Citizenship: Some Political Consequences of Economic Marginality. *Signs : Journal of Women in Culture and Society* 10(2): 209–31.
1990   The Origins of the Two-Channel Welfare State: Workmens Compensation and Mothers' Aid. In Linda Gordon, ed., *Women, the State, and Welfare.* Madison: University of Wisconsin Press.
Neubeck, Kenneth J. and Jack L. Roach
1981   Income Maintenance Experiments, Politics, and the Perpetuation of Poverty. *Social Problems* 28(3):308–20.
Oakley, Ann
1981   Interviewing Women: A Contradiction in Terms. In Helen Roberts, ed., *Doing Feminist Research.* London: Routledge and Kegan Paul.
Ong, Aihwa
1991   The Gender and Labor Politics of Postmodernity. *Annual Review of Anthropology* 20:279–309.
Ortner, Sherry Nelson B.
1984   Theory in Anthropology Since the Sixties. *Comparative Studies in Society and History* 26(1):126–66.
1991   Reading America: Preliminary Notes on Class and Culture. In Richard G. Fox, ed., *Recapturing Anthropology: Working in the Present.* Santa Fe, NM: School of American Research.
Parker, Seymour
1973   Poverty: An Altering View. In Thomas Weaver, ed., *To See Ourselves: Anthropology and Modern Social Issues.* Glenview, IL: Scott, Foresman.
Pearce, Diana
1984   Farewell to Alms: Women's Fare Under Welfare. In Jo Freeman, ed., *Women: A Feminist Perspective.* Mountain View, CA: Mayfield.
1990   Welfare Is Not *for* Women: Why the War on Poverty Cannot Conquer the Feminization of Poverty. In Linda Gordon, ed., *Women, the State, and Welfare.* Madison: University of Wisconsin Press.
Personal Narratives Group
1989   *Interpreting Women's Lives: Feminist Theory and Personal Narratives.* Bloomington: Indiana University Press.
Philipson, Ilene J. and Karen V. Hansen
1990   Women, Class, and the Feminist Imagination: An Introduction. In Karen V. Hansen and Ilene J. Philipson, eds., *Women, Class, and the Feminist Imagination: A Socialist Reader.* Philadelphia: Temple University Press.
Piven, Frances Fox
1984   Women and the State: Ideology, Power, and the Welfare State. *Socialist Review* 74(14):11–19.
Piven, Frances Fox and Richard A. Cloward
1971   *Regulating the Poor: The Functions of Public Welfare.* New York: Random House.

1977   *Poor People's Movements.* New York: Pantheon Books.
1987   The Historical Sources of the Contemporary Relief Debate. In Fred Block,
        Richard A. Cloward, Barbara Ehrenreich, and Frances Fox Piven, *The
        Mean Season: The Attack on the Welfare State.* New York: Pantheon.
1988   Welfare Doesn't Shore Up Traditional Family Roles: A Reply to Linda Gor-
        don. *Social Research* 55(4):631–647.
Polanyi, Livia
1989   *Telling the American Story: A Structural and Cultural Analysis of Conversational
        Storytelling.* Cambridge, MA: MIT Press.
Pope, Jacqueline
1989   *Biting the Hand That Feeds Them: Organizing Women on Welfare at the Grass
        Roots Level.* New York: Praeger.
Prottas, Jeffrey M.
1979   *People-Processing: The Street-Level Bureaucrat in Public Service Bureaucracies.*
        Lexington, MA: Lexington Books.
Ramazanoglu, Caroline
1989   *Feminism and the Contradictions of Oppression.* London and New York: Rout-
        ledge.
Rosaldo, Renato
1989   *Culture and Truth: The Remaking of Social Analysis.* Boston: Beacon Press.
Scott, James C.
1985   *Weapons of the Weak: Everyday Forms of Peasant Resistance.* New Haven, CT:
        Yale University Press.
Scott, James C.
1986   Everyday Forms of Peasant Resistance. In James C. Scott and Benedict J.
        Tria Kerkvliet, eds., *Everyday Forms of Peasant Resistance in South-East Asia.*
        London: Frank Cass.
1990   *Domination and the Arts of Resistance: Hidden Transcripts.* New Haven, CT:
        Yale University Press.
Shortridge, Kathleen
1984   Poverty Is a Woman's Problem. In Jo Freeman, ed., *Women: A Feminist Per-
        spective.* Mountain View, CA: Mayfield.
Shultz, Jeffrey J.
1975   *The Search for Comembership: An Analysis of Conversations Among Strangers.* Un-
        published dissertation, Harvard University Graduate School of Education.
Sklar, Kathryn Kish
1993   The Historical Foundations of Women's Power in the Creation of the
        American Welfare State, 1830–1930. In Seth Koven and Sonya Michel,
        eds., *Mothers of a New World: Maternalist Politics and the Origins of Welfare
        States.* New York and London: Routledge.
Smith, Dorothy E.
1987   *The Everyday World as Problematic.* Boston: Northeastern University Press.
Smith, Ruth L.
1990   Order and Disorder: The Naturalization of Poverty. *Cultural Critique* 14:
        209–29.
Stacey, Judith
1990   Sexism by a Subtler Name? Postindustrial Conditions and Postfeminist
        Consciousness in Silicon Valley. In Karen V. Hansen and Ilene J. Philipson,
        eds., *Women, Class, and the Feminist Imagination: A Socialist-Feminist Reader.*
        Philadelphia: Temple University Press.

Stack, Carol B.
1974 *All Our Kin: Strategies for Survival in a Black Community.* New York: Harper.
U.S. Bureau of the Census
1992 *Statistical Abstract of the United States, 1992.* Washington, DC: U.S. Government Printing Office.
Warren, Mark
1990 Ideology and the Self. *Theory and Society* 19:599–634.
Weedon, Chris
1987 *Feminist Practice and Poststructuralist Theory.* Oxford: Basil Blackwell.
Wertkin, Robert A.
1990 *Assistance Payments Worker Job Satisfaction: A Study of Michigan Workers.* Lansing: Michigan Department of Social Services.
West, Guida and Rhoda L. Blumberg
1990 Reconstructing Social Protest from a Feminist Perspective. In Guida West and Rhoda L. Blumberg, eds., *Women and Social Protest.* New York and Oxford: Oxford University Press, pp. 3–35.
Wineman, Steven
1984 *The Politics of Human Services: A Radical Alternative to the Welfare State.* Boston: South End Press.
Withorn, Ann
1984 For Better and For Worse: Social Relations Among Women in the Welfare State. *Radical America* 18(4):37–47.
Witz, Ann and Mike Savage
1992 The Gender of Organizations. In Mike Savage and Ann Witz, eds., *Gender and Bureaucracy.* Oxford: Blackwell / The Sociological Review.
Yeatman, Anna
1990 *Bureaucrats, Technocrats, Femocrats: Essays on the Contemporary Australian State.* Sydney: Allen and Unwin.
Zopf, Paul E., Jr.
1989 *American Women in Poverty.* New York: Greenwood Press.

Index

Abramovitz, Mimi, 3, 18, 19, 21, 22, 31, 70, 81

Accommodation, 29, 32, 42, 61, 157–59; and "Pollyannas," 118–20; and AP production of policy, 129–30; and comembership, 154–56; and mixed narratives, 28, 31; and status quo narratives, 27–28; and welfare rights groups, 69–70, 72; definition, 7; mixed forms, 7; relationship to resistance, 7, 70–71; theory of, 7

Aid to Dependent Children (ADC), 19. *See also* Aid to Families with Dependent Children

Aid to Families with Dependent Children (AFDC): and poverty threshold, 3; benefits, 20–21; eligibility, 19–21; funding and administration of, 20–21; growth in rolls, 31; history, 19–20; inadequacy of benefit levels, 29

Assistance Payments (AP) workers: and "burn-out," 140; and domestic responsibilities, 87; and ethic of care, 86; and gender roles, 83; and limited job opportunities, 85–87; and occupational segregation, 3, 83–84, 132, 171–74; and office culture, 168; *see also* Blues Boulevard, Pollyannas; and office restructuring, 94; and pressure from clients, 90; and production of policy, 124–30, 147, 160–61, 186–88; and stress leave, 96; as boundary workers, 83, 136–37; as street level bureaucrats, 83; background of, 82–83; backgrounds of as compared with recipients, 131–32, 152–53; case loads, 87; discretionary power of, 137; job description, 1–2; job pressure, 98–99; and men-

tal health, 95–97; and physical health, 95–97; low status of, 83–84; motivations for taking the job, 82–83, 86; official relationship to policy formation, 88–89; proletarianization of, 88–89; recipients' constructions of, 72–75, 140–42; relationships with supervisors, 91–93, 95–96, 133; responsibilities of, 184–86; salary levels, 186; status vis-a-vis clients, 95; time constraints on the job, 87–88

Berger, Peter L. and Thomas Luckmann, 4

"Blues Boulevard," 117, 120–23, 183–84; and AP supervisors, 122; and resistance, 120–22, 183–84; management views of, 120

Blumer, Herbert, 11

Bookman, Ann and Sandra Morgen, 6, 7, 161

Bourdieu, Pierre, ii, 4

Briggs, Charles, 23, 84

Bush, George, 22

Child protective services, 106–11, 115

Childcare: and education, 27; and employment, 24–26, 53

Citizenship, 34

"Clients,": AP workers' constructions of and face-to-face interaction, 99; and deserving/undeserving dichotomy, 114–17, 146–48; AP workers' constructions of as criminals, 104–5, 180–83; as unclean, 103; as child abusers, 105–11, 125; as cunning, 142–43, 146; as dishonest, 99–101, 106, 124–26, 147–48, 174–76, 188; as lazy, 101–2, 176–80; as manipu-